The Condition of the Working Class in Turkey

The Condition of the Working Class in Turkey

Labour Under Neoliberal Authoritarianism

Edited by
Çağatay Edgücan Şahin and Mehmet Erman Erol

First published 2021 by Pluto Press
New Wing, Somerset House, Strand, London WC2R 1LA

www.plutobooks.com

British Library Cataloguing in Publication Data
A catalogue record for this book is available from the British Library

ISBN   978 0 7453 4312 9   Hardback
ISBN   978 0 7453 4311 2   Paperback
ISBN   978 0 7453 4315 0   PDF
ISBN   978 0 7453 4313 6   EPUB

Typeset by Stanford DTP Services, Northampton, England

Simultaneously printed in the United Kingdom and United States of America

Contents

Abbreviations

AIA – Automotive Industrialists Association
AKP – Justice and Development Party (Adalet ve Kalkınma Partisi)
AMECO – Annual macro-economic database of the European
  Commission's Directorate General for Economic and Financial
  Affairs
ANAP – Motherland Party (Anavatan Partisi)
ARIP – Agricultural Reform Implementation Project
CBRT– The Central Bank of the Republic of Turkey
DİSK – Confederation of Progressive Trade Unions
EES – European Employment Strategy
ESM – European Social Model
ESOP – Employee stock ownership plans
EU – European Union
FAO – Food and Agriculture Organization of the United Nations
FDI – Foreign Direct Investment
HAK-İŞ – Confederation of Turkish Real Trade Unions
HRW – Human Rights Watch
ILO – International Labour Organization
IMF – International Monetary Fund
IRA – Independent Regulatory Agency
ISI – Import Substitution Industrialisation
ITUC – International Trade Union Confederation
KESK – Confederation of Public Employees' Trade Unions
MESS – Turkish Employers Association of Metal Industries
MFSP – Ministry of Family and Social Policies
MOD – Ministry of Development (DPT)
MOLSS – Ministry of Labour and Social Security
MOENR – Ministry of Energy and Natural Resources
MÜSİAD – Independent Industrialists and Businessmen's
  Association
NES – National Employment Strategy

OECD – Organisation for Economic Co-operation and Development
PEA – Private Employment Agencies
PETKİM – Petrokimya Holding Inc.
PKK – Kurdistan Workers' Party
QE – Quantitative Easing
SAP – Structural Adjustment Policies
SEKA – General Directory of Turkey's Cellulose and Paper Factories
SGK – Social Security Institution
SOE – State Owned Enterprise
TEKEL – Turkish Tobacco and Alcoholic Beverages Company
TİSK – Turkish Confederation of Employer Associations
TTSİS – Turkish Textile Employer's Union of Turkey
TÜRK-İŞ – Confederation of Turkish Trade Unions
TurkStat – Turkish Statistical Institute
TÜSİAD – Turkish Industry and Business Association
UIF – Unemployment Insurance Fund
WB – World Bank
WHO – World Health Organization
WSM – Workers' Self-management

Acknowledgements

We are grateful to Immanuel Ness for his encouragement and support for this project since the very beginning. We would like to thank David Shulman and everyone at Pluto Press for all their help and guidance. We are grateful to Christopher Shim for his help in preparing the index. We would like to thank our contributors without whose hard work this book would not have been possible. Finally, special thanks go to Fiona and Duygu for their support throughout the development of this project.

Introduction

Mehmet Erman Erol and
Çağatay Edgücan Şahin

But the bourgeoisie defends its interests with all the power placed at its disposal by wealth and the might of the State. (Friedrich Engels, *The Condition of the Working Class in England*)

In the aftermath of the Soma mining disaster in Turkey where 301 workers died in 2014, the then Turkish Prime Minister Recep Tayyip Erdoğan cited nineteenth-century Britain to prove that these accidents are 'usual'. 'I went back to British history' he said, 'some 204 people died there after a mine collapsed in 1838. In 1866, 361 miners died in Britain. In an explosion in 1894, 290 people died there' (*Hurriyet Daily News*, 2014). These anachronistic comments were shocking; but the comparison with the 'savage capitalism' of nineteenth-century Britain also exposed the modus operandi of Turkish capitalism in the twenty-first century.

This 'savage capitalism' of nineteenth-century Britain was most famously analysed by Friedrich Engels in *The Condition of the Working Class in England*, originally published in 1845. Having been completed on the 200th anniversary of Engels' birth, and in the context of President Erdoğan's comments, this book project takes its inspiration from Engels, and specifically his above-mentioned work, as the title of this book suggests. Written in the heyday of the industrial revolution, young Engels' impressive study and his documentation of the condition of the English working class reflected the brutal exploitation of labour in Victorian England. He was appalled by widespread child labour, low wages, miserable conditions, poor health, death rates and environmental destruction, as well as the English bourgeoisie.

1

Looking at the condition of the working class in Turkey in the twenty-first century, we share a similar sentiment, which led us to edit this volume. We wanted to document and analyse the condition of the working class in Turkey in the twenty-first century, as we are appalled by widespread 'work murders', low wages, miserable conditions, widespread precarity and insecurity, commodification, extractivism, systematic violation of labour rights, and practices of gendered division of labour. The developments since the Covid-19 pandemic have so far proven that this condition will be worsened as the pandemic is seen as an economic 'opportunity' by the capitalists and the state; and that Turkey could seek to 'capitalise on a possible shake-up of global supply chains' (Pitel, 2020) through its cheap labour.

Turkey's political economy since the twentieth century has never been truly pro-labour, as the country embraced capitalist development which relied on the exploitation of labour. However, as capitalism developed, so did class struggle. The labour movement intensified its struggle against the bourgeoisie and the capitalist state during the 1960s and 1970s. This period was also marked by import-substitution industrialisation and development planning which entailed certain improvements on the condition of labour. However, this condition unsettled Turkish capitalists and the state; and their response was the transition to neoliberalism in 1980 via a brutal military coup which aimed to 'put an end to class-based politics' (Yalman, 2009). Hence, the last four decades which were marked by neoliberalism dismantled the gains of labour and paved the way for the above-mentioned condition of the working class in Turkey in the twenty-first century. Against this background, the aim of this volume is to make sense of 40 years of neoliberal restructuring of labour; with an extensive framework that deals with various aspects of this restructuring.

A significant part of this neoliberal restructuring of labour was carried out under the AKP (Adalet ve Kalkınma Partisi – Justice and Development Party), in power since 2002. Much like the contemporary 'authoritarian populist' parties and 'strongman' leaders that benefited from the discontent following the 2008 global financial crisis; Turkey's AKP and its leader Erdoğan capitalised on the discontent and the legitimacy crisis that was caused by the country's 'lost decade' of the 1990s and the infamous 2001 crisis (Madra & Yılmaz, 2019). However, like most of these leaders and parties, the AKP decisively implemented the neoliberal framework in the last two decades.

In conventional analyses which dismiss the significance of class relations, the AKP period is generally assessed in terms of a rupture from the earlier periods of Turkey's political economy. Some other accounts also make a distinction within the AKP era; i.e. the 'good AKP years' (2002–07 or pre-2011) and the later 'authoritarian turn', 'democratic backsliding' and 'bad economic management' (cf. Erol, 2019; cf. Tansel, 2018). However, we contend that, as far as the restructuring and management of labour is considered, there has been a direct continuity with earlier periods (since the 1980s) in terms of neoliberal authoritarianism, attempts at labour market flexibilisation, deunionisation, insecurity, precarity, privatisation, commodification, financialisation and restructuring in many sectors. Hence, while recognising the pecularities of the condition of Turkey's working class under AKP rule, the aim of this volume is to make sense of 40 years of neoliberal restructuring of labour in its *totality* and *continuity*. It is important to emphasise, however, that the AKP governments managed to be more decisive and overcome the legitimacy issues that previous governments faced, through various containment mechanisms and populist cushions (Akçay, 2018) such as financial 'inclusion', neoliberal social assistance strategies or identity-based politics, as well as promoting pro-government unionisation.

Nevertheless, in recent years, Turkey's political economy under the AKP has become crisis-ridden and this 'successful' management of contradictory capitalist social relations became increasingly difficult. Concomitantly, this was complemented by an unprecedented authoritarianism beyond the already authoritarian political economy of Turkey. This arguably reflects the weakening hegemony of the AKP (as seen in local elections in 2019 and frequent 'currency crises') and the tensions between the ruling classes and the AKP. Against the background of this crisis-ridden condition and Erdoğan's authoritarian-Islamist 'one-man rule', there are calls for a return to the 'good AKP years' (i.e. 2002–07) or the post-2001 rule-based neoliberal market framework rather than the 'statist' or 'crony' political economy of recent years. However, we contend that this state-market dichotomy is a false one and that it explicitly removes the notion of class from the analysis. Therefore, class-based analyses are of vital importance in the debates in the context of Turkey's crisis-ridden political economy.

The contributors to this volume do not share an overarching common theoretical framework. However, relying on a broadly Marxist and critical political economy tradition, the overarching concept that they share and prioritise is 'class', and particularly 'labour'. All chapters develop a labour-centred perspective, and labour and class struggle understood as the constitutive category of capitalist social relations. Hence, various aspects of the 'condition of the working class' are researched and analysed thoroughly from the standpoint of labour (see Burnham et al., 2008, pp. 330–1 for 'working class standpoint research'), with rich empirical data and fieldworks/interviews for most of the chapters.

STRUCTURE OF THE BOOK

The book is organised in three parts. These parts reflect the general characteristics and the condition of labour in the contemporary political economy of Turkey. Part I focuses on the *restructuring* of state and labour since the 1980s. Divided into two sections, the chapters in this part deal with various aspects of neoliberal restructuring since the military dictatorship of the 1980s to the AKP years.

This part starts with Mehmet Erman Erol's chapter on neoliberalism and the AKP. Drawing upon critical International Political Economy (IPE) and state theory, the chapter first discusses the meaning of neoliberalism and its emergence in the late 1970s as a response to both crisis-ridden capitalism and class-based democratic demands. It then provides a trajectory of neoliberalism in Turkey from the 1980s to the 2000s and its crisis-prone nature. The chapter argues that the AKP era since 2002 represents a continuity with earlier periods in terms of the broad objectives; i.e. putting labour in its place. However, it also takes the AKP's peculiarities into account and discusses the conditions which provided a significant degree of legitimacy to the

AKP and Erdoğan and the restructuring of class relations. Against conventional accounts, this chapter holds the argument that authoritarianism is not a recent development in Turkey, but it is intrinsic to neoliberalism. Its intensification in recent years does not necessarily represent a shift from neoliberalism but reflects its crisis-ridden condition.

The second chapter in this part is Kerem Gökten's *Turkey's Labour Markets Under Neoliberalism: An Overview*. Through a rigorous analysis of the main indicators of labour markets such as wages, unemployment, labour force participation, women and youth, informality, dynamics of sectoral transformation, Gökten reveals the general condition of labour in Turkey. The chapter also examines the main pillars of the labour policies implemented by the governments and the main dynamics of transformation in labour relations, as well as recent agendas of further restructuring in the late AKP era. Thus, this chapter provides a critical framework for the political economy of labour market restructuring since the 1980s to the AKP period.

In the next chapter, *Commodification and Changing Labour in Turkey: The Working Class in the Public Sector*, Koray Yılmaz focuses on the transformation of labour in the public sector. He emphasises the importance of the concept of 'commodification' to understand neoliberal transformation. The main argument of the chapter is that these commodification tendencies invigorated a structural transformation in the characteristics of public labour and that this transformation in Turkey has been accelerating ever since the 1980s. The chapter first focuses on the commodification process and structural transformation of Turkish public labour at a conceptual level, drawing upon Marx and his *Capital*. The chapter then continues with a look at the historical background and the practices related to this transformation process within this conceptual framework. The chapter concludes with the impact of the recent political and economic developments (such as the state of emergency and crisis) on the transformation of the public labour.

Sebiha Kablay's *Neoliberal Transformation of Turkey's Health Sector and Its Effects on the Health Labour Force* focuses on neoliberal transformation in the health sector as part of a wider restructuring in public employment and health policies. She argues that healthcare is one of the most significant fields in which attempts have been made to activate market mechanisms in neoliberal Turkey. In addition, the systematic changes in public labourers' working regime started first in the public healthcare sector. The chapter starts with the development of neoliberal health policies in Turkey, and then continues to the discussion of changing employment models and various aspects related to the conditions of the health labour force, based on the data obtained from various field researches, including that of the author. As the outbreak of the Covid-19 pandemic has significant effects on the healthcare workers, Kablay briefly documents its impact on Turkey's healthcare workers with a postscript and argues that the existing problems of the healthcare workers has worsened with the pandemic.

The second section of this part (Gender, Migration and Rural Aspects of Neoliberal Restructuring) starts with Demet Özmen Yılmaz's chapter titled *Between Neoliberalism and Conservatism: Recent Developments and New Agendas in Female Labour Policies in Turkey.* Özmen-Yılmaz focuses on gender and female labour policies in late Turkey mainly under the AKP governments from the perspective of paid and unpaid labour. Following a presentation of the general condition of female labour in Turkey, the chapter addresses recent labour policies in three sections: (1) flexible employment and informality, (2) demographic opportunity and protection of family, and (3) poverty and social policies. She argues that the dominant patriarchal structure and the gender-based division of labour in Turkey cause lower female participation in the labour force and employment. In relation to this dominant structure and conservative agendas of the AKP, women are considered to be responsible for housework and care.

In Chapter 6, Coşku Çelik's *The Making of the Rural Proletariat in Neoliberal Turkey* analyses the formation of the rural proletariat in neoliberal Turkey through proletarianisation of small-scale agricultural producers, feminisation of agricultural labour, and reproduction of ethnic structure of the country in the rural labour markets. The chapter theoretically draws upon Marxist approaches to agrarian change under neoliberalism. Çelik argues that neoliberalisation in the countryside is marked by the 2001 crisis and the subsequent AKP rule and led to impoverishment, dispossession and therefore proletarianisation of small-scale agricultural producers. Although this led to migration to big cities for wage work, she argues that neoliberal transformation in the countryside of Turkey does not merely indicate de-agrarianisation. The main transformation has been the elimination of the smallholder-based agrarian structure, and increasing dominance of agribusiness firms. She highlights that the composition of rural labour is characterised by sexual division of labour and ethnic discrimination (i.e. Kurdish and Syrian) which, alongside extractivism, have important impacts in terms of the reproduction of the AKP's hegemony and lack of resistance to it.

This part of the book ends with Ertan Erol's *Burden or a Saviour in the Time of Economic Crisis? AKP's 'Open-Door Migration Policy' and Its Impact on Labour Market Restructuring in Turkey.* Erol analyses the AKP's controversial 'open-door' migration policy and its meaning for the capitalist relations of production in Turkey. He argues that the integration of migrants (mostly Syrian) into the country had a 'positive' effect in alleviating and holding off the inevitable disruption of the AKP's growth model, which, among other things, relies on cheap labour for competitiveness. He further argues that Turkey's open-door policy should not be seen as an ideological choice or a rupture from previous policies, but a perfect fit in the existing accumulation model and a quick – but critical and temporal – fix to the deepening economic crisis. Without this perspective, he argues that it is not possible to understand fully why the AKP government cannot give up on the open-door migration policy even though it generates substantial electoral opposition and discontent.

Part II of the book is entitled *Containment*; that is, specific strategies and mechanisms that aim to manage and contain contradictions stemming from labour market restructuring. In this regard, one of the most important techniques of the AKP governments has been implementing a 'neoliberal social policy regime'. In this context, Denizcan Kutlu's chapter *Social Assistance as a Non-Wage Income for the Poor in Turkey: Work and Subsistence Patterns of Social Assistance Recipient Households* sheds light on this phenomenon in Turkey, based on the field research he conducted in Ankara. Kutlu discusses social assistance recipient households and social assistance as a policy tool in labour market structure and policies. He locates labour market, wages and cash needs of the household at the centre of the analysis. Thus, the author assesses the formation of the new poverty as part of the relations among labour market, wages and cash with both qualitative and quantitative data.

One of the most important impacts of the neoliberal labour restructuring has been the global rise of precarity. In Chapter 9, *A View of Precarisation from Turkey: Urban-Rural Dynamics and Intergenerational Precarity*, Elif Hacısalihoğlu examines the precarity experiences of the working class in the context of Turkey. She argues that the concept has remained Western-oriented so far and the unique and immanent features of late capitalist countries are eschewed. Then she discusses the extensive fieldwork she conducted and reveals that urban-rural dynamics and intergenerationality are defining characteristics of precarity amongst the working class in Turkey. As such, the intergenerational transmission of precarity on the one hand has an impact on the life cycles of the new generations, and on the other it functions as an adaptation strategy in the context of the transmitted experience. Also, the lack of formal and secure labour relations of precarious workers make them more dependent on employers, serving as a containment mechanism.

In the following chapter, one of the most salient characteristics of the labour regime under the AKP governments is discussed by an experienced labour lawyer, Murat Özveri. In his chapter, *When the Law Is Not Enough: 'Work Accidents', Profit Maximisation and the Unwritten Rules of Workers' Health and Safety in New Turkey*, Özveri draws upon Engels' concept of 'social murder', and prefers the concept of 'work murder' to the term 'work accident'. Through his detailed analysis of the legal framework and its practical implementations (i.e. court cases) in the context of 'work murders' and occupational diseases, he reveals that under neoliberal conditions which prioritise profit maximisation, legal principles and framework are ignored by the authorities and capitalists. Long judicial processes and 'unwritten rules' are also crucial in terms of subordinating workers' health and safety to capital accumulation imperatives. Finally, against this background, the chapter analyses the political economy of the major Soma Coal Mine Disaster.

The last chapter in this part is Yeliz Sarıöz Gökten's fresh analysis of the impact of the Covid-19 pandemic on Turkey's political economy, and specifically the working class. In *Are We All in the Same Boat? Covid-19 and the Working Class in Turkey*, Gökten first analyses the condition of global political economy under the pandemic. She then argues that, despite claims that Covid-19 is class-blind, the pandemic has different implications for different classes. As the existing inequalities made sure, the working class is negatively affected globally. In the Turkish case, the state and capitalists assessed the situation as an opportunity, and various disciplining and control mechanisms are already being implemented, with the health of workers again subordinated to the capital accumulation and crisis-resolution processes. Hence, the pandemic has made the condition of the working class in Turkey worse.

The third and last part of the book focuses on *Resistance*; that is, different cases of labour struggles against the neoliberal restructuring of labour. The first chapter in this part is Berna Güler and Erhan Acar's *Reconsidering Workers' Self-Management in Turkey: From Resistance to Workers' Self-Management Possibilities/Constraints*. Their chapter first introduces the conceptual framework and the meaning of workers' self-management. With historical references and the impact of broader resistances such as Gezi, the chapter discusses a recent prominent factory occupation: the case of Kazova Textile Corporation Workers' Self-Management. The authors analyse the case based on qualitative data obtained through a number of semi-structured in-depth interviews. The chapter concludes with some remarks on the differences and similarities with earlier workers' self-management practices in Turkey, constraints (i.e. limits to solidarity) and future possibilities both in this case and for workers' self-management in Turkey more broadly.

In the last chapter of the book, *Organised Workers' Struggles Under Neoliberalism: Unions, Capital and the State in Turkey*, Çağatay Edgücan Şahin focuses primarily on organised labour struggles within a broader political-economic context. He starts with an overview of union movement and the material condition of the working class in neoliberal Turkey. The chapter points out that there are macro-level dynamics which directly affect the trade union movement in Turkey such as union-political party relationships, employers' union busting strategies and government's strategy of postponement of strikes with the aim of achieving deunionisation. Hence, the chapter analyses the relationships between the state and the unions, capital and the unions and finally the working class and the unions mostly based on major worker movements and actions in the neoliberal era.

Conventional (and partly critical) approaches to Turkey's political economy generally focus on popular dichotomies of democracy and authoritarianism, secularism and Islamism, and state and market. As demonstrated in the structure of the book, however, this volume offers a very different perspective. It has a direct and comprehensive focus on the 'condition of the working class' in Turkey in the last four decades of neoliberalism; from the military dictatorship of the 1980s to the AKP years. It centralises and prioritises the category of labour and class struggle. In this context, the contributors to this volume offer a wide array of subjects pertinent to the 'condition of labour' in Turkey; from gender dynamics to refugee workers, from agrarian labour relations to workers' health and safety, from the politics of labour restructuring to factory occupations, and from precarity to organised labour. This breadth of coverage and rigorous empirical analysis are provided by researchers whose work has long focused on the issue of labour in Turkey. Within this framework and beyond the popular dichotomies, this book enables a full grasp of the political economy of Turkey; a rising regional capitalist power, and a country consistently listed in the ten worst countries in the world for working people.

BIBLIOGRAPHY

Akçay, Ü. (2018) 'Neoliberal Populism in Turkey and Its Crisis', Working Paper No. 100/2018, Institute for International Political Economy Berlin, www.econstor.eu/bitstream/10419/175884/1/1015691811.pdf (accessed July 2020).

Burnham, P., Lutz, K.G., Grant, W. and Layton-Henry, Z. (2008) *Research Methods in Politics*, 2nd edn, London: Red Globe Press.

Engels, F. (2008) [1845] *The Condition of the Working-Class in England in 1844*, trans. F. Kelley-Wischnewetzky, New York: Cosimo Classics.

Erol, M.E. (2019) 'State and Labour under AKP Rule in Turkey: An Appraisal', *Journal of Balkan and Near Eastern Studies*, 21 (6), 663–77.

Hurriyet Daily News (2014) 'Turkish PM Cites 19th Century Britain to Prove Mine Accidents are "Typical"', www.hurriyetdailynews.com/turkish-pm-cites-19th-century-britain-to-prove-mine-accidents-are-typical-66472 (accessed July 2020).

Madra, Y. and Yılmaz, S. (2019) 'Turkey's Decline into (Civil) War Economy: From Neoliberal Populism to Corporate Nationalism', *South Atlantic Quarterly*, 118 (1), 41–59.

Pitel, L. (2020) 'Turkey's Logistic Providers Adjust to the Strains of Covid-19', *Financial Times*, Special Report: Coronavirus and Logistic', www.ft.com/content/24db45c0-9393-11ea-899a-f62a20d54625 (accessed August 2020).

Tansel, C.B. (2018) 'Authoritarian Neoliberalism and Democratic Backsliding in Turkey: Beyond the Narratives of Progress', *South European Society and Politics*, 23 (2), 197–217.

Yalman, G. (2009) *Transition to Neoliberalism: The Case of Turkey in the 1980s*, İstanbul: İstanbul Bilgi University Press.

PART I

Restructuring

*Neoliberal Restructuring of Labour and the State:
From Military Dictatorship to the AKP Era*

1

Not-So-Strange Bedfellows: Neoliberalism and the AKP in Turkey

Mehmet Erman Erol

1.1 INTRODUCTION

The neoliberal transformation of Turkey began with the military coup in 1980 and has continued uninterrupted since then. It was uninterrupted in the sense that it reflected the broader policy preferences of state managers; however, it also faced frequent and significant impediments and instabilities. Following a major economic crisis in 2001, political Islamist AKP has been the agent of neoliberalism in Turkey. Enjoying 'strong' majority governments since 2002, the AKP played a significant role in restructuring of the state and economy; and achieved the implementation of unaccomplished parts of neoliberal reforms such as massive privatisations, flexibilising the labour market, restructuring of social security and the health system, and imposition of market imperatives in general. This process, however, was not without problems and, especially with the outbreak of the global financial crisis of 2008, the AKP's neoliberal path became crisis-ridden; marked by various domestic and external crises and ever-growing Islamist and authoritarian practices.

This chapter locates the rise of political Islam in general, and the AKP in particular, within the neoliberal transformation of Turkey since the 1980s. The chapter starts with making sense of the meaning of neoliberal state and economy, both theoretically and historically. Then Turkey's encounter and experience with neoliberalism in the 1980s is dealt with. Following this, the crisis-ridden 1990s is discussed in terms of financial and political turmoils; ending up with the major 2001 crisis, and the 2002 elections which the AKP won by a landslide. The AKP era is periodised as 2002–07 (the first term, the so-called 'golden age') and post-2007 (crises and intensified authoritarianism). The overall argument of the chapter is that neoliberalism is most significantly a (political) project that aimed to curb the power of labour; and Turkey's transition to neoliberalism reflects this ambition. AKP governments, in that sense, represent a direct continuity as far as management of labour power is considered. However, the chapter takes the AKP's peculiarities and contradictions into account as well, in the context of unprecedented authoritarianism and Islamist politics.

1.2 MAKING SENSE OF NEOLIBERALISM: FREE ECONOMY AND STRONG (AUTHORITARIAN) STATE

It would not be an overstatement to argue that the global political economy has been governed within the parameters of a neoliberal framework in the last four decades. Despite legitimacy problems arising from the 2008 global financial crisis,[1] neoliberalism survived and 'in some respects strenghten[ed] as a response to that crisis' (Kiely, 2017: 725). This chapter conceives neoliberalism as a form of political economy or a particular organisation of capitalism (Saad-Filho and Johnston, 2005: 3) that entails a 'free economy' and a 'strong state' simultaneously (see Gamble, 1994; Bonefeld, 2017a). The reason why this couplet came to the fore should be understood in the context of politicised social relations (i.e. intensified class struggle) and the crisis of Keynesian/developmentalist political economy in the 1970s in both the Global North and the Global South.

As Bonefeld (2017b: 754) explains, 'during the 1970s, neoliberal interpretation of the then crisis of capitalist accumulation focused either explicitly or implicitly on the crisis of state authority'. Hence, to achieve the aims of the neoliberal paradigm, i.e. removing barriers to capitalist accumulation and curbing the power of labour for a 'free economy', restoring state authority via the 'strong state' was of vital importance. The crisis of the 1970s manifested itself in the form of escalating inflation, rising real wages, slowing of the pace of global capitalist accumulation, and difficulty of financing the ever growing government budget deficits (Clarke, 2005: 58). However, the crisis, by the neoliberals, was conceived of as not a crisis of 'economy' per se; it was in fact the crisis of 'political' economy. It was argued that at the heart of the crisis were the 'economic consequences of democracy' and a 'weak state' (crisis of 'governability') that was surrendered to the special interests (i.e. trade unions) and mass democratic demands for welfare, full employment and employment protection (Bonefeld, 2017b). In such a situation, social relations were politicised, as well as economic management. Strong trade unions, excess of (social) democracy, accompanied by a 'weak state' were seen to be the main reasons of the crisis and also the main impediments to achieving *free economy*.

Hence, as Andrew Gamble (1994: 40) points out, the strong state was needed 'firstly to unwind the coils of social democracy and welfarism that had fastened around the free economy; secondly to police the market order; thirdly to make the economy more productive; and fourthly to uphold social and political authority'. For the state to be strong enough to materalise such objectives, neoliberal thinkers such as Hayek and Friedman believed that the economy should have been freed from political interference, and the economic relations should have been depoliticised such that the market could self-regulate (Macartney, 2013). As David Harvey describes, 'neoliberal theorists are … profoundly suspicious of democracy' (2005: 66). Thus, the 'democratic overload' on the state should have been removed via depoliticisation (i.e. insulating key institutions such as the central bank from democratic pressures). Hence the argument over the 'separation of politics and economics', or the attempts to separate the 'economy and state into distinct forms of social organisation' (Bonefeld, 2017b).

As such, active public economic policy and strong trade unions were to be avoided as their intervention would create perverse (i.e. inflationary) consequences (Macartney, 2013). In that sense, by constantly attempting to insulate policy-making processes from the trade unions and other democratic pressures, it could be well argued that neoliberalism is an *authoritarian form of governance*. As Bruff (2014) notes, authoritarianism is not solely the exercise of brute coercive force: it 'can also be observed in the reconfiguring of state and institutional power in an attempt to insulate certain policies and institutional practices from social and political dissent'. This does not mean that 'coercion' or 'use of force' would not be practised. It 'is justified when it is employed to defeat and contain those interests, organisations and individuals that threaten the survival of the free economy, either by flouting its rules or resisting the outcomes that flow from market exchanges' (Gamble, 1994: 39).

Neoliberalism is commonly associated with 'globalisation', such that the term 'neoliberal globalisation' is frequently used. Indeed, the globalisation of economic and financial relations give the capitalist states a very strong justification for implementing the neoliberal policies. Faced with the competition to attract capital to their territories or to be competitive in the world market, states particularly targeted labour markets and attempted to make them flexible and competitive (Harvey, 2005). Also, this process led to the transformation of the 'welfare state' into a 'workfare' state. In the neoliberal globalisation era, therefore, the result of such a shift has been curbing and dismantling various social expenditures in the context of greater fiscal discipline and austerity (Rogers, 2014: 66).

These developments, i.e. less visible involvement of the state in some areas, privatisation, dissolution of the welfare state, increased significance of global markets, led some accounts in International Political Economy (IPE) to argue that the state lost its autonomy and surrendered to market forces. However, this view is too simplistic. As Bonefeld outlines, 'the depoliticization of the economy, the curtailment of trade union power, the transformation of the welfare state into a workfare state, and the liberalization of the economy, creating, maintaining and sustaining free economy, are all a matter of a *practice of government*' (2017b: 755, my emphasis). Furthermore, this means these processes are reflections of a political project; and amount to a 'strong, authoritarian state'. This is the essence of neoliberalism.

Without doubt, there would be variations in neoliberal policies 'from place to place as well as over time' (Harvey, 2005: 70). However, wherever implemented, neoliberalism essentially focused on the 'question of labour' for a free economy and 'restoration of (capitalist) class power' (Harvey, 2005: 70), and establishing a 'strong state' to sustain this free economy and the domination of capital over labour.

Turkey's experience with neoliberalism since the 1980s reflects these tendencies well.

1.3 TURKEY'S EXPERIENCE WITH NEOLIBERALISM UNTIL THE AKP PERIOD

1.3.1 Military Dictatorship and ANAP Governments: 1980–91

Against the background of the crisis-ridden political economy of Turkey between the 1977 and 1980 period, which was marked by the crisis of Import Substitution Industrialisation (ISI), intensified class struggle and political instability, the Turkish Army staged a coup on 12 September 1980. It is important to note hereby the explicit and implicit calls and pressures of the Turkish bourgeoisie for authoritarian solutions before the coup. The military junta's first concern was 'restoring law and order, and state authority'. This entailed the 'strong state as a guarantor of economic individualism' (Aydin, 2005: 54) as well as the 'free economy' of neoliberalism, instead of the collective demands of organised labour. Hence, state-economy and/or state-society relations needed to be restructured through a new legal, political and economic framework, which was in sharp contrast to the pre-1980 economic and politico-legal structure.

The military dictatorship, which lasted until 1983, had certain political and economic objectives. Economically, the International Monetary Fund (IMF) and World Bank (WB)-backed 24 January 1980 stabilisation programme[2] would be implemented immediately, as Turkish capitalism was suffering from foreign currency constraints, external debt, balance of payment problems, high inflation and a shortage of crucial commodities. The stability programme consisted of a devaluation of Turkish lira, removal of price controls, trade liberalisation, removal of restrictions on imports and encouragement of exports (Duman, 2014: 81). Although there was no direct reference to labour-related issues, the aim was to change the way Turkey integrated with the world market, from ISI to an export-oriented strategy based on competitiveness, which would necessitate the disciplining of labour and dramatic wage reductions (Duman, 2014: 81).

In order to achieve the objectives of this anti-labour neoliberal economic orientation, the military aimed 'to put an end to class-based politics' (Yalman, 2009). Under the military dictatorship, all trade union activity was banned. The labour front was completely excluded from any policy-making process. This amounted to an authoritarian trade union policy and an authoritarian neoliberal restructuring of the state. In this context, the 1982 Constitution was quite functional. In line with its general anti-democratic character, the Constitution 'institutionalized measures intended to de-politicize, de-mobilize, de-radicalize, and de-unionize society' (Marois, 2012: 102). The right to strike was curtailed and could only take place under carefully defined circumstances. Hence, the military regime 'ensured through the authoritarian 1982 constitution that the working class would not challenge capital in the foreseeable future' (Aydın, 2005: 53). In the following year, the new labour legislation furthered restrictions on unionisation and labour movement (see Chapter 13).

As far as authoritarian neoliberal restructuring of the state and policy-making is concerned, there has been a shift within the branches of the state. Following the new constitution, the executive power was strengthened at the expense of legislature, and power had been centralised within the executive (Öniş and Webb, 1992). The right-wing ANAP governments between 1983 and 1991 continued these authoritarian political and economic orientations of the military dictatorship. However, it lost power in the 1991 elections. Nevertheless, this defeat 'did not mean ... the demise of the pro-structural adjustment or the pro-liberalisation coalition. The long period of ANAP rule helped consolidate reforms to such a degree that all the principal parties agreed on a broadly similar economic program' (Öniş and Webb, 1992: 48), namely *neoliberalism*. There would be significant economic and political instabilities in the 1990s, however, which would make it 'a lost decade'.

1.3.2 Crisis-Ridden Neoliberalism: The Long 1990s and the 2001 Crisis

Although the neoliberal economic policies brought some stability mainly thanks to the disciplined labour power and massive external support through the 'credibility' of the regime, this process brought its own contradictions. Indeed, from 1987 onwards, the labour movement and unions revitalised, partly due to the limited transition to 'democracy', and challenged the anti-labour stance of the ANAP government. Hence, towards the end of the decade, distributional pressures made themselves felt again, growth was declined, and other economic indicators worsened (see Chapter 2).

Under these conditions, the main macroeconomic policy response of the ANAP government was complete deregulation of financial markets and capital account liberalisation in 1989 (Aydın, 2005). The expectation was to attract short-term capital inflows to restore economic growth and finance the deficits. However, this move made the Turkish political economy once again crisis-prone led by a financial and speculative capital accumulation regime, which marked the 1990s. In this context, the increasing fiscal and current account deficits, the shaky nature of the political environment, and the deterioration of external and internal debt stocks ended up with a massive capital outflow in April 1994 (Aydın, 2005). The 5 April 1994 IMF-backed orthodox stabilisation measures attempted to impose discipline on the economy, but remained limited against the background of labour unrest and political legitimacy issues, as well as favourable world market conditions which pave the way for achieving 'easy growth'. Nevertheless, the privatisation process slightly gained momentum and the gains made by labour since the late 1980s in wage terms were reversed post-crisis.

Politics as well became crisis-ridden in the 1990s. In contrast to the 1980–91 era, which was characterised by 'strong neoliberal governments', the 1991–2002 period was characterised by 'weak' coalition politics. This period also saw the radical rise of political Islam. The military was concerned with the rise of radical Islamism – they rather preferred the 'moderate' Islamism in the 1980s against the socialist left. The Kurdish question came to the fore as well, manifesting itself in the armed struggle between the PKK (Kurdistan Workers' Party) and the military. These processes led to the 'securitisation of politics' through the increased role played by the army (Akça, 2014).

The rise of the Islamist movement was mostly a result of the post-1980 political economy of Turkey. Neoliberal policies since the 1980s had increased inequalities in society; and the working class and urban poor were affected negatively. The social democratic left, which was the coalition partner from 1991 to 1995, could not represent the interests of the working class. The socialist left was not able to function in the same manner since it was destroyed by the military in the early 1980s. Hence, the Islamist Welfare Party's (WP) discourse which was named 'Just Order' (*Adil Ekonomik Düzen*) implied a stance against neoliberalism, 'garnering the political support of the growing informal proletariat' (Yörük, 2014: 239).

The Islamist movement was also supported by the so-called Islamic bourgeoisie which flourished in the post-1980 era through the export-oriented growth strategy, based in Anatolia. The organisational manifestation of this 'fraction of capital' was the establishment of MÜSİAD (Independent Industrialists and Businessmen Association) in 1990. The rise of the MÜSİAD, and the Islamist movement and WP, however, alarmed the Turkish army and TÜSİAD (Turkish Industry and Business Association) in particular. In the National Security Council meeting of 28 February 1997, the military declared that some measures should be taken by the WP-DYP (centre right True Path Party) coalition against radical Islam. Following this 'postmodern coup', the Islamist PM Erbakan resigned.

The new coalition government focused on economic woes, as following a brief recovery post-1994, the economy was on shaky grounds again; against the backdrop of decreased capital inflows and declined growth as well as chronic high inflation and increased public debt. Hence, the government approached the IMF for a three-year standby agreement, covering the period 2000–02. The aim was to reduce inflation through tight fiscal and monetary policy. Despite its initial success, the programme soon led to serious economic imbalances, combined with the political problems. This process resulted in November 2000–February 2001 crises.

The February 2001 crisis led to serious discontent among the disadvantaged segments of society, and political legitimacy issues came to the fore. However, on the other hand, 'the 2001 financial crisis acted as a catalyst for further neoliberal reforms' (Dufour and Orhangazi, 2009: 117). In this context, a major IMF-backed restructuring programme was launched in the aftermath of the crisis, under the guidance of Kemal Derviş, who was brought from the WB to serve as a technocrat minister of economy. Derviş was a firm believer of neo-liberalism and the so-called 'second wave of reforms' (i.e. 'regulatory neoliberalism'). He sustained the discourse of 'separation of politics and markets'. With this aim, the 2001 reforms depoliticised monetary policy by ceding operational independence to the CBRT with the aim of inflation targeting. The depoliticisation of policy-making was also extended to other areas through Independent Regulatory Agencies (IRAs).

The implementation of the restructuring programme, however, did not resolve the general discontent of the masses. In the early general elections of November 2002, all coalition partners were punished at the ballot box. The AKP, on the other hand, had a cautious but critical discourse on the state of affairs and aimed to reassure capital and labour. Hence, it was able to win the elections which provided the first majority government since 1991, and was seen as an opportunity to facilitate the imposition of further neoliberal reforms.

1.4 AKP TAKES OVER NEOLIBERAL RESTRUCTURING

1.4.1 AKP's First Term and the 'Golden Age' of Neoliberalism, 2002–07

When it won a decisive victory in the 2002 elections, the AKP was only a one-year old political party. Its establishment was mostly a result of the clashes between the 'reformist' and 'radical' wings that the '28 February process' created within the political Islamist movement in Turkey. Failing to win the leadership within the Islamist movement, the reformist wing then established the AKP in August 2001, under the leadership of Erdoğan. The AKP defined itself as 'conservative democrat', in order to emphasise its 'break' from the Islamist National Outlook movement (Akça, 2014: 29).

AKP's pragmatic discourse amounted to a full-hearted embrace-ment of neoliberalism with some populist characteristics. The party read political and economic developments both domestically and globally well and in the absence of a leftist popular alternative, it 'suc-cessfully targeted the excluded peoples in Turkish society' (Marois, 2012: 177), while assuring both domestic and international capital circles that it did not envisage any radical break with neoliberalism. Thus, 'unlike the *National Outlook* parties, the AKP was ready to engage itself with the neoliberal rules, which ... brought the party a wider appeal than the religio-conservative electoral support would have provided' (Coşar, 2012: 82).

Despite paying lip service to popular demands in terms of softening the IMF programme, the first AKP government had a clear preference for continuing with the IMF and it 'tied its hands' under the pre-existing IMF conditionality for further neoliberal restructuring (Uğur, 2008). Furthermore, it renewed the IMF standby agreement in 2005, which lasted until 2008. Within this framework, the first AKP government's economic policy consisted of a tight fiscal policy, inflation targeting via an 'independent' central bank; high interest rates for the sustainability of foreign capital flows, and an export-led growth strategy (see Bekmen, 2014: 60). During its first term, the AKP remained loyal to this framework in general; despite some 'micro' deviations and favouring of close (Islamist) business groups at times (Boratav, 2009).

Another external anchor, the European Union (EU), also played a significant role in pursuing the government's restructuring agenda in this term. Alongside its political conditionality, the EU also became an 'economic anchor' in the post-2001 crisis period through the Copenhagen economic criteria (Öniş and Bakır, 2007), thus intensifying the deepening of the restructuring process. Moreover, the approach of the EU to the post-2001 economic reforms, and the references to economic reforms in progress reports were always within the framework of the IMF programme (Sönmez, 2007). As such, the widespread support for EU membership within Turkish society in the early 2000s worked as a legitimisation mechanism for the neoliberal reforms imposed as part of the EU conditionality.

Within this broader economic policy framework, and relying on the 'strong majority government' and political legitimacy, the AKP government started to deal with the more unaccomplished areas of neoliberalism in Turkey, such as privatisation and labour market flexibilisation. The AKP had an aggressive privatisation policy. This was due to both the party's committment to neoliberalism, the party's political bargaining with sceptical capital groups (the so-called big bourgeoisie or TÜSİAD), as well as the IMF conditionality. Against this background, the AKP resolved the legal, administrative and bureaucratic stalemate in the area of privatisation. As a result, privatisation revenues increased to over US$ 20 billion in only three years following 2004 – double the amount of revenues between 1985 and 2002.

Another important area of neoliberal restructuring during the AKP's first term in office was the flexibilisation and re-regulation of labour markets. The objective of this policy was to increase competitiveness and productivity of the labour power. Significant in this context was Law No. 4857, enacted in May 2003, which introduced new forms of control on labour power, re-regulated the conditions of work, and facilitated flexibility and new types of contract. This restructuring further paved the way for precarity, insecurity and deunionisation in the labour market, and an increase in the rate of exploitation.

The AKP kept the post-1980 authoritarian neoliberal union policy and legal framework intact during this term, despite its ostensible discourse on the 'democratisation' of state-society relations. Hence, the union density further decreased. This was due to privatisation, increase of precarious employment, informality, subcontracting, the repressive legal and political context, and union-busting strategies of employers (Çelik, 2015). Reflecting the authoritarian neoliberal management of labour in this period, the AKP government did not hesitate to use its legal powers to ban strikes; thus between 2002 and 2006, five important strikes were banned on the grounds of 'national security' and 'public health' (Çelik, 2015).

Despite this assault on labour and further neoliberal reforms to the detriment of workers, as well as stagnant wages and persistent double-digit unemployment, the AKP enjoyed significant support from the working class. Apart from the promotion of 'identity-based politics' at the ideological level, two socio-economic containment mechanisms helped in securing the legitimacy and popularity of the AKP during this period. These mechanisms are the so-called 'financial inclusion'; that is, the financialisation of everyday life and rising indebtedness of workers as a compensation mechanism for the deteriorating living standards; and 'neoliberal social policy regime' which consisted of social assistance based on local municipalities, faith-based charitable organisations and public poverty reduction programmes (Özden, 2014). That is why some accounts decribe the political economy of the AKP as 'neoliberal populism' (Akçay, 2018) to draw attention to the co-existence of neoliberal accumulation and containment strategies.

Apart from these mechanisms, the global economic conditions and the overall crisis-free atmosphere helped the AKP government to increase its popularity among the electorate. Chronic high inflation was taken under control through the new 'inflation targeting' system, and the new depoliticised monetary policy increased AKP's room for manoeuvre vis-à-vis the various demands from capital and labour. Concomitantly, the availability of cheap money and the relatively high interest rates Turkey offered, as well as the IMF-EU anchors helped sustain capital inflows in the form of both short-term 'hot money' and foreign direct investment (FDI). These processes also increased the AKP's bargaining power with the big bourgeoisie as the 'strong majority' government achieved most of its demands. As a result, as the party's popularity increased and it gained the trust of domestic capital and international financial capital, the opposition of the 'old establishment' (such as the Turkish military) was gradually marginalised.

The accounts which assess the AKP's first term as a 'golden age' associate this period with a process of democratisation and reforming of the infamous anti-democratic 'state tradition' in Turkey (see Keyman and Öniş, 2007). However, this argument is maintained 'through the denial of class reality' (Yalman, 2012). The so-called 'democratisation via Europeanisation process' in the first term of the AKP was very selective and limited, and focused on the areas which would improve the AKP's legitimacy and bargaining power vis-à-vis the old establishment (such as civil-military relations and some identity-based demands).

As discussed, the AKP took over the authoritarian management of labour power and deepened the process of 'putting an end to class-based politics' (Yalman, 2009), which was the defining character of neoliberalism in Turkey since the 1980s. Furthermore, the AKP's statecraft in its first term mostly relied on technocratic and depoliticised governance (i.e. insulated from democratic processes) which is an authoritarian tendency in itself (Erol, 2019). However, as mentioned above, the sustained high growth rates, crisis-free atmosphere, neoliberal containment strategies, favourable global conditions and the support of international as well as domestic actors helped the AKP to win another victory in the 2007 general elections, with almost 47 per cent of the votes, forming another majority government.

1.4.2 Neoliberalism, Crises, Explicit Authoritarianism: Political Economy of Post-2007 AKP

The period which started after the 2007 general elections was not as easy for the AKP government as it was for the 2002–07 era. The post-2007 period brought about contradictions in neoliberal governance, political confrontation and crises. The AKP government increasingly relied on more coercive forms of governing, and increased the tone of Islamism against the background of social discontent and crises. In this context, as debated by various authors, there seems to be a gradual shift from 'authoritarian statism' to an 'exceptional state form' – in the Poulantzian sense – especially in the third third term of the AKP, from 2011 onwards (Oğuz, 2016; Kaygusuz, 2018).

Concomitantly, the depoliticised and rather rule-based governing strategy which marked the first AKP government to a great extent gradually shifted to a more politicised/centralised (discretionary) governing strategy (Erol, 2016). As such, the role of the executive further increased in decision-making processes; hence insulation from democratic pressures took a more politicised form, but still kept its authoritarian tendency. The more politicised and discretionary governance brought some contradictions and discontent in state-capital relations as well, as big business fractions such as TÜSİAD repeatedly expressed their concerns over the Public Procurement Law, fiscal rule debate, IMF and EU anchors, and overall influence of the government on the 'independent' regulatory institutions as well as the attacks on the 'independent' central bank (Dönmez and Zemandl, 2019).

I further argue that, faced with a military memorandum in 2007, a party closure case in 2008, and also the effects of the global crisis which put the AKP in a politically precarious position; the party attempted to consolidate its power and confronted the 'old secularist establishment' within the state. These developments increased the contradictions in the AKP's management of capitalist social relations, and led to further crises in AKP's third term. Hence, the significant events that marked the character of *neoliberal authoritarianism* post-2007 in Turkey were the 2008 global financial crisis, 2008 party closure case against the AKP, operations against the military, 2010 constitutional referendum, 2013 Gezi Uprising, 2014 presidential election, two general elections in 2015, 2016 military coup attempt and the following state of emergency regime which ended up with a political *regime change* and Erdoğan's consolidation of his 'one-man rule'.

1.4.3 Global Financial Crisis and Further Neoliberal Restructuring

The 2008 global financial crisis had a direct impact on the Turkish economy. The crisis manifested itself in the declined financial capital inflows and FDI, economic contraction, decline in production and exports, and increased unemployment (Marois, 2012). The AKP government's response was fiscal loosening, increasing liquidity and introducing some stimulus measures. Also, the government sustained negotiations with the IMF until 2010, in order to enhance the credibility of economic policy-making and therefore used the IMF as a quasi-anchor in this process (Öniş and Güven, 2011).

Another important response of the AKP government to the crisis was pertinent to labour market restructuring. The AKP government attempted to further the flexibilisation process in the labour market, as a 'solution' to rising unemployment (Çelik, 2015). New regulations enabled employers to hire and fire workers more easily, and also made them exempt from some contributions and taxes in terms of hiring workers. The National Employment Strategy (NES) was brought to the agenda, as well as the 'private employment agency' regulation, which meant the crisis led the government to have a more systematic approach to flexibilisation and introduce more capital-friendly measures in order to increase competitiveness. Furthermore, real wage decline and increased labour productivity played an important role in the recovery from the crisis.

Thanks to this restructuring and (neoliberal) state intervention, the economy showed signs of quick recovery starting from 2010. However, the most significant reason was perhaps the crisis-ridden world market. The monetary policy of the developed countries in the aftermath of the crisis facilitated the conditions for the 'emerging markets' to attract foreign capital. In particular, the Quantitative Easing (QE) policy of the US Federal Reserve made cheap money available and, combined with low growth and interest rates in advanced capitalisms, led to inflows of capital to 'developing' economies such as Turkey (Marois, 2012: 195). Thanks to this, economic growth reached record levels in 2010 and 2011 which helped the AKP government to win another landslide victory in the June 2011 general elections.

1.4.4 The Road to Gezi and Resistance to Neoliberal Authoritarianism

The authoritarian tendencies which gradually increased in AKP's second term became less concealable following the 2011 elections. With its majoritarian understanding of democracy, the AKP leadership and political Islamist movement set out to consolidate their power. In terms of policy-making, the centralisation of decision-making processes in the hands of the executive was strengthened. Concomitantly, in the aftermath of the 2008 crisis, the AKP government relied on the construction sector for boosting economic growth. In an attempt to restore growth, significant urban transformation projects were developed. This mechanism – through various amendments and deviations in 'regulatory reforms' and rule-based policy – has also facilitated and enhanced profit-making opportunities for pro-government and mostly 'Islamist' business circles. The authoritarian neoliberal policies of the AKP further combined with increased Islamist motivations, reaching significant levels by 2013. These included the restructuring of the education system, new union legislation which made organisation more difficult, an authoritarian stance towards Kurds and Alevis, Islamisation of everyday life, a 'neo-Ottomanist' foreign policy stance in the Middle East, increased control on the media, and increased police brutality and criminalisation of almost every oppositional movement.

Against this background, in June 2013, a spontaneous popular uprising emerged, which was initially against a decision to demolish Istanbul's Gezi Park as a part of a neoliberal urban development project. The protests rapidly became a country-wide wave of anti-AKP insurrection. Police violence and the unresponsive attitude of the Erdoğan government radicalised and politicised the wider population against the AKP's authoritarian neoliberal Islamist rule. The government assessed and presented these protests as a part of a 'global conspiracy' and an 'attempt of *coup d'état*', in an attempt to legitimise its repression of protesters. Thus, the 'neoliberal security state' practices were strengthened, and repression and authoritarianism increased further in the aftermath of the Gezi uprising (Kaygusuz, 2018), as the AKP was determined to prevent further uprisings in the future.

1.4.5 Clash of the Islamists and the 'Permanent State of Emergency'

In December 2013, another unprecedented political development unsettled the AKP government. A corruption probe (reflecting the intra-Islamist clash within the state between the Gülenists and the AKP) regarding Erdoğan, his bureaucrats, ministers and various close businessmen showed the extent of corrupt practices. The AKP government presented these developments as the continuation of the conspiracy that started with Gezi. This was used as another excuse to justify authoritarian practices. Simultaneously, the government's credibility in financial markets was shaken as Erdoğan's endless criticisms towards the central bank for not delivering lower interest rates for growth increased concerns over monetary policy, and combined with a crisis within the state, led to capital flight in early 2014.

However, against all these developments, Erdoğan benefited from the polarisation in society (which he aimed to create in any event), increased the tone of Islamism, and secured victory in the presidential election in August 2014. Following this, authoritarian and coercive practices gained further momentum, as the negotiation process with the Kurdish movement came to an end in early 2015, and a controversial 'Law on Internal Security' was introduced which gave enormous powers to the police and security forces (Kaygusuz, 2018: 14). However, rather surprisingly, the AKP lost its majority in the Parliament for the first time since 2002, in the June 2015 elections. This result shocked the AKP leadership, and following a short period of hesitation, President Erdoğan's 'me or chaos' strategy was put into practice. As peace negotiations came to an end with the PKK, and several ISIS attacks occured as a result of the state's ineffective struggle with the organisation, society and politics were paralysed with terror attacks and military operations (Kaygusuz, 2018). Hence, security became a common concern. Simultaneously, economic problems and instability came to the fore as well which raised concerns of the voters. In this context, as a government was not formed following the June elections, a 'repeat election' took place in November 2015. President Erdoğan's strategy proved to be successful and the AKP won the elections, forming a 'strong majority government', vital for 'neoliberal stability'.

This de facto state of emergency took a formal form following the unexpected coup attempt by the Gülenist faction within the army in July 2016. This development was a turning point in Turkey's political economy, as the measures and restructuring during the two years of the state of emergency (July 2016–July 2018) 'finalised the passage to an exceptional state form' (Kaygusuz, 2018). Under the state of emergency, and with the support of ultra-nationalist political parties (such as the Nationalist Movement Party – MHP, and Great Unity Party – BBP), a referendum took place in April 2017, which changed Turkey's political regime and introduced the presidential system with enormous centralised powers. Also, the AKP ruled by decree during these two years, and the decrees went beyond the causes of the coup attempt. These decrees worked as a disciplining mechanism to repress the dissident voices and movements. Strikes were banned, economic and political restructuring was carried out in a non-transparent and anti-democratic fashion. Although the formal state of emergency came to an end in the summer of 2018, Erdoğan's re-election as president in the June 2018 elections and the victory of the Islamo-nationalist AKP-MHP-BBP bloc (known as People's Alliance – Cumhur İttifakı) in Parliament meant that the 'state of emergency' became permanent with enormous powers at Erdoğan's disposal.

1.5 RETREAT FROM NEOLIBERALISM OR ISLAMO-NATIONALIST NEOLIBERALISM?

According to some accounts, these turmoils in the political sphere were complemented by the restructuring of Turkey's political economy which amounted to a retreat from neoliberalism. Particularly from the 'currency and debt crisis' of summer 2018 onward, Turkey's economy became crisis-ridden with a recession in 2019 and recurrent and frequent currency shocks, complemented with high inflation and unemployment. The AKP's erratic management of crises/economy, and more visible role of the state through further 'politicisation' of management of capitalist social relations (i.e. recently established Sovereign Wealth Fund, 'de facto' end of central bank independence, 'soft' capital controls, increased crony practices, ongoing regional military involvement, and warming to Russia-China axis of 'authoritarian capitalism') led to various conceptualisations such as 'state capitalism' (Öniş, 2019), neo-mercantilism (Erensü and Madra, 2020) and 'post-neoliberalism' (Akçay, 2020) to define this 'new' political economy of the AKP and its nationalist allies.

It is important to critically analyse the incoherent and inconsistent economic direction of Turkey's Islamo-nationalist ruling coalition in recent years. However, as Copley and Moraitis (2020) argued recently, it is not possible to declare paradigms such as neoliberalism dead when governments tilt to one side under the threat of capital outflows or other pressures. Even though the AKP's political economy became more ambigious, in the context of the ongoing insulation of economic management from popular-democratic pressures (a key neoliberal principle (Watkins, 2021)), extremely flexible and cheap labour markets, the pro-business stance of the AKP,[3] persistence of financialisation (Bedirhanoğlu, 2020), reluctance to implement full capital controls, ongoing free trade agreements and pro-privatisation and pro-marketisation logic, I find it difficult to argue that there has been a 'qualitative shift'. Hence, I find the above-mentioned conceptualisations rather hasty and contend that the defining parameters of neoliberalism remain broadly intact. Its crisis-ridden condition, however, creates ever-increasing legitimacy problems which the ruling coalition confronts with increased repression and attempts to consolidate the 'exceptional state form', which amounts to neoliberalism with Islamo-nationalist characteristics.

1.6 CONCLUSION

This chapter analysed Turkey's experience with neoliberalism, focusing particularly on the AKP period since 2002. I argued that neoliberalism came to the fore in the late 1970s, as a response to the crisis of global political economy, and against the background of rising class struggle and failed state-led political economy. As a result, the ruling classes contended that the economy had to be 'free' and the state had to be 'strong'. Turkey's transition to neoliberalism was in line with these developments and the state attemped to put an end to class-based politics (Yalman, 2009).

In the first decade of neoliberalism in Turkey, attempts were made to discipline labour both politically and economically. This authoritarian management of labour power was briefly challenged by the revitalised labour movement in the late 1980s and early 1990s. However, financial crises in the 1990s worked as a further disciplining mechanism, although they also amounted to legitimacy problems. Under these conditions, and against the backdrop of the failures of neoliberal policies, political Islam gained momentum in the 1990s, and further with the rise of the AKP in 2002 elections. I argued that the first AKP government (2002–07) imposed unprecedented neoliberal reforms while securing its legitimacy through a crisis-free atmosphere, support of the external anchors, and domestic and international capitalist circles. Most importantly, the financial inclusion mechanism and neoliberal social policy regime helped contain labour unrest. Authoritarian management of labour power, however, remained intact; and the depoliticised governing strategy meant that economic governance remained undemocratic.

The period which began with the 2007 elections was marked by various crises, however. Despite continuities in neoliberal authoritarianism, this period represented a 'rupture within continuity'. Against the backdrop of political crises and events like Gezi, as well as economic woes, authoritarianism, Islamism, 'securitisation of politics', violence, coercion, and instability gradually increased. This process ended up with a (de facto) 'permanent state of emergency' under a political regime resembling an 'exceptional state form'. Although this might seem to be in contradiction with neoliberalism, it is a direct result of neoliberalism which increasingly relies on coercion, as is seen elsewhere. As Slobodian (2018) argued, the neoliberal project's focus is 'to inoculate capitalism against the threat of democracy'. Hence, real democratisation could not be achieved without challenging neoliberalism, and that entails a labour-centred struggle.

BIBLIOGRAPHY

Akça, İ. (2014) 'Hegemonic Projects in Post-1980 Turkey and the Changing Forms of Authoritarianism', in Akça, İ., Bekmen A. and Özden, B.A. (eds), *Turkey Reframed: Constituting Neoliberal Hegemony*, London: Pluto Press, 13–46.

Akçay, Ü. (2018) 'Neoliberal Populism in Turkey and Its Crisis', *Institute for International Political Economy Berlin*, No. 100/2018. www.econstor.eu/bitstream/10419/175884/1/1015691811.pdf (accessed June 2020).

—— (2020) 'Erdoğan's One-Way Ticket: Authoritarian Consolidation Attempt', www.birartibir.org/international/584-erdogan-s-one-way-ticket-authoritarian-consolidation-attempt (accessed July 2020).

Aydin, Z. (2005) *The Political Economy of Turkey*, London: Pluto Press.

Bedirhanoğlu, P. (2020) 'Social Constitution of the AKP's Strong State Through Financialization: State in Crisis, or Crisis State?', in Bedirhanoğlu, P., Dölek, Ç., Hülagü, F. and Kaygusuz, Ö. (eds), *Turkey's New State in the Making: Transformations in Legality, Economy and Coercion*, London: Zed Books, 23–40.

Bekmen, A. (2014) 'State and Capital in Turkey during the Neoliberal Era', in Akça, İ., Bekmen A. and Özden, B.A. (eds), *Turkey Reframed: Constituting Neoliberal Hegemony*, London: Pluto Press, 47–74.

Bonefeld, W. (2017a) *The Strong State and the Free Economy*, London and New York: Rowman & Littlefield International.

—— (2017b) 'Authoritarian Liberalism: From Schmitt via Ordoliberalism to the Euro', *Critical Sociology*, 43 (4–5), 747–61.

Boratav, K. (2009) 'AKP'li Yıllarda Türkiye Ekonomisi', in Uzgel. I and Duru, B. (eds), *AKP Kitabı: Bir Dönüşümün Bilançosu*, Ankara: Phoenix, 463–72.

Bruff, I. (2014) 'The Rise of Authoritarian Neoliberalism', *Rethinking Marxism*, 26 (1), 113–29.

Çelik, A. (2015) 'Turkey's New Labour Regime under the Justice and Development Party: Authoritarian Flexibilization', *Middle Eastern Studies*, 51 (4), 618–35.

Clarke, S. (2005) 'The Neoliberal Theory of Society', in Saad-Filho, A. and Johnston, D. (eds), *Neoliberalism: A Critical Reader*, London: Pluto Press, 50–9.

Copley, J. and Moraitis, A. (2020) 'Neoliberalism's Many Deaths and Strange Non-deaths', https://developingeconomics.org/2020/06/18/neoliberalisms-many-deaths-and-strange-non-deaths/ (accessed July 2020).

Coşar, S. (2012) 'The AKP's Hold on Power: Neoliberalism Meets the Turkish Islamic Synthesis', in Coşar, S. and Yücesan-Özdemir, G. (eds), *Silent Violence: Neoliberalism, Islamist Politics and the AKP Years in Turkey*, Ottawa: Red Quill Books, 67–92.

Dönmez, P.E. and Zemandl, E.J. (2019) 'Crisis of Capitalism and (De-) politicisation of Monetary Policymaking: Reflections from Hungary and Turkey', *New Political Economy*, 24 (1), 125–43.

Dufour, M. and Orhangazi, Ö. (2009) 'The 2000–2001 Financial Crisis in Turkey: A Crisis for Whom?', *Review of Political Economy*, 21(1), 101–22.

Duman, S.Ö. (2014) *The Political Economy of Labour Market Reforms: Greece, Turkey and the Global Economic Crisis*, Basingstoke: Palgrave Macmillan.

Erensü, S. and Madra, Y.M. (2020) 'Neoliberal Politics in Turkey', in Tezcür, G.M. (ed.), *The Oxford Handbook of Turkish Politics*, doi: 10.1093/oxfordhb/9780190064891.013.17

Erol, M.E. (2016) 'AKP Döneminde İktisadi Politika Yapımının Siyaseti: Süreklilik ve Kopuş Bağlamında Bir Tartışma', in Tören, T. and Kutun, M. (eds), *Yeni Türkiye: Kapitalizm, Devlet ve Sınıflar*, İstanbul: SAV, 280–328.

—— (2019) 'State and Labour under AKP Rule in Turkey: An Appraisal', *Journal of Balkan and Near Eastern Studies*, 21 (6), 663–77.

Gamble, A. (1994) *The Free Economy and the Strong State*, Basingstoke: Palgrave Macmillan.

Harvey, D. (2005) *A Brief History of Neoliberalism*, New York: Oxford University Press.

Kaygusuz, Ö. (2018) 'Authoritarian Neoliberalism and Regime Security in Turkey: Moving to an "Exceptional State" under AKP', *South European Society and Politics*, 23 (2), 281–302.

Keyman, F. and Öniş, Z. (2007) *Turkish Politics in a Changing World*, İstanbul: İstanbul Bilgi University Press.

Kiely, R. (2017) 'From Authoritarian Liberalism to Economic Technocracy: Neoliberalism, Politics and "De-democratization"', *Critical Sociology*, 43 (4–5), 725–45.

Macartney, H. (2013) *The Debt Crisis and European Democratic Legitimacy*, Basingstoke: Palgrave Macmillan.

Marois, T. (2012) *States, Banks and Crisis: Emerging Finance Capitalism in Mexico and Turkey*, Cheltenham, UK: Edward Elgar.

Oğuz, Ş. (2016) 'Yeni Türkiye'nin Siyasal Rejimi', in Tören, T. and Kutun, M. (eds), *Yeni Türkiye: Kapitalizm, Devlet ve Sınıflar*, İstanbul: SAV, 81–127.

Öniş, Z. (2019) 'Turkey under the Challenge of State Capitalism: The Political Economy of the Late AKP Era', *Southeast European and Black Sea Studies*, 19 (2), 201–25.

Öniş, Z. and Bakır, C. (2007) 'Turkey's Political Economy in the Age of Financial Globalization: The Significance of the EU anchor', *South European Society and Politics*, 12 (2), 147–64.

Öniş, Z. and Güven, A.B. (2011) 'Global Crisis, National Responses: The Political Economy of Turkish Exceptionalism', *New Political Economy*, 16 (5), 585–608.

Öniş, Z. and Webb, S. (1992) 'Political Economy of Policy Reform in Turkey in the 1980s', Policy Research Working Paper Series. World Bank, WPS 1059.

Özden, B.A. (2014) 'The Transformation of Social Welfare and Politics in Turkey: A Successful Convergence of Neoliberalism and Populism', in Akça, İ., Bekmen, A. and Özden, B.A. (eds), *Turkey Reframed: Constituting Neoliberal Hegemony*, London: Pluto Press, 157–73.

Rogers, C. (2014) *Capitalism and Its Alternatives*, London: Zed Books.

Saad Filho, A. (2020) 'From COVID-19 to the End of Neoliberalism', *Critical Sociology*, 46 (4–5), 477–85.

Saad Filho, A. and Johnston, D. (2005) 'Introduction', in Saad-Filho, A. and Johnston, D. (eds), *Neoliberalism: A Critical Reader*, London: Pluto Press, 1–6.

Slobodian, Q. (2018) *Globalists: The End of Empire and the Birth of Neoliberalism*, Cambridge, MA: Harvard University Press.

Sönmez, M. (2007) 'İlerleme Raporu: AB'nin Referansı IMF', https://bianet.org/bianet/ekonomi/102829-ilerleme-raporu-ab-nin-referansi-imf (accessed 10 March 2019).

Uğur, M. (2008) 'Turkish Economic Policy under AKP government: An Assessment', *Biblioteca della Liberta*, 43(191), 1–15.

Watkins, S. (2021) 'Paradigm Shifts', *New Left Review*, 128, 5–22.

Yalman, G. (2009) *Transition to Neoliberalism: The Case of Turkey in the 1980s*, İstanbul: İstanbul Bilgi University Press.

—— (2012) 'Politics and Discourse under the AKP's Rule: The Marginalisation of Class-based Politics, Erdoğanisation, and Post-secularism', in Coşar, S. and Yücesan-Özdemir, G. (eds), *Silent Violence: Neoliberalism, Islamist Politics and the AKP Years in Turkey*, Ottawa: Red Quill Books, 21–41.

Yörük, E. (2014) 'Neoliberal Hegemony and Grassroots Politics: The Islamists and the Kurdish Movements', in Akça, İ., Bekmen, A. and Özden, B.A. (eds), *Turkey Reframed: Constituting Neoliberal Hegemony*, London: Pluto Press, 234–46.

2

Turkey's Labour Markets Under Neoliberalism: An Overview

Kerem Gökten

2.1 INTRODUCTION

At the end of the 1970s, neoliberalism became the dominant form of capitalism as the response of the ruling classes to the crisis-ridden global political economy. Turkey was not an exception and was rapidly involved in neoliberal policies. Although 24 January 1980 stabilisation measures are generally considered as the beginning of the neoliberal programme in Turkey, radical implementation was made possible with the military coup that took place on 12 September 1980. The pro-bourgeoisie military coup brutally crushed the unified opposition which would resist the restructuring of capital accumulation and the labour markets. Labour organisations were among the most important components of the opposition front. During the three years of the military coup regime, militant worker organisations such as DİSK (Confederation of Progressive Trade Unions) were banned and also several legal regulations were introduced to prevent the organisation of workers in the long term and to secure the uninterrupted accumulation of capital.[1] In the years following the coup, neoliberalisation of Turkey's labour markets deepened, and the working class lost a significant amount of social, economic and political rights as a consequence. Labour organisations could not overcome the crisis they faced, and their struggles rarely went beyond the singular and short-lived resistances.

Against this background, this chapter aims to reveal the general condition of labour in Turkey, relying on the primary indicators of the labour market dynamics since the 1980s. The chapter also aims to focus on the key pillars of the labour policies implemented by the governments and the main dynamics of the transformation in labour relations. A particular focus is given to the AKP era, which deepened neoliberal labour market restructuring.

2.2 OVERALL CHARACTERISTICS OF THE POST-1980 LABOUR REGIME

As observed throughout the world, neoliberalism in Turkey also amounted to deregulation of labour markets, deunionisation, liberalisation of foreign trade and capital movements, reducing public expenditures and privatisation. The IMF and World Bank crafted Structural Adjustment Policies (SAP) in the 1980s had an additional meaning for countries such as Turkey: the end of the 'national development' agenda. Instead of import substitution industrialisation, export-oriented growth strategy was adopted, foreign trade restrictions and currency controls were reduced and a real interest rate was implemented (Öngen, 2004: 82–3; Köymen, 2007: 127).

However, the key element of this orientation was a regressive wage policy in the 1980s, both under military dictatorship and subsequent ANAP governments. The Turkish state and the bourgeoisie conceived that, without a disciplined and cheap labour force, it would not be possible to boost exports and increase the competitiveness of Turkish goods in the world market by only relying on exchange rate adjustments and export promotion incentives (Marois, 2012: 101). Under these conditions, where political opposition of labour was eliminated via the coup, real wages in the manufacturing industry declined by a striking 32 per cent between 1978 and 1988. While the purchasing power of the workers was declining, production and productivity gains increased in the manufacturing industry (Boratav, 2004: 164–5). Keynesian linkage between productivity and wage was broken in Turkey as it was throughout the world. The policy of securing profits and foreign competitiveness by suppressing wages continued until the late 1980s.

1989 was the year of two critical developments. The first one was 'Decision No. 32 on the Protection of the Value of the Turkish Currency' which liberalised capital movements, representing the final stage of Turkey's integration into global capitalism.[2] The second development was a historical milestone in terms of class struggle. With the 'Spring Mobilisations' in 1989, the working class overcame the post-coup inertia. These actions, started by the public workers spread to many sectors, resulted in wage gains and these gains were spread to the public sector.[3] Other forms of resistance, such as solidarity visits, marches and the strike activity also rose in the private sector (Akkaya, 2002: 91; Doğan, 2010: 13). This meant that the counter-attack of the capitalist class since the early 1980s slowed down. The protests also became the pioneer of relative democratisation and liberalisation attempts in the early 1990s.

2.3 CRISES AND RESTRUCTURING OF THE LABOUR MARKETS BETWEEN 1991 AND 2002

The Turkish economy became crisis-ridden in the 1990s. One of the key triggers of the 1994, 1999 and 2001 crises was the fluctuations in capital flows. Turkey's gross domestic product (GDP) shrunk by 4.7 per cent, 3.3 per cent and 5.7 per cent, in each crisis year, respectively (World Bank, 2021). In the context of volatile coalition governments, the growth model was based on the budget deficit and public borrowing until the 2000s, which made Turkey one of the biggest debtor nations in the world.

Starting particularly with the 1994 crisis, relative gains of labour after the Spring Mobilisation have diminished during this period. The state and capital tried to overcome the real wage pressure through the global financial capital flows. Pursuing inflationary policies and informalisation were other tools used in this process. Concomitantly, financial crises, stabilisation programmes and privatisations damaged the union movement. The gains of the labour movement in the 1989–93 period could not be kept as they could not be tied to institutional guarantees. In the mid-1990s the labour share in GDP declined again, and after the 2001 crisis it decreased to 43.3 per cent, almost back to 1988 level where it was 41.1 per cent. The unionisation rate, which was 42.5 per cent in 1990, fell below 20 per cent in 2000 (Akkaya, 2002: 96; Boratav, 2004: 176, 194; Topak, 2012: 234).

Table 2.1   Main Labour Market Indicators (1988–2002)

Years	1988	1991	1994	1997	2000	2002
Non-institutional Working Age Population (000)	33.74	37.15	40.32	43.55	46.21	48.04
Total Employment (000)	17.75	19.20	20.02	21.08	21.58	21.35
Labour Force Partipication Rate (%)	57.5	56.5	54.1	52.2	49.9	49.6
Unemployment Rate (%)	8.4	8.5	8.3	6.8	6.5	10.3
Non-agricultural Unemployment (%)	14.4	14.7	13.2	11	9.3	14.5
Unemployment, female (%)	10.6	7.1	8	7.7	6.3	9.4
Youth unemployment rate (%)	17.5	17	16.2	15.2	13.1	19.2
Unemployment Rate (%)*	11.6	10.1	9.7	9.2	11.4	14.6
Sectoral Distribution of Employment (%)						
Agriculture	46.5	47.8	44	41.7	36	35
Industry	15.8	15.2	16.5	17.5	17.3	18.5
Services	32	32	33.4	34.6	40.4	42.1
Construction	5.7	5.1	6	6.2	6.3	4.6
Adjusted wage share (% of GDP)	41.1	64.7	48.1	44.5	46.5	43.3

Source: CBRT Labor Statistics database, AMECO database.

Note: * Broadly defined. Calculated by adding the discouraged workers to the standard unemployed.

This decline in the labour movement occurred because of newly introduced and more sophisticated methods – compared to the 1980s – implemented by capital. As such, all the protective measures of labour were considered as manifestations of a 'rigid labour market'. The firms (especially in automotive, defence and metal industries) had undergone a structural transformation towards flexible accumulation and the labour legislation was also changed in this direction. The union movement could not organise an effective resistance to neither privatisations and flexibility policies nor stratification and subcontracting tendencies. As a result, the industrial relations system which was shaped by Fordism gradually declined and has been restructured (Özkaplan, 2008: 174; Topak, 2012: 231–9, 298).

Table 2.1 contains the main indicators of the labour market in the period 1988–2002. The first striking indicator is the labour force participation rate. While it was close to the OECD average in 1988 (60.5 per cent),[4] this situation changed in the 1990s. The process of urbanisation and the decrease in agricultural development were effective in this decline. As some argued, the female workforce who migrated to the urban areas were discouraged to participate in the labour force. The reasons for this are the difficulty of women to find jobs in the non-agricultural sector, sexual division of labour and cultural values against the participation of women in the labour force (Özkaplan, 2008: 201; Olhan, 2011: 6; Gürsel & Uysal-Kolaşin, 2012).

Another important indicator, unemployment, become sticky at the level of 8 per cent during this period, but did not reach dramatic levels. In this period, Turkey's unemployment rate remained above the average of the upper middle-income countries group, but did not deviate much from the average of the OECD countries, except for the 2001 crisis. In this period, female unemployment did not differ much from both the general unemployment rate of the country and the world average. Again, the female unemployment rate of Turkey remained below the OECD average until the 2001 crisis.[5]

During this period, structural changes occurred in the sectoral distribution of employment. The share of agricultural employment in total employment has declined rapidly since the mid-1990s. With the 2000s, the service industry took over from the agricultural sector in terms of sectoral distribution of employment. Concomitantly, this had a direct effect on the rise of informality. Because of the conflict in eastern Turkey, a significant population of the Kurds left the region and agriculture and migrated to Western metropolitan cities where they became a major part of the informal labour (Yörük, 2014; see also Chapter 6). As such, more than 30 per cent of the non-agricultural labour force was informal in the second half of the 1990s.

The late 1990s and early 2000s were marked by economic crises, as mentioned. The weak coalition governments attempted to resolve these crises under the IMF and World Bank support, which urged for labour market flexibilisation and privatisation, among other things. These policies would be 'successfully' implemented post-2001 crisis, but especially under the AKP rule, following the 2002 elections.

2.4 NEOLIBERALISM AND LABOUR MARKETS
UNDER THE AKP RULE

2.4.1 International political economy and Turkish labour markets in 2002–10

The AKP took over the institutional structure created after the 2001 crisis and carried it to the 2010s. In contrast to the fragmented coalition politics of the 1990s, the AKP had a comfortable majority that enabled it to continue with the 'regulatory neoliberalism' framework uninterruptedly in the 2000s (Öniş, 2012: 139). In the first period the AKP government benefited from the favourable external conditions such as the expansionary stage of global economic conjuncture between 2002 and 2007. Indeed, with the year 2002, capital flows from the core countries to the top 30 peripheral economies started to increase, and reached US\$ 919 billion in 2007; whereas it was only \$169 billion in 2001. Turkey has taken its share from this cycle and had a capital inflow of \$184 billion between 2003 and 2007 (Boratav, 2009: 464). As a result, the AKP did not change institutional structure that was established before it came to power and capitalised on the global financial expansion.

The labour policies were also restructured legally, socially and economically under these developments. While the damage caused by the 2001 crisis in the national income was compensated by the growth rate of the first period of the AKP government, it is not possible to argue the same for labour and the relations of distribution indicators. The official unemployment rate remained almost unchanged at around 9–10 per cent, while the broadly defined unemployment increased and the decline in real wages continued. The decline in real wages in 2002 was 10.5 per cent, and in 2007 it was 12 per cent, when the year 1998 was taken as a basis (Boratav, 2009: 471). The wage share in GDP decreased from 43.3 per cent in 2002 to 31.5 per cent in 2012 (AMECO, 2017). The ongoing decline in agricultural employment led to the abundance of labour in the urban labour market. As Boratav emphasises, this process was triggered by the price depression in agriculture, and created negative consequences for the working classes (2009: 472).

In 2003, a new Labour Law (No. 4857) and in 2006 a new Social Security Law (No. 5510) were introduced; thus, two important common interests of the different fractions of the Turkish bourgeoisie materialised: a more flexible labour power and an increased retirement age. Indeed, with Law No. 4857 the AKP government adopted the neoliberal labour market mentality fully. The government established a legal infrastructure in line with the flexible accumulation regime with this law: different types of flexibility and new forms of work, and institutional innovations such as the wage guarantee fund and private employment agencies have been arranged (Topak, 2012: 252–3). Law No. 4857 defined atypical forms of employment, and also aimed to eliminate the 'rigidities' of the labour market by creating legal grounds for part-time work, casual work and compensatory work. Hence, the capitalists gained full control over the labour process and labour has become overdependent on the production process (Topak, 2012: 253–6; BSB, 2015: 60). The working class, however, could not organise against these regulations effectively, except for some short-lived campaigns and resistances.

Throughout the 2000s, informal and flexible work have become essential elements of the state labour regime as well. There has been a shift from secure and permanent employment to precarious employment through legal and institutional changes, and these changes led to the establishment of different groups of workers in the public sector. The differences between the various strata of dependent classes have deepened, and that fragmentation led to the working class move away from class identity. These legal and institutional changes directly affected the organisation of labour and the common struggle of the working class, which became paralysed during this period (Topak, 2012: 262–3).

Hence, the labour politics in Turkey in the 2000s was based on precarisation and commodification. Job insecurity, precarious employment patterns, social insecurity and income insecurity were the determinants of the labour politics of this period. The commodification process manifested itself through the elimination of public intervention in the labour markets, as well as transferring health, retirement, education services to market forces (BSB, 2015: 73–7). In the period 2002–10, the influence of neoliberalism on the society has been intensified, and social consent was manufactured with the wider possibilities offered by the expansionist conjuncture through credit-fuelled growth.

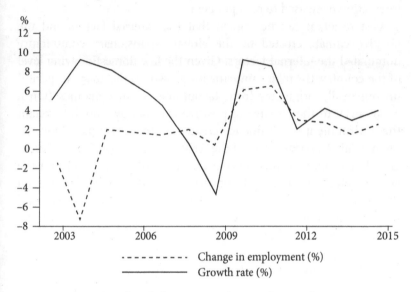

Figure 2.1   GDP Growth and Change in Employment (2003–15)
Source: TurkStat Statistical Database.

However, this growth was rightly identified as 'jobless growth' by many commentators (see, for instance, BSB, 2015). As seen from Figure 2.1, the Turkish economy experiences difficulties in creating new jobs despite the increase in growth and exports. Despite the 7 per cent growth on average in the 2003–07 period, the average employment increase was –0.5 per cent. As a result, the unemployment rate has remained at around 10 per cent. The main characteristic of this period was the capital inflows triggered by relatively high real interest rates. Foreign exchange inflows have cheapened imports, and domestic production and employment have been adversely affected as a consequence. The new inflation targeting strategy also meant unemployment level was not prioritised. In sum, the employment creation capacity of the national economy weakened in the 2000s. This situation is also reflected in employment elasticities. Employment elasticity was only 0.14 in the 2002–08 period, while it was

0.39 in the 1989–2000 period. In non-agricultural sectors between 1989 and 2000 a 1 per cent increase in national income created an employment increase of 0.68 per cent; between 2002 and 2008 this interaction decreased to 0.48 per cent.

As a result, it can be argued that the external factors and the positive climate created by the global expansionary conjuncture dominated the internal factors. Given the low domestic saving level of the country, the major impetus for growth in the 2003–10 period unequivocally originates from favourable global dynamics (Öniş, 2009: 425). In the absence of positive external dynamics, to retain the environment of confidence created by the single-party government would be harder. Also, if the AKP had found itself in a different global environment, the internal dynamics of the country and the class alliance surrounding the government could not have prevented the 2008 crisis from being more damaging and the 2009 electoral failure would not easily be overcome without a new wave of capital flows to emerging markets.

2.4.2 AKP and the Labour Markets in the 2010s

With the high growth rates in 2010 and 2011 due to increased capital inflows as a result of Quantitative Easing (QE) in crisis-ridden advanced capitalist countries, the AKP secured a referendum victory to control the judiciary and also won the 2011 elections with a strong majority. Hence, it set out to consolidate its power for the 2010s and authoritarianism increased significantly, without deviating much from neoliberalism, despite its crises. These developments paved a way for a further capital-friendly investment environment and labour market restructuring.

Against this background, the first indicator to look at is wages and labour's share in GDP. Despite its slight increase in the 2010s, if the overall AKP period is taken into account, labour's wage share in GDP in 2019 is significantly lower than the 2003 level (Table 2.2). In the Global Wage Report 2018/19 of the International Labour Organization (ILO), financial and trade liberalisation, higher capital inflows and competition from low-wage economies are shown as the reasons for the decline of labour income share of Turkey. Interestingly, in these usual explanations, the bargaining power of the labour, unemployment and barriers to the use of union rights are not mentioned (ILO, 2018).

Table 2.2   Main Labour Market Indicators During AKP Era

Years	GDP (billion USD)	Share of Labour in GDP	Labour Force Participation Rate	Unemployment Rate	Employment Rate	Informal Employment Rate	Female Labour Force Participation Rate
2003	312	42.27	48.3	10.5	43.2	51.75	26.6
2007	677	33.82	44.3	9.2	40.3	45.44	23.6
2011	730	30.14	47.4	9.1	43.1	42.05	28.8
2015	855	33.96	51.3	10.3	46	33.57	31.5
2019	749	36.03	53	13.7	45.7	34.52	34.2

Source: Created by the author from the data of TurkStat (2020) and AMECO (2017).

As it can be seen in Table 2.2, informal employment, which represents those who are not enrolled in the social security system and who are not employers or self-employed, seems to decrease in the late AKP government. However, Turkey has a fluctuating appearance in terms of labour force participation rate and also for labour force participation rates of women, even though there is a gradual increase in more recent years. For this indicator, the country ranked last in the emerging market economies a few years ago, and surpassed only India by 2019.

Turkey's unemployment levels continued to be a problem in the 2010s. As mentioned, unemployment had risen to double digits with the 2001 crisis and remained around 10 per cent. Even when the crisis was over and high growth rates were achieved, it did not improve, and as of 2019, the official unemployment rate reached 13.7 per cent (TurkStat, 2019). This level is close to the 2009 rate, when the global financial crisis conditions were severe. Overall, in the 2003–19 period, the unemployment rate of Turkey remained above the average of the upper middle-income countries just as before 2003. However, the difference is getting bigger.[6]

Furthermore, as of 2019, Turkey's female unemployment rate is 16.7 per cent, well above the 5.7 per cent OECD average and 6 per cent upper middle-income countries average (World Bank, 2020). If the labour force participation rates of women in Turkey were close to the group of countries where the comparison is made, this difference would be much greater. Indeed, the female labour force participation rate was in the 30–35 per cent range until 2000, declining to a low level of 23.6 per cent in 2007 during the so-called 'Turkish miracle'. The rate exceeded 30 per cent by 2013, and finally reached 34.2 per cent in 2019, but still remained lower than the level of the early 1990s. Despite the considerable decline in migration from the rural to the urban areas in the last decade, the low rates of participation suggest that cultural reasons and conservative attitude towards women remain important barriers. It is difficult to say whether the increase in the attainment of education and decreasing fertility rates are enough to overcome the conservative obstacles.

Table 2.3   Employment by Industry (thousands / %)

Year	Agriculture	Industry	Construction	Services
2003	7165 / 33.8	3746 / 17.7	965 / 4.5	9271 / 43.8
2007	4546 / 22.5	4403 / 21.8	1231 / 6.1	10 029 / 49.6
2011	5412 / 23.3	4842 / 20.8	1680 / 7.2	11 332 / 48.7
2015	5483 / 20.6	5332 / 20	1914 / 7.2	13 891 / 52.2
2019	5097 / 18.2	5661 / 19.80	1550 / 5.5	15 872 / 56.5

Source: Created by the author from the data of TurkStat (2019, 2021).

The proportional distribution of employment by industry is also another important indicator to understand the transformation of the labour market in Turkey in the AKP era. The most striking data in Table 2.3 is the decreasing share of the labour force in agriculture. Also, since the employment creation capacity of the industrial sector is limited, employment has intensified in services and the construction sector, where informality, insecurity and also lack of foreign competition are common (Kolsuz and Yeldan, 2014: 54–5; BSB, 2015: 50–3). It is known that the proportional distribution of employment by industry transforms and the share of the agriculture decreases as the economies develop. However, the process experienced in Turkey is beyond the limits of the concept of structural transformation. If we put into the analysis agriculture's share in GDP, which was 9.88 per cent in 2003 and 5.76 per cent in 2018, the dissolving of agriculture and embeddedness of poverty will be proper evaluation marks for the era.

Turkey has the longest average weekly working time among the OECD and European countries. According to OECD data, the average weekly working time in Turkey was 46.4 hours in 2019, only Colombia is above with 47.6 hours, and it is well above the OECD average of 37 hours (OECD, 2020). The average weekly working time was the worst among the OECD countries with 52.6 hours during the 'Turkish miracle' of 2002–07. For the periods exceeding 45 hours, overtime pay is not paid or only regular hourly wages are paid. Without doubt, the weekly working time of informal workers is worse.

The factors causing the weakness of the unions continued under the AKP government, and especially in the 2010s. By 2020, the unionisation rate was 12.14 per cent, while in 2003 it was 22.3 per cent. In recent years, the trade union membership process has become available via the internet. Some argue this practice has been carried out to increase unionisation rates. However, significant inconveniences and misuses draw our attention. Employers can easily put pressure on workers' free will, who can be registered in different trade unions instead of organised unions in the workplace. With the rate of unionisation at 12.14 per cent and the collective bargaining coverage 7.8 percent, Turkey is the worst amongst the OECD countries (OECD, 2020). In addition, one third of the unionised workers are outside the collective bargaining agreement. The most fundamental reason for this is the sectoral and workplace threshold and the anti-democratic collective bargaining authorisation mechanisms (ILO, 2017; DİSK-AR, 2020; see also Chapter 13).

Finally, we can focus on the three most striking arrangements of recent times: private employment agencies, severance payment and pension reform. The private employment agencies are the organisations that act as intermediaries to find jobs, and additionally, they provide worker hiring services. In Turkey, the legal basis of the intermediary activity was established in 2003, and with the 2016 amendment, these organisations were allowed to hire workers. With these private employment agencies, the traditional employment relationship has been abolished and a triangular business agreement has emerged. While there is a contract establishing supply of workers between the agency and the employer, there is also a labour contract between the worker and the agency. It emerges as a model of increased flexibility; and all responsibilities stemming from the employment relationship are undertaken by agencies instead of employers. The employer who uses temporary workers shall not be the employer according to labour law, but can give instructions to the worker. Thus, wages and social benefits and tax payments, social security and other similar payments will be paid by the agencies (Çelik, 2016; Özveri, 2017: 436). The system causes many problems. When the agency bankrupts, wages are at risk of not being paid by the bankrupt agency, and the workers cannot claim their wages from the employer because the joint liability of the agency and the employer has been lifted. The worker hired by an agency cannot benefit from the collective bargaining agreement because he is not directly employed by the employer.

The severance pay is another important step in the 'National Employment Strategy' (NES) initially announced in 2011. Along with private employment offices, it is the most controversial field of labour relations in Turkey. The public authorities addressed this issue in the context of lack of flexibility. Severance payment has become 'a nightmare' for employers in the Turkish labour market. Employers use a variety of methods[7] to avoid paying this when they fire a worker. It has been strongly argued by a wide circle of unions, activists, academics and lawyers that the severance payment must be secured as it would be the last element of security that a worker has got (Özveri, 2017: 426). The draft law, on which the government is working as of 2020, foresees the establishment of a fund that will guarantee severance pay. However, various official policy texts, particularly the NES, view seniority compensation as an obstacle to flexibility. It is safe to argue that the conditions for entitlement to the severance payment will be made more difficult, and the amount of compensation and the employer's liability will be reduced (Çelik, 2017). The fund, like other funds in Turkey, could also be used for different reasons as well. The logic and structure of the current severance payment system will continue to be a controversial issue in the coming years between unions, capitalists and the state.

The pension reform is the third most important agenda regarding the restructuring of the labour markets. The pension reforms[8] started with the experiment held in Chile – the laboratory of neoliberalism under Pinochet, where public pensions have been privatised. With the World Bank's powerful incentive for the reforms, the experiment has spread to over 30 countries (Oran, 2017: 49–50). The pension reform campaign has mainly concentrated on Latin America and post-Soviet countries. Turkey remained out of this tendency until recently, but it implemented a mandatory individual pension system in 2017. Thus, retirement has been restructured just like education, health and housing. It is not a coincidence that the system operating on personal responsibility and investments is realised under the conditions of the increasing flexibility and precarity in labour markets (Oran, 2017: 52–5). This practice will open new profit areas for financial actors and subordinate retirement income to fictitious capital relations. The transformation of retirement from a social right to a financial investment has the potential to further increase this inequality between retirees in Turkey, where income differences are already high (Oran, 2017: 189–90).

2.5 CONCLUSION

This chapter analysed Turkey's labour markets under the neoliberal form of the state since the 1980s. This form of state, which makes a class preference in favour of capital, has brought serious legal and practical constraints to the organisation of labour. The working class in Turkey could not develop a strong resistance to the class struggle intensified by capital, similar to other examples in the world. As a result, there has been a significant restructuring of labour markets in Turkey to the benefit of *capital in general.*

Since the 1980s, first the power of organised labour was eliminated for integration to the world market via a disciplined and cheap labour force. Hence, labour's share in national income declined significantly, despite increases at times. Turkish state managers are still trying to use the low-wage economy and long working hours as an advantage in terms of competition in the world market. The problems of unemployment (especially for the youth), informality and labour force participation could not be resolved. These issues continued to be exploited during the AKP era since 2002, and priority was given to labour market flexibilisation during this period. Ever increasing new agendas for further labour restructuring come to the fore with increasing economic difficulties faced by Turkish capitalism.

Today, the traditional layers of the working class and the new layers concentrated in the service sector are under the pressure of neoliberalism. The obstacles stem not only from the legal regime and reluctance to organisation; the mechanism of 'debt and discipline' also leads to an insufficient struggle.[9] The conventional trade unions have not yet succeeded to analyse today's complex class structure and also have not developed creative solutions to prevent labour from losing power. There is a very poor performance in preventing worker deaths, which has become a business crime on a daily basis. According to the *ITUC Global Rights Index* 2020, Turkey is among the worst ten countries for workers along with Bangladesh, Brazil, Colombia, Egypt, Honduras, India, Kazakhstan, the Philippines and Zimbabwe (2020: 6). This condition of the labour market in Turkey is a result of 40 years of neoliberal restructuring. A progressive, labour-centred 'restructuring' of the labour market is urgently needed for the 2020s, after 40 years of neoliberal destruction.

BIBLIOGRAPHY

Akkaya, Y. (2002) 'Türkiye'de İşçi Sınıfı ve Sendikacılık II', *Praksis*, 6, 63–101.
AMECO (2017) 'Adjusted Wage Share: Total Economy, Percentage of GDP at Current Market Prices', https://tinyurl.com/y2hnupqa (accessed 17 January 2017).
Boratav, K. (2004) *Türkiye İktisat Tarihi*, Ankara: İmge.
—— (2009) 'AKP'li Yıllarda Türkiye Ekonomisi', in Uzgel, İ. and Duru, B. (eds), *AKP Kitabı*, Ankara: Phoenix, 463–72.

BSB (Bağımsız Sosyal Bilimciler) (2015) *AKP'li Yıllarda Emeğin Durumu*, İstanbul: Yordam.

Çelik, A. (2016) '10 Soruda Özel İstihdam Büroları ve Kiralık İşçilik', *T24*, 20 April 2016, https://tinyurl.com/yyrbw97p (accessed 16 May 2017).

—— (2017) 'Bir Truva Atı Olarak Kıdem Tazminatı Fonu', *Birgün*, 24 April 2017.

DİSK-AR. (2020) *Covid-19 Salgını Günlerinde Türkiye'de Sendikalaşmanın Durumu Araştırması*, Türkiye Devrimci İşçi Sendikaları Konfederasyonu Araştırma Dairesi, https://tinyurl.com/y5256whd (accessed 16 May 2020).

Doğan, M.G. (2010) 'When Neoliberalism Confronts the Moral Economy of Workers: The Final Spring of Turkish Labor Unions', *European Journal of Turkish Studies*, 11, 1–20.

Gürsel S. and Uysal-Kolaşin, G. (2012) *İstihdamda Dezavantajlı Grupların İşgücüne Katılımını Artırmak*, BETAM Research Report, 29 July 2012.

ILO (2017) 'Key Indicators of the Labour Market Database', https://tinyurl.com/y3y9dowu (accessed 23 June 2017).

—— (2018) *Global Wage Report 2018/19: Wages and Income Inequality*, Geneva: ILO.

ITUC (2020) *2020 ITUC Global Rights Index: The World's Worst Countries for Workers*, Brussels: ITUC, https://tinyurl.com/ya8sjglq (accessed 20 July 2020).

Kolsuz, G. and Yeldan, E. (2014) '1980 Sonrası Türkiye Ekonomisinde Büyümenin Kaynaklarının Ayrıştırılması', Çalışma ve Toplum, 40 (1), 49–66.

Köymen, O. (2007) *Sermaye Birikirken: Osmanlı, Türkiye, Dünya*, İstanbul: Yordam.

Marois, T. (2012) *States, Banks and Crisis: Emerging Finance Capitalism in Mexico and Turkey*. Cheltenham, UK: Edward Elgar.

OECD (2020) 'Average Usual Weekly Hours Worked on the Main Job', https://tinyurl.com/ycq5l79h (accessed 10 July 2020).

Olhan, E. (2011) *Türkiye'de Kırsal İstihdamın Yapısı*, Ankara: FAO.

Oran, S.S. (2016) *Financialisation and Turkish Pension Reform*, PhD Thesis, SOAS, University of London.

—— (2017) *Sermayeyi BES'lemek*, İstanbul: NotaBene.

Oyan, O. (1998) 'Neo-liberal Politikaların Gelişimi', in *Türk-İş Yıllığı 97*, Ankara: Türk İş Yayınları, 25–31.

Öngen, T. (2004) 'Türkiye'de Siyasal Kriz ve Krize Müdahale Stratejileri: Düşük Yoğunluklu Çatışmadan Düşük Yoğunluklu Uzlaşma Rejimine', in Balkan, N. and Savran, S. (eds), *Sürekli Kriz Politikaları*, İstanbul: Metis, 76–104.

Öniş, Z. (2009) 'Beyond the 2001 Financial Crisis: The Political Economy of the New Phase of Neo-liberal Restructuring in Turkey', *Review of International Political Economy*, 16 (3), 409–32.

——(2012) 'The Triumph of Conservative Globalism: The Political Economy of the AKP Era', *Turkish Studies*, 13 (2), 135–52.

Özkaplan, N. (2008) 'Türkiye'de İşgücü Piyasasının Dönüşümü (1980–2007)', in Elmas-Aslan, G. (ed.), *Çeşitli Yönleriyle Cumhuriyetin 85. yılında Türkiye Ekonomisi*, Ankara: Gazi Üniversitesi Yayını, 161–212.

Özveri, M. (2017) 'Türkiye'de Güvencesiz Çalışmanın 'Hukuki' Dayanakları', in Makal, A. and Çelik, A. (eds), *Zor Zamanlarda Emek*, Ankara: İmge, 411–53.

Soederberg, S. (2014) *Debtfare States and the Poverty Industry: Money, Discipline and the Surplus Population*, Oxon: Routledge.

Topak, O. (2012) *Refah Devleti ve Kapitalizm*, İletişim: İstanbul.

TurkStat (2019) 'İstihdam Edilenlerin Yıllara Göre İktisadi Faaliyet Kolları (NACE Rev.2)', https://tinyurl.com/y4kfc87e (accessed 3 May 2019).

——(2020) 'Labour Force Statistics', https://tinyurl.com/y3gqqgpw (accessed 1 July 2020).

TurkStat (2021) 'İşgücü İstatistikleri', https://biruni.tuik.gov.tr/isgucuapp/isgucu.zul (accessed 25 May 2021).

World Bank (2020) 'World Bank Open Data', http://data.worldbank.org/ (accessed 1 July 2020).

World Bank (2021) 'Data', https://data.worldbank.org/indicator/NY.GDP.MKTP.KD.ZG?locations=TR (accessed 25 May 2021).

Yeldan E. (2004) *Küreselleşme Sürecinde Türkiye Ekonomisi*, İstanbul: İletişim.

Yörük, E. (2014) 'Neoliberal Hegemony and Grasroots Politics: The Islamists and the Kurdish Movements', in *Turkey Reframed: Constituting Neoliberal Hegemony*, Akça, İ., Bekmen, A., and Özden, B.A. (eds), London: Pluto Press, 234–46.

3

Commodification and Changing Labour in Turkey: The Working Class in the Public Sector

Koray R. Yılmaz

Public servants consider themselves under guarantee until they retire and this perception of security prevents their development. We aim to implement a system that breaks this perception.[1]

3.1 INTRODUCTION

The crisis of capitalism in the 1970s, the dissolution of the welfare state, and the collapse of the Soviet Union in 1991 all led to the rapid growth of commodity relations within new areas and a global widening of the geography of capital. The neoliberal policies of Britain and the US accelerated these tendencies on a world scale. These developments have affected the working class the most.

The 24 January 1980 decisions made by the Turkish government marks Turkey's adoption of neoliberal policies; an event that was only made possible following the military coup of 12 September 1980. The short-medium term direct class results of the neoliberal era of Turkey, like the suppression of the working-class struggle, suspension of trade unions and repressed wages, were followed by the medium-long-term results of deunionisation, the rise of subcontractors, undeclared work, precarity and unemployment. On the other hand, the neoliberal policies on exchange rates, interest rates, foreign trade regime and financial movements, all of which made the country vulnerable to frequent economic crises, served to further lower the social status of the working class. Moreover, the policies and implementations related to privatisation, reduced state intervention, creating independent regulatory agencies, tightening of public spending, reshaping of public policies like healthcare and education, and flexibilisation in the public personnel regime reflected the transformation of the state apparatus and had a major impact on the working class.

In this period, similar reforms which were executed in the public sector and associated areas can be observed not only in Turkey but also in many developed and developing countries from Europe, Asia and Latin America. These reforms have been implemented through the discourses of a new public management approach, governance, engagement, transparency, accountability and efficiency. One of the most significant aspect of these implementations is their intended outcome on the public policies, public services and the public employees responsible for providing these services.

Besides the Turkish military coup attempt, the power of discourse on the state failures lent legitimacy to the post-1980 transformation, and the policies implemented for the changing role of the Turkish state. It was this discourse that set the ideological basis of the transformation and helped to foster and promote the narrative that the Turkish state was cumbersome, with excessive bureaucracy and an ineffective structure, that there was an excess number of public service personnel, that the state was the source of corruption, that excessive public spending and State Owned Enterprises (SOEs) were responsible for various economic problems, that politics disrupted the economic process, and finally, that the government was too big and should be minimised.

A few key events shaped the transformation of the state; the first being the shift in class dynamics that took place in the 1980s and intensified as the implementations spread in their range. Next, the legal and institutional reforms within the framework of the 'Transition to the Strong Economy Programme', which was put in place in the aftermath of the 2001 crisis, had a significant impact on further cementing the neoliberal agenda. Closely related to this was the privatisation initiatives enacted by the AKP governments, which came to power in the aftermath of the 2001 crisis, and 'the Draft Law on the Public Administration Basic Law', which the Parliament agreed to adopt in 2003. However, the draft law was implemented gradually and fragmentally because it was not fully approved by the President at the time.

Against this background, this chapter focuses on the public sector working class in Turkey, by arguing in particular the impact of the post-1980 transformation, and of the structural transformations of public labour that took place in relation to this transformation. The general public sector transformation specifically intended for public labour has been discussed at length in many critical studies. In these studies, different arguments have emerged, depending on the perspective from which the issue has been approached. For instance, nationalist approaches conceived this transformation as imposed by international organisations and imperialists, whose objectives were to erode the nation-state. Leftists have analysed the transformations as outputs of neoliberalism. Approaches that highlighted class dynamics in their analyses discussed the transformation in terms of differentiation in the capital accumulation regime. Looking at the transformation in terms of its impact on public personnel, which is the subject of this chapter, the implementations carried out are interpreted as being convenient for the post-Fordist regime of accumulation.

Without neglecting the contributions of these approaches in providing a comprehensive understanding of the issue in question, this chapter emphasises the importance of inherent capitalist tendencies to understand this transformation. Within this framework, 'commodification', one of the basic tendencies of capitalism, will be looked at closely in this chapter, and the argument will be made that commodification tendencies invigorated a structural transformation in the characteristics of public labour and that this transformation in Turkey has been accelerating ever since the 1980s, and particularly since the 2000s.

In the section that follows, the commodification process and structural transformation of Turkish public labour will be addressed at the conceptual level, based on certain points made by Marx in his *Capital*. The section after that looks at the historical background; and the practices related to this transformation process will be considered within this conceptual framework.

3.2 COMMODIFICATION AND TRANSFORMATION
OF PUBLIC LABOUR

In the beginning of the first section of *Capital*, Marx underlined the importance of the commodity for the capitalist system, stating that 'the wealth of those societies in which the capitalist mode of production prevails appears as an immense collection of commodities' (Marx, 1992 [1867]: 125). In the analysis of the capitalist mode of production, the fact that commodity as collection is presented at the beginning of the book should not be taken to mean that the commodity is a simple object. Commodity is a rather complex social/class relation which Marx analysed in detail in *Capital*. Therefore, the phenomenon of commodification should not be considered as simply an increase in commodity accumulation, but rather be regarded as a *process* in which these social/class relationships become deeper and more widespread. Furthermore, this process is continuing even in advanced capitalist countries. This point, that commodification is an ongoing historical/social/class process, is important to keep in mind, because it points at different and changing concrete labour types that produce the commodity. To be clearer, in the commodification process, historically and geographically there are diversified concrete labours used for commodity production, and these concrete labours may have similar or different class positions. These diversifications also indicate the presence of institutionally and legally differentiated labour, such as paid labour, unpaid labour, peasant, agricultural labour, small bourgeoisie, civil service labour, subcontractor labour, temporary work labour, part-time labour etc. These all are observed in the historical development process of commodification in each capitalist country.

However, in a capitalist society, there is also labour that does not produce a commodity. These include subsistence labour, domestic labour and the labour whose product is not sold on the market. This leads to the second point; the opening of new areas for commodity relations. The opening of new areas for commodity relations is an inherent tendency in capitalism and *this process also creates a differentiation in the social characteristics of labour*. The main importance of looking at commodification as a process stems from this creation of differentiation in the social characteristics of labour. Returning to Marx to analyse this issue, in *Capital* he presents an important concept, 'useful labour', which he defines as 'the labour, whose utility is represented by the use-value of its product, or by the fact that its product is a use-value' (Marx, 1992 [1867]: 132). Therefore, the use-value of each commodity has useful labour. However, as understood from this definition, useful labour is not just a sub-category of the capitalist mode of production, nor are useful products only commodities. It can be pointed out that, on the one hand, useful labour is also included in the pre-capitalist societies, while on the other, the utility of a product is identified in different ways, even under the capitalist mode of production. The opening of new areas for commodity relations changes the social characteristics of labour and mode of determination of labour's usefulness.

It is well known that under the capitalist mode of production although there is labour which does not gain revenue, the principal labour is the waged labour. The latter could be defined as professional labour. Professional labour[2] produces the product for others, not for the labourers' own use. Therefore, a professional labour product can be thought of as useful for others, or stated otherwise, it is *socially useful labour*. How the utility of this labour is determined is a fundamental question for this chapter. This idea of social labour suggests that each type of labour whose utility is accepted by the market is an *indirectly social labour*. However, the utility of each type of useful labour cannot be determined through the market indirectly. In contrast, each type of labour whose utility is accepted by the central authority, independent from the market, has the status of *directly social labour*. In the former situation, the division of social labour depends on the market-dependent decisions of enterprises, while in the latter, the central authority distributes employees in different areas, the social utility of the labour is known in advance, and the effects of market forces are not considered.

No society operates according to only one of these two situations, yet the largest part of social labour is constituted by indirectly social labour in the capitalist mode of production. In other words, the utility of social labour is defined by the market. However, even in capitalist societies, the saleability of the product in the market is not the only condition of the utility. There are many activities featuring the characteristics of directly social labour, and the production of non-commodity goods and services are included in this group. Public labour, which is the main subject of this chapter, is also mainly considered within this category. Activities such as providing public order, education or healthcare are useful only where they are considered so according to the decisions made by the public authority. The utility of such services is not determined by the market.

As an inherent dynamic of capitalism, the commodification process establishes new commodity relations for non-commodity areas within the development process of capitalism. Commodification, or the transformation of products into commodities, which can involve differences in speed, scope and emergence, in terms of time and space, functions perhaps as the greatest magic act of the capitalist mode of production. The best historical example of this is when people who had been engaged in subsistence production met their needs from the market and produce for the market at an increasing rate. A more recent example would be the transformation that has been observed in the public sector.

The effect of commodification in the Turkish public sector was primarily observed in public service production. This tendency, as observed by the opening of public services to new providers in the private sector, not only transformed public services into a commodity but also led to a structural transformation in the social character of labour in public services. Whereas the type of labour previously producing these services in the public sector had largely been directly social labour, with the opening of these services to the private sector, today it has the characteristics of indirectly social labour. Therefore, the commodification process has created an *explicit* transformation on the social characteristics of labour within the areas of public services. Another significant point, in terms of the characteristics of labour in the privatisation of public services, is the degradation of the status of indirectly social labour that produces commodities in the public sector, i.e. in the SOEs.

On the other hand, it is also important to understand that the commodification process led to a transformation in the social character of the labour employed in the public sector. As public services open up to private enterprises, the social character of the labour producing these services in the public sector also transforms. An explicit transformation to indirectly social labour is not relevant to this labour because it does not produce any commodities. But it is possible to argue that there is an implicit transformation from directly social labour to indirectly social labour in terms of the adaptation process of working conditions, legal and institutional regulations and differentiated utility criteria of labour. Following an outline of the historical background, the rest of this chapter will focus on the social transformation of public labour that started in Turkey after 1980 but accelerated in the 2000s.

3.3 PUBLIC LABOUR AND ITS TRANSFORMATION IN TURKEY

The Turkish Republic was established in 1923 from the ruins of the Ottoman Empire. The continuity and disengagements between the Ottoman Empire and the Turkish Republic had been one of the most important topics of debate for the Turkish intellectuals for a long period. But looking at the facts alone, it can be concluded that the nineteenth-century reforms enacted by the Ottoman state underlie the processes of building a 'Western style' state and society. Although there are differences, it can be stated that a similar trend has been at work in the Republic of Turkey.

In terms of the present study, it is significant to state that the Ottoman Empire's increasing integration into the global capitalism paved the way for the reorganisation of the Ottoman state structure and public personnel system. The Imperial Edict of Reorganisation in 1839, the Imperial Reform Edict in 1856, and the Ottoman Constitution of 1876 mark the milestones of the capitalist transformation of the Ottoman state and the establishment of modern public labour in the Ottoman Empire on legal grounds.

There have been two watershed moments in the Republican era that helped to shape public labour. The first was the 1926 Legislation (Law No. 788) on State Employees, which was an output of the 1924 Constitution and remained in force until 1965. This law dealt with status, employment rights and the responsibilities of public labour –

civil servants, which constituted the largest sub-group. The second was the 1965 Legislation (Law No. 657) on Civil Servants, an output of the 1961 Constitution, which is still in force with minor revisions, but regularly pressed to be changed. The period covering the Law of Civil Servants No. 657 can also be divided into two periods. The first period was the pre-1980 period, which was marked by the high social status of civil servants, on account of their greater job security. The post-1980 period is seen as a period marked by greater flexibility and insecurity in the public sector and a rise in the number of contracted employees. The post-2000 era has been evaluated in terms of an intensification of the post-1980 trends.

As argued by Öktem (1992: 86), the period of State Employees (1926 legislation) posed several problems for public personnel. These problems mainly emerge from the aim to establish a functional synthesis between the old Ottoman implementations and the new regulations based on the new Republic's goals and policies, and personnel management systems based on the Western Europe and Anglo-Saxon models. In this period, the detailed reports on public management and personnel arrangements frequently demanded by foreign experts attest to the ongoing pursuit of integrating these new models and regulations. Şaylan (2000: 106) stated that in this law period 'the laws passed for arranging the personnel system did not go beyond the arrangement of pre-defined requirements of salaries and positions of civil servants, and the system inextricably deteriorated with each legal arrangement.' However, it can be stated that Law No. 788 on State Employees provided security for civil service workers. Acar (2009: 92) was less optimistic about this matter, stating that 'some new arrangements that had been practiced since 1949 had weakened the working guarantees of civil servants ... Therefore, the main discussion area of public personnel management had focused on the employment security of civil servants within the period extending up to 1960.' After the transition to the multi-party system, the aforementioned problems of the prior period continued to be observed, with significant losses in the working conditions, salary arrangements and social status of civil servants.

As mentioned, Law No. 657 was introduced in 1965 and is still in force. Although it was enacted in 1965, because of various reasons, it did not come into force until Law No. 1327 in 1970. This law, which passed as a new implementation to address the losses experienced by civil servants in the 1950s, was a significant breaking point for the public personnel regime. This law provided stronger employment security, trade union rights and a higher social status, but it is important to note that this law was changed in various ways later on. The main tendency of these changes has been a transformation of the secure employment provided by public labour and based on the status law to contracted and more precarious employment based on private law. Today, the main aim, as expressed by persons in positions of authority, is to dismantle Law No. 657 and ultimately stamp out worker-civil servant distinction to enable all workers to be referred to as employees. If this transformation is successful, there would be an extensive change in public labour. With this change, the process, which started in the 1980s and accelerated in the 2000s, is expected to reach its logical end, where the secure work prescribed by status law will be replaced by the more precarious work of contracted employment. This will lead to legal, political and economic losses for public workers, which are part of the working class.

The transformation process mentioned above led to certain structural transformations in the character of public labour. A detailed mapping of this transformation is beyond the scope of this chapter; therefore, only the most significant and prominent implementations of this process will be addressed. In line with the conceptual framework of this study, these implementations will be discussed under two headings that reflect the structural transformations in the main character of public labour: (1) explicit transformation from directly social labour to indirectly social labour, and (2) implicit transformation from directly social labour to indirectly social labour.

3.4 THE EXPLICIT TRANSFORMATION OF DIRECTLY SOCIAL LABOUR TO INDIRECTLY SOCIAL LABOUR

Since the 1980s, most public institutions and services throughout the world have undergone a significant transformation. Specifically, the scope of public service was narrowed, with some public sector jobs being taken on by the private sector. Turkey was not an exception.

Although certain concepts and regulations of privatisation had been observed in the Turkish legal system starting from the mid-1980s, the enacted Law No. 4046 in 1994 (following the 1994 crisis) was the first privatisation law. The purpose of this law was to regulate the principles on privatisation. An amendment (No. 4446) to the law in 1999 has re-regulated Article 47 of the 1982 Constitution and finalised the law. This legislation process in Turkey paved the way for public sector privatisation, giving private legal entities the right to carry out public services (Avcı, 2014). This process not only ushered in the privatisation of public sector institutions, but it also opened traditional public sector areas to private investment. This can particularly be seen in the sectors of education and healthcare where there has been a strong privatisation trend.

Opening of public service institutions and public sector areas to the private sector has led to the rapid commodification of public services. This commodification process also triggered a structural transformation in labour's qualification to produce these services: public labour which has the characteristics of being directly social labour transformed into indirectly social labour. This means that the utility of labour is no longer publicly determined, but rather determined by the market. In other words, the utility of this labour is not given anymore and needs to be approved by the market. So a civil servant, who before had long-term employment security because of the utility of his/her labour is accepted in advance by the government, has now been transformed into an employee who must continuously prove the utility of his/her labour; or put differently, he/she has to sell his/her service in the market for proving the utility of his/her labour. The necessity of continued approval of the utility of labour transforms a secured employee into a contracted employee with little or no long-term employment security. The renewal of the employment contract is based on this verification. The areas where civil servants had produced the service whose utility was publicly determined have been transformed into new areas, where contracted employees are employed, whose utility is defined by the market. This transformation has resulted in significant losses in the legal, economic, political and class status of public employees.

The most striking examples of the commodification of public service areas include the commodification of education, health-care, communication, transportation and security. For instance, the commodification of healthcare intensified after the 2000s. Table 3.1 shows the extent of commodification and how the scope of the public sector was reduced after the increased presence of the private sector in this area. This transformation shows that the healthcare industry went from being a common public service in the directly social labour category, where there was employment security and protec-tions under status law, to a less secure work area subject to the law of contract.

Table 3.1   The Ratio of Private Sector Inpatient Medical Institutions in Total

Years	1970	1976	1982	1988	1994	2000	2006	2012	2018
Ratio	0.10	0.10	0.15	0.14	0.15	0.22	0.27	0.36	0.39

Source: TurkStat (2014, 2019).

The same trend becomes more apparent in the context of the number of hospital beds (Table 3.2).

Table 3.2   The Ratio of Number of Hospital Beds of Private Sector Inpatient Medical Institutions to Total Number of Beds

Years	1970	1976	1982	1988	1994	2000	2006	2012	2018
Ratio	0.05	0.03	0.04	0.04	0.05	0.09	0.08	0.17	0.21

Source: TurkStat (2014, 2019).

Education, like healthcare, is another prominent area. After the 1980s, the opening of private schools at all levels including univer-sities was encouraged by means of incentives under various legal regulations. As a result of these implementations, the number of private schools throughout Turkey increased from a little over 300 in the mid-1980s (Uygun, 2003: 117) to 10,053 in 2016–17 (MEİ, 2017: 35). As seen from the numbers above, the public services sector is getting smaller as the private sector has brought a new understanding to service labour, an understanding based on low employment security contracted work. These processes have been implemented in various services once provided by the public sector, such as security, communication and transportation services.

State Owned Enterprises (SOEs) are another prominent feature of the privatisation of public services. As known, the concept of public service includes the production of goods and services. SOEs are public enterprises that usually produce commodities and services in the economic field. However, after the 1980s the reduction in the relative importance of the state sector in Turkey led to the privatisation of many SOEs. With the legal development mentioned above, the privatisation process was accelerated during the AKP era. Privatisation revenue for the period between 1986 and 2003 was US$ 8240 million, and in 2013 alone, Turkey realised a revenue of $12,486 million from privatisation. Table 3.3 presents more detailed information on privatisation.

Table 3.3   Privatisation Implementations by Year in Turkey

Years	1986–2003	2004–08	2009–13	2014–19
Million USD	8240	28 119	22 222	11 815

Source: Privatization Administration of Turkey (2020).

Evaluating this process in terms of the labour employed in the SOEs, it is important to point out that the labour employed in the SOEs already produces commodities with indirect social characteristics. However, this process has led to outcomes capable of degrading the employed labour in the SOEs. The privatisation process of SOEs not only led to unemployment but also to a change in the status of the SOE workers who were securely employed under the civil servant status into contracted employees. In 1984, civil servants working for SOEs constituted 36 per cent of the total employment, while in 2010, this figure decreased to 5 per cent. The proportion of contracted employees increased from 0.1 per cent to 35 per cent in the same period (Aslan, 2012: 27). This process ended with either layoffs or obligatory retirement of most of these employees. Some employees like Tekel Inc. workers also transferred to open positions of other SOEs as contracted workers according to Article 4/C of Law No. 657.

3.5 THE IMPLICIT TRANSFORMATION OF DIRECTLY SOCIAL LABOUR INTO INDIRECTLY SOCIAL LABOUR

The second dimension of the transformation of public labour is the *implicit transformation* of directly social labour in the public sector into indirectly social labour, a labour that produces commodities, and the in-market determination of the utility of labour involved in the production of public services. In more concrete terms, in public service institutions today, there has been a widespread increase in the number of employees under insecure contract work as compared to the number of civil servants subject to status law and who have secure employment. This rising shift is one of the most important transformations intended for public labour. The employment of new workers under contracted personnel status, instead of a secure civil servant status, or the offering of incentives to transform civil servants into contracted personnel, has become widespread in contemporary Turkey.

According to the 1982 Constitution, the employment of contracted personnel was permitted for only secondary and temporary tasks. However, as Aslan (2012: 7) states, although this employment form was exceptional in the pre-1980 period, it practically became the rule for some public institutions in the post-1980 period. Although it has been observed that contracted employees are occasionally promoted to the position of civil servants during the election periods, when popular policies are trumpeted, the rise in the status of contracted personnel shows that the main tendency after 1980 has been to use contracted personnel. This tendency would be more clearly recognised in the longer term. TurkStat data on personnel positions in the general budget institutions show that there were 1,008,183 civil servants and only 3557 contracted personnel in 1980. The number of civil servants doubled in 2011 and increased to 2,027,206, while the number of contracted personnel increased by more than 60-fold, increasing to 217,656 (TurkStat, 2014: 162).

Although the contracted employment was only a matter of secondary and temporary work, as time has passed, the service area defined as primary and permanent work to be carried by civil servants has been narrowed. Aslan (2012: 11–12) states that

> tasks carried out by the Subsidiary Services in the Law of State Employees were defined as secondary and temporary in the second half of the 1980s, and they were subjected to be purchased from the market instead of conducted by civil servants. Again, in the second half of the 1980s, primary and permanent tasks in the SOEs were organized only as executive tasks, with the remaining tasks being left to contracted personnel to be purchased from the market. Primary and permanent works in regulatory agencies were opened for contracted labour in the 1990s. In the 2000s, through legislative action, it was legally permitted for contracted or subcontracted personnel to carry out primary and permanent tasks. Initially this was implemented by local authorities, but then gradually, ministries like the Ministry of National Education and the Ministry of Health began to make use of this new legislation.

In summary, after the 1980s, the working class, which before had been securely employed in public institutions under the status of civil servant and was subject to status law, was increasingly placed under the insecure work and became subject to the law of contract.

This transformation was mostly observed in the healthcare and education sectors. Sayan and Küçük's study (2012), which focused on the transformation of public personnel employment in the healthcare sector, argued that practices like 'family medicine' and 'public hospital associations' reflect the change that has taken place in healthcare organisations, as they are models of employment based on a contractual system. Furthermore, service contracts protected under the private law paved the way for outsourcing to third parties, or 'employing subcontractor personnel', to develop private hospital management and secure cheap labour. It has been argued that the transition taking place within health services, where the employment of health personnel and a public-private partnership staff under a contractual system have been observed, will further pave the way for personnel outsourcing. Subcontractors tend to be more common in the healthcare sector (Ciğerci-Ulukan and Özmen-Yılmaz, 2016), and this sector is the first area in which the performance assessment system was implemented. This shift has been substantially aided by the Healthcare Transformation Program in 2003 under the AKP government's first term (see next chapter for a detailed analysis of this transformation).

Education is another area where the working class employed in the public sector has experienced serious losses. For example, teachers, who traditionally had employment security as civil servants and were subject to status law, were employed as contracted workers with less job security. After a series of legal regulations were enacted, a range of new employment forms emerged for the hiring of teachers who had been previously employed as civil servants. Acar (2009: 191) defined some different employment styles adopted, referring to them as contracted teacher, contracted teacher under temporary personnel status, tuition fee-based teacher, and deputy teacher. He emphasised that 'as a result of this process, some differences among the employees within the same profession have emerged in terms of the rights of employment security, pay, and retirement, etc.'

Subcontracted personnel, which is taking up a larger proportion of jobs within the public sector, are one of the most significant components of this growing tendency towards less employment security. The subcontracting tendency in the public sector began with the 1988 Statutory Decree, which affected subsidiary services such as cleaning, cafeteria, transportation and security; but as stated by Aslan (2012: 27), 'in the 2000s it has had the tendency to be also utilised in the primary and permanent services, and it has become widespread particularly in the municipality and healthcare services'. This is considered by Aslan (2013: 39) to be one of the basic implementations of the flexibilisation seen in the public personnel regime. Similarly, Özmen (2017: 277) also suggests that subcontractors are the primary but invisible elements of the public personnel regime, the ones who carry out public services in public institutions without being occupied in any official staff or position in the sector. The idea behind subcontracting is to use subcontractors to carry out subsidiary work in an effort to reduce personnel costs. Therefore, the working conditions and salary levels of these employees are extremely poor, and they do not have any union rights in practice or employment security. In this regard, subcontracted workers are the weakest element of the precariat. The true number of subcontracted workers is relatively uncertain, but it has been reported that in both the private and the public sector the number was 1,611,204 in 2011. The Confederation of Public Employees Trade Unions (KESK, 2017) data indicated that the number of subcontracted workers in the public sector was 3183 in 2004 and has increased to 850,000 in 2017.

Another significant phenomenon within this framework is the utility criteria of the service. As emphasised above, direct social labour is labour whose utility is accepted by the public authority, and public services are usually included in this category. However, this process led to a deterioration in determining the utility criteria of public services. Today, there is an increasing tendency for the public utility to be subjected to the market utility criteria. The performance system adopted in the healthcare service is the most striking example of this.

The performance system is most clearly defined in the Draft Law on the Public Administration Basic Law (KYTK)[3] dated 2003, which has also guided the post-2000 transformation in public administration. This draft law was sent to the Parliament at the end of 2003. In July 2004, its title was changed and passed by the Parliament, but it was rejected by the President and sent back to the Parliament in August 2004. However, according to Albayrak (2017: 2), 'although this law did not enter into force, its scope and content have been implemented in parts over time'. This draft law declared that 'public services will be conducted by civil servants, and other full-time and part-time public personnel and workers, and civil servants and other public personnel will be evaluated for their performance criteria', which means that the performance system has been implemented in public services. Acar (2009: 111) stated that 'the expression of full-time and part-time work here points to contracted personnel and allows the use of a flexible working system in public services'.

Another significant text regarding the transformation in the public personnel regime is the Public Personnel Regime Draft Law dated August 2004. As stated by Acar (2009: 112), 'in this text, many civil servants are proposed to be transfered into a contracted position'.

Therefore, it could be argued that the main aim of this draft law was to reduce the scope of civil service – which had previously been seen as fundamental on a permanent and secure basis subject to the status law – and to extend the scope of the contracted personnel. The Public Personnel Law Proposal Draft dated October 2005 presented a text with a similar approach. This draft proposal aimed to transform the contracted work into a fundamental element of the public personnel regime, and also aimed to reduce the scope of the public personnel through the implementation of subcontracting (Acar, 2009: 114).

3.6 A FINAL REMARK

There have been significant developments in Turkey since the July 2016 attempted coup. Following the coup attempt, the controversial referendum held in April 2017 changed the country's political regime from a parliamentary democracy to a kind of presidential system. With the early parliamentary and presidency elections on 24 June 2018, the result of the 2017 referendum entered into force.

In the run-up to the election, the Turkish economy was suffering from high unemployment, high inflation, depreciating national currency, rising interest rates and persistent current account deficit. In this context, the AKP government pursued some 'populist' policies in the election atmosphere. Within this framework, the AKP government stated that there would be a regulation to remove the subcontractor system in the public sector and that all subcontracted employees working in the public sector would be given full staff status. Turkey was under a state of emergency, therefore, the content of this regulation had not been announced until the last day. However, it was announced with the Statutory Decree No. 696 that was issued on 24 December 2017, without any prior negotiations with labour unions and with the omission of parliamentary procedure. Having a considerable number of members in the public sector, the Confederation of Public Employees' Trade Unions – KESK – made a public announcement to show the truth regarding this regulation, namely that the subcontractor system in the public sector would be removed and that all subcontracted employees working in the public sector would have a full staff status. The KESK announcement shows that this regulation does not involve all subcontracting workers. Although it is quite long, it is worth citing the relevant section.

> The Statutory Decree no. 696 deprived a majority of subcontracted employees from having full staff status. According to these regulations, 450 thousand subcontracted employees who work in municipalities and provincial special administrations will not have a full staff status but will be transferred to the public economic enterprises, where there will be serious differences in terms of union-social and financial rights and wages compared with staffed employees. A significant number of the 400 thousand subcontracted labour in public – it was said that they would have permanent employment – were left out of the scope. According to this, subcontracted employees worked in 26 institutions under the scope of SOE and in 26 privately held institutions, they were left out of the scope of this regulation.

The list goes on.

> … workers could only be included in the scope provided that they had security clearance and had passed written-oral or applied exams … In addition, in the case that contracted workers were changed into permanent employees after they had fulfilled the necessary conditions (i.e. passed security clearances and exams), they were to retain their 'current rights and salaries'. In other words, even though subcontracted employees are transferred into full staff, there would not be any changes in their working conditions, and also, they would not have the same wages and rights as their co-workers who made up the permanent working staff. Even after all these conditions are met, these subcontracted employees would not be entitled to utilizing the rights afforded by collective bargaining agreements that the current permanent employees are entitled to utilizing (KESK, 2017).

This new regulation once again shows that should the working class, which through this regulation will lose job security and enjoy no protections, not mount collective resistance, then the secure working conditions of public employees, who are subject to status law in Turkey will continue to evolve into contracted and insecure working conditions. At the beginning of this chapter, the cited discourse of the former Minister of Labour also clearly indicates this. The practical purpose is the removal of Law No. 657. It is crucial that the working class, as a collective power, challenge the potential losses they face from these developments.

Today, the AKP seems to be stuck in a narrow corridor between right-wing authoritarian populist policies and the rationality of capital. This narrow path either leads to postponing the regulations which will adversely affect many workers or to carry out these regulations through ideological manipulations based on religion and nationalism.

Although it was on the agenda at least during the past five years, the new regulations that will lead to civil servants becoming contracted workers can be considered to be an example of the first scenario. Factors such as weakening political power, rising economic crisis and the Covid-19 outbreak seem to keep the AKP away from such radical changes for now. But all these regulations in the last instance are subject to the needs of capital and the results of class struggle.

BIBLIOGRAPHY

Acar, A. (2009) *Türkiye'de Kamu Personel Rejiminde 1980 Sonrasında Yaşanan Dönüşüm: Eğitim Sektörü Örneği*, Unpublished PhD Thesis, Dokuz Eylül University, Izmir.

Albayrak, S.O. (2017) 'Kamu Yönetimi Temel Kanunu Sonrası Kamu Personel Rejimi', Memleket Siyaset Yönetim Dergisi, Cilt 12, Sayı 26, 1–18.

Aslan, O.E. (2012) *Kamu Personel Hukuku*, Anadolu Üniversitesi Yayınları.

—— (2013) 'Subcontracting in the Public Sector as the Capital Accumulation Process', in Kendir-Özdinç, H. and Güzelsarı, S. (eds), *Flexibility*, London: Ijopec, 39–50.

Avcı, M. (2014) 'İdarenin Kamu Hizmeti Faaliyetlerinde Daralma ve Dönüşüm: Özelleştirme ve Regülasyon', *TAAD*, Yıl 5, Sayı 16, 105–39.

Ciğerci-Ulukan, N. and Özmen-Yılmaz, D. (2016) 'Kamu Sağlık Sektöründe Çalışan Taşeron Kadın İşçiler: Samsun ve Ordu Örneği', *Çalışma ve Toplum Dergisi*, 48, 87–114.

Gouverneur, J. (2005) *The Foundations of Capitalist Economy*, Po Louvain. Louvain-la-Neuve, Diffusion Universitare Ciaco. Bruxelles.

Güler, B.A. (2005) *Devlette Reform Yazıları*, Paragraf Yayınevi.

KESK (Kamu Emekçileri Sendikaları Konfederasyonu) (2017) 'Basın Açıklaması', 26 December 2017.

Marx, K. (1992) [1867] *Capital I*, trans. B. Fowkes, London: Penguin Books.

MEİ (2017) *Milli Eğitim İstatistikleri*, Resmi İstatistik Programı Yayını.

Öktem, M.K. (1992) 'Türk Kamu Personel Yönetiminin Gelişimi', *AMME İdaresi Dergisi*, Cilt: 25, Sayı, 2, 86–105.

Özmen, A.Ö. (2017) *Kamuda Güvencesizlik Uyum ve Direniş*, İstanbul: Notabene Yayınları.

Privatization Administration of Turkey (2020) *Özelleştirme İdaresi Başkanlığı 2019 Faaliyet Raporu*, https://tinyurl.com/y34e68tg (accessed 17 July 2020).

Sayan, İ.Ö. and Küçük, A. (2012) 'Türkiye'de Kamu Personeli İstihdamında Dönüşüm: Sağlık Bakanlığı Örneği', *Ankara Üniversitesi SBF Dergisi*, Cilt 67, No. 1, 171–203.

Şaylan, G. (2000) *Devlet Reformu: Kamu Personel Yönetiminden İnsan Kaynakları Yönetimine Geçiş: Kritik ve Reform Önerileri*, TESEV Yayınları, 18.

TurkStat (Turkish Statistical Institute) (2014) 'İstatistik Göstergeler, 1923–2013', TÜİK Yayınları.

—— (2019) 'Sağlık İstatistikleri', www.tuik.gov.tr/PreTablo.do?alt_id=1095 (accessed 1 June 2020).

Uygun, S. (2003) 'Türkiye'de Dünden Bugüne Özel Okullara Bir Bakış: Gelişim ve Etkileri', *Ankara Üniversitesi Eğitim Bilimleri Fakülte Dergisi*, Cilt 36, Sayı 1–2, 108–20.

4

Neoliberal Transformation of Turkey's Health Sector and its Effects on the Health Labour Force

Sebiha Kablay

4.1 INTRODUCTION

Neoliberal policies were generated as a solution to the crisis of accumulation experienced in the 1970s, and they have affected many areas. Perhaps they most significantly affected labour. In Turkey, similar to other country examples, one of the most important manifestations of this transformation came to the fore in the form of flexibility and precarity. As seen in Turkish Labour Law No. 4857 introduced by the AKP government in 2003, it led to the flexibilisation of regulations that were once considered strict; in favour of capital. This has not only occurred in the private sector but also in the public sector.

The direct productive, distributive and regulatory roles of the state in various fields have been eliminated by neoliberal policies, and were left to the market actors. These not only include economic investments but also public services such as education, healthcare and social security. The remains of the welfare state were transformed and the areas previously covered by it were left to the market principles. As such, services that were once civil rights have become customer-oriented because they are now marketed as commodities.

Healthcare is one of the most significant fields in which attempts have been made to activate market mechanisms. The changes in healthcare are generally influenced by the programmes regarding transformation in health in addition to the change in public employment. In this context, this chapter examines the change in the health labour force caused by neoliberal policies in Turkey within the framework of the changes in public employment and health policies.

4.2 FROM WELFARE STATE TO NEOLIBERALISM: TRANSFORMATION OF HEALTHCARE POLICIES

The World Health Organization (WHO) defines health as: 'a state of complete physical (bodily), mental or social well-being and not merely the absence of disease or infirmity'. The physical and mental well-being in the definition is the known state of health (Fişek, 1982). Based on this definition, humans are assessed on their physical, mental and social integrity. Social environment is a significant factor in health, including places where people live or work. Indeed, problems in the work environment can have significant impacts on people's health. Occupational accidents and occupational diseases make this clear. Work environment can cause sickness, accident, permanent disabilities and even death.

Paying for medical services has been considered normal for a long time in order to benefit from these services. However, in the nineteenth century, workers in Germany reacted against this situation, and after these struggles the health insurance system came into existence. Similar developments occurred in other European countries. A group of physicians also argued that everyone has the right to healthcare services, and that the state must ensure them. After the establishment of the United Nations (UN), it was recognised with the Universal Declaration of Human Rights proclaimed in 1948 that everyone has the right to well-being without discrimination (Fişek, 1982). The expansion of welfare state practices and the recognition of well-being as a human right in many other international documents published afterwards increased the involvement and effectiveness of governments in healthcare. Thus, the state became the sole authorised and responsible unit in various healthcare-related activities from production to financing of health services, and from training to recruiting the health labour force.

However, the notion of reforms in health has changed the field of healthcare since the 1980s. A comprehensive reform process was generally implemented through a standard policy framework in most capitalist countries. These reforms were in line with several international agreements and international organisations of global capitalism such as the World Bank (WB) and the International Monetary Fund (IMF). The common point of these reforms is that they are based on the needs of capital accumulation processes rather than the needs of labour (Atalay, 2015). In fact, the very notion of 'reform' amounts to neoliberal policies in the area of healthcare. Leading international organisations such as the IMF and the WB imposed the implementation of neoliberal policies in the form of structural adjustment programmes (SAP), particularly in developing countries (Aka et al., 2012). These programmes have three main goals: the domination of market mechanisms, putting an end to the delivery of goods and services by the public (leaving these areas to the private sector) and reducing the regulatory power of the state (Hamzaoğlu, 2007).

Since the implementation of neoliberal policies in healthcare, the state is no longer a prominent healthcare provider in many countries and it has taken on a role in financing health services. Health is no longer considered a human right, but a service that can be produced based on supply and demand in the market (Kablay, 2011), which leads to basic changes in the delivery of health services, service preferences and the performance of services by the labour force. These changes lead to many other changes both for citizens, who benefit from the right to well-being, and for the labour force workers, who deliver health services.

4.3 DEVELOPMENT OF NEOLIBERAL HEALTH POLICIES IN TURKEY

In Turkey, the effect of neoliberal policies in the health sector began after the 1980s with several projects conducted with the support of the WHO and WB. In this period, the notion of autonomy was the basis for transformation. Hospitals were allowed to remain legal entities, while the incorporation of all elements of the management into hospitals was envisaged. A legal basis was to be created for the healthcare field to become marketable with the 1987 Turkish Fundamental Law on Health Services (Law No. 3359). This regulation allowed the hospitals affiliated with the Turkish Ministry of Health to become 'autonomous health enterprises'. Several articles of the law were cancelled later by the Constitutional Court. Due to delays in the new regulations, legal gaps have occurred in the field. As per Article 9 of the law, 'A Regulation on the Management of Health Enterprises of Public Institutions and Organisations and Their Working Procedures and Principles' was enacted on 29 November 1994, and the Türkiye Yüksek İhtisas Hastanesi (Turkey Postgraduate Research and Training Hospital) in Ankara was turned into a health enterprise on 7 March 1995 (Kablay, 2002). Thus, the first concrete step was accomplished with a programme introduced as a reform.

Law No. 3359 allowed individuals who worked in various services (general administration, technical, health and allied health, training and education, legal, religious and allied services) of the health institutions that were transformed into health enterprises 'to be employed in the status of contracted personnel' on condition of being permanent employees and without being subject to the provisions of Civil Servants Law (CSL) No. 657 and other laws on the employment of contracted personnel (Kablay, 2002). In fact, this brought a significant exception to the implementation of essential and permanent functions by civil servants as stated by constitutional law and Law No. 657, and caused important disturbances in healthcare employment models. Changing the legal status of public officials in their profession is one of the most important ways to make public employment flexible (Kablay, 2014a). After the Turkey Postgraduate Research and Training Hospital became a health enterprise, the number of its employees that were employed as workers in the services specified and the number of contracted personnel in the public official employment type 4B-DSS instead of type 4A (civil servants) increased.

Law No. 3359 includes regulations that allow physicians who do not freely practise their profession in the institutions to perform special diagnosis and treatment. These regulations include paying premiums to the physicians and giving incentive bonuses to the staff who work on contract in the institutions and from whom allied health, health and other services are bought in proportion to the business conducted. The regulations are not limited to payments. In addition to the rates, determining other personal rights by the Council of Ministers was facilitated by the Turkish Ministry of Health's proposal and the opinions of relevant ministries, as needed. Constitutional Court has cancelled several articles regarding this issue and partially prevented the intended flexibilisation (Kablay, 2002). However, Article 4 of the CSL regarding public officials states: 'Civil servants are individuals who are charged with carrying out essential and permanent public services executed by the state and other statutory bodies regardless of the existing structure.' Although providing healthcare is an essential and permanent function of the state, opening this field to contracted employment contradicts the essence of the CSL. Civil servants are bound by statute, which can be a law, ordinance or directive (Tortop, 1992), but this provision violates the statute legislation, and the scope of contractual employment in the public sector is being expanded.

The Regulation on Healthcare Enterprises has likened the management structure to that of enterprises with its adjustments and also tried to allow hospitals to be managed based on the principles of enterprises. For example, meeting operating incomes and expenses became an objective for private sector enterprises. However, the essential objective of institutions and organisations providing public services is giving this service for the public interest rather than balancing income and expenses or being profit-oriented. It is clear that the principles of private enterprise have been gradually implemented in the area of healthcare with these regulations, which affected not only health service users, but also the health labour force. This effect has been primarily observed in employment models, then it progressed towards performance payments, wage systems and the pace of work.

Turkey's healthcare is the sector that has been affected mostly by the changes in public service law. It could even be claimed that the first practices regarding flexibility in employment were carried out in the healthcare sector. Using subcontractors particularly in sub-services, increasing the use of temporary staff instead of permanent staff in public official employment, even expecting hospitals to employ personnel with their own revolving fund incomes, and flexible wage systems with performance-based revolving fund premium practices are among the examples of this. These practices in healthcare resulted in flexibility in the public sector to spread to other areas, such as education.

The most recent practice of neoliberal policies in healthcare is the 'Health Transformation Programme' (HTP) which was introduced by the AKP government in 2003. Its intention is said to be: 'organising, financing and presenting health services in an effective, efficient and fair manner'. It is also claimed that the effectiveness of its policies will improve public health. 'Preventing people from becoming sick, reducing maternal-infant mortality rates and increasing life expectancy at birth' are considered to be the parameters for achieving these goals. Reducing costs and providing more services with the same resources are intended to ensure efficiency; so careful attention is to be paid to: 'the distribution of human resources, materials management, rational drug use, health management and preventive medicine practices'. To maintain equality, HTP intends to reduce the differences between diverse social groups, urban and rural districts, and eastern and western Turkey regarding 'access to health services and health indicators', enable them to access as much health services as they need and contribute to financing of services in accordance with their financial possibilities (Turkish Ministry of Health, 2007: 24).

The Turkish Ministry of Health's (2007: 25) list of the Transformation in Health Programme's basic principles are as follows: human centeredness, sustainability, continuous quality improvement, participation, openness to consensus, volunteerism, division of power, decentralisation and finally competition in services. These basic principles are in compliance with the 'individualism, free market and decentralisation' approaches that mark the neoliberal policies of the HTP (Görmüş, 2013: 173).

The HTP has eight basic components (Turkish Ministry of Health, 2007): a Ministry of Health for planning and supervision, General Health Insurance that covers everyone under a single roof, a widespread, accessible and friendly health service system, enhanced primary health services and family practice, effective and staged referral chains, healthcare facilities with administrative and financial autonomy, manpower in the health sector with knowledge, skills and high motivation, educational and scientific support institutions, quality and accreditation for highly qualified and effective health services, institutional structuring in rational drug and materials management, access to effective knowledge for decision making from the Health Information System.

These HTP regulations bring radical changes to the delivery and financing of health services and the functions of health institutions. First, the organisational structure of the Turkish Ministry of Health has been changed from a healthcare provider to an institution that makes policies, supervises and maintains standards. For example, primary healthcare has been left to family practice centres, and its financing has been transferred to general health insurance. Hospitals providing the service have been left to the public hospital associations; and became decentralised health institutions with autonomous administrative and financial structures (Görmüş, 2013: 173). Public hospital associations were established on 2 November 2011 by the Decree Law 663 Concerning the Organisation and Duties of the Ministry of Health and its Subsidiaries. However, they did not last long due to problems at the point of service delivery. The previous Ministry of Health system was brought back with Decree Law 694, and the general secretariats of the public hospitals were closed. The General Directorate of Public Health and the General Directorate of Public Hospitals were also established[1] (MY, 2017).

The Turkish Medical Association (TMA) (2008) reported that these policies reduced the responsibilities of the state regarding health to 'planning and standard setting'. Thus, the state was turning into a rule maker rather than a healthcare provider. These policies also prevented stability in healthcare because they changed frequently. Healthcare workers are excluded from the social safety net and forced to be contractors – just another set of market actors. While the general budget's contributions to health services are being dramatically reduced, patients' financial contributions are increased day by day in the form of premiums, out-of-pocket payments and additional contributions. The units that produce and finance services in the health sector are forcibly separated and left to market conditions as well. Hospitals are obliged to collect the fees for the services they provide as revolving funds. This leads to healthcare service production under market conditions and increases subcontracting. Revolving funds are used in particular to employ contracted personnel. When the share allocated for primary healthcare is reduced, the focus becomes healing diseases instead of preventing them. In reality, prevention is always more cost-effective. These developments in the Turkish health sector have increased both total healthcare expenses and public health expenses since the year 2000. The share of the public sector increases in financing, while the share of the private sector increases in service delivery.

4.4 TURKEY'S HEALTHCARE LABOUR FORCE

The health labour force is one of the most significant components of enabling the health system to operate well and achieve its goals. The WHO (2006) defines the health labour force as: 'people who work to protect and promote community health'. Health services involve the intensive use of technology in particular and require specialised professional knowledge and intensive teamwork. They are affected by advances in medicine, which require both updated pre-service training for health professions and in-service training. Certain occupational groups such as physicians already receive specialised training while practising their professions after receiving basic education. Health services require several occupational groups to work in a coordinated manner. The organisation of the labour force affects not only healthcare professionals but also the health of patients. Health services and thus the health labour force should be well organised for community health.

According to the Regulation on the Job and Function Descriptions of Health Professionals and Other Professionals Working in the Health Services,[2] health professionals include: doctors and specialists, dentists and dental specialists, pharmacists, midwives, nurses, clinical psychologists, physiotherapists, physiotherapy technicians, audiologists, audiometry technicians, dietitians, language and speech therapists, podologists, health physicists, radiotherapy technicians, anaesthesia technicians (vocational high school graduates/vocational school of higher education graduates), medical laboratory technicians (vocational high school graduates), medical laboratory and pathology technicians, medical imaging technicians (vocational high school graduates/vocational school of higher education graduates), oral and dental health technicians, dental prosthesis technicians, medical prosthesis and orthosis technicians (vocational high school graduates/vocational school of higher education graduates), operating room technicians, forensic science technicians, dialysis technicians, perfusionists, pharmacy technicians, occupational therapists (ergotherapists), occupational technicians (ergotherapy technicians), electro neurophysiology technicians, mammography technicians, opticians, emergency medical technicians (vocational high school graduates), emergency medical technicians, nursing aides, midwife assistants and healthcare technicians (Annex-1 of the regulation). Since some other professionals also have important roles in health services, Annex-2 of the regulation also recognised the functions of psychologists, biologists, child development specialists, social workers/social service specialists, health educators/medical technologists, health administrators, environmental health technicians (vocational high school graduates/vocational school of higher education graduates), geriatric care technicians/home patient care technicians, medical secretaries, and biomedical device technicians in the health services.

The health policy choice of a country consists of financing, organisation and manpower; and practices in these fields affect each other. The health policy choice, in general, and financing systems, organisational forms and manpower practices, in particular, affect and shape each other. Thus, all these changes in health policy cause changes in these fields as well (Akdur, 2018). After the establishment of the Republic, policies related to the health labour force were intended to increase the number of the workforce, improve the quality, encourage work in the public sector and the balance between specialists and basic healthcare providers (general practitioners, midwives, public health nurses, etc.). Although improvements were observed in the number and quality of physicians until the 1960s, imbalances in the distribution of physicians in urban and rural areas, specialists and general practitioners and physicians in public and private institutions were not eliminated. The Law No. 224 on the Socialization of Health Services was enacted to reorganise the field of healthcare in 1961. This regulation introduced 'high wages via contracted status and deprivation grant, socialization scores for primary healthcare centre employees in specialty examinations and giving scholarships during student years in exchange for compulsory service' (Yılmaz, 2017: 53; Akdur, 2018). Its actual contribution was taking health services to remote corners of Turkey with the primary healthcare centre system and providing staged (referral chain) health services. This new system integrated preventive and therapeutic health services (Fişek, 1992). However, Law 224 was amended significantly at the end of the 1960s, which again led to imbalances in the distribution of physicians, decreases in wages and a lack of qualified personnel in rural areas (Akdur, 2018).

After the transition to neoliberalism in 1980, health services were commodified and market mechanism started to dominate healthcare. As part of the neoliberal policies, privatisation in this period led to the reduced significance of public institutions and the entrance of the private sector in the field of healthcare. Since health services became commodities, the rate of investment increased in therapeutic health services instead of preventive health services, which are more cost-effective. Healthcare is turned into an important area of investment for global capital. Articulation of this sector to the international economy facilitated the integration of the health labour force into the market. The service sector constitutes one fifth of international trade, and the health sector is its fastest growing component. Of the health labour force professionals, 33 per cent work in private sector therapeutic services (The Turkish Medical Association, 2008). According to 2015 data, 31.3 per cent of inpatient treatments and 33.6 per cent of surgeries took place in private health institutions (TOBB, 2017).

As mentioned, neoliberal policies in the 2000s emerged as the Transformation in Health Programme, introduced by the AKP government. This programme comes with many changes in the healthcare service. Almost all the new, resulting practices have effects on the health labour force. However, this study examined the practices that have *direct* effects on the health labour force.

4.4.1 Employment Models and the Health Labour Force

Health services are delivered by civil servants, permanent workers, contracted personnel or subcontracted workers because they are provided by both public and private sectors and by public-private partnerships (city hospitals) in Turkey today. This fragmentation is also observed when the public sector itself is considered. In fact, there are employees in the public sector who perform the same jobs, but are employed in different positions. This fragmentation manifests itself in dichotomies such as civil servants and contracted personnel in healthcare professions (nurses, technicians, etc.), and permanent-temporary workers (subcontracted workers) in assistance services. It creates groups that perform the same jobs, but have different rights[3] and sometimes wage differentials. The starkest difference in rights is related to the leave of absence. For example, a civil servant whose wife gives birth is given ten days of leave of absence with pay, but a worker only gets five days of leave. This leads to several problems for health personnel. For example, the payment of the revolving fund premiums to those excluded from the civil servant status (workers) was to be prevented due to the employment models created by Law No. 3359, which led to inquiries by the court of accounts. Autonomous institutions tried to resolve this problem by making the same payments, but calling them bonuses. This problem was eliminated by enacting the relevant regulation (in 2004 with budget law) after a long period of time.

Employment models that should normally be exceptional in public institutions were used as essential employment models (Kablay, 2014a). The employment of contracted personnel in essential and permanent functions increased since Law No 4924,[4] introduced in 2003. The employment of personnel known as fixed staff is based on this law. Contracts were signed with these employees. In the 2005 Law No. 5413,[5] the Fundamental Law on Health Services and the Law on the Modifications in the Decree Law on the Organisation and Functions of the Ministry of Health allow the recruitment of contracted personnel for health services and allied health services according to CSL 4/B through a central examination and with contracts to be paid by revolving funds (Yazıcı, 2018). These employees are permanent staff, and although their work conditions and pay are the same as those of the civil servants, they have less job security. The 2011 Decree Law 663 modified the organisational structure of the Turkish Ministry of Health, and although Turkish Public Hospitals Institution was established, Decree Law 663 was revoked in 2017 by Decree Law 694 under the state of emergency. The organisation of health services turned into a puzzle with this restructuring. The employment of contracted personnel was made possible also by this regulation.

Leaving certain fields (catering, security, cleaning, etc.) of health services to subcontractors also affects the health labour force. These groups do not provide direct health services. However, in case of failure in the employment of allied health personnel from time to time, cleaning staff are employed as aides in patient care. Allocating certain tasks to subcontractors through service procurement bids is a practice that has recently become more popular. Imaging services such as magnetic resonance imaging (MRI) or computerised tomography (CT) scans, in particular, are performed through service procurement bids, which is the most significant example of opening up health services to subcontracting. The employment of contracted personnel or subcontractors in healthcare is affected particularly by elections, and a part or a great number of these employees are made permanent before elections for political gains.

City hospitals have most recently influenced the employment model in healthcare. They are a type of public-private partnership that offers medical support and non-medical services. The operation of trading areas is transferred into the private sector in block and the state only does core medical services (Karasu, 2011). Increased numbers of beds lead to centralisation, particularly in metropolitan cities, which also accounts for the centralisation of the health labour force. Increase in productivity and effectiveness are prioritised to enable the private sector to make a profit which leads to downsizing the health labour force and reduced costs. Fewer employees and larger hospitals indicate increased workload of the health labour force. Including the private sector increases the number of contracted labour models, transfers the public sector to private business administrators and increases the number of employees who do the same job, but have different employment statuses (Yavuz, 2018).

In public employment, including the health sector, the government switched to a flexible employment model based on a neoliberal 'governance' structure in the 1980s, and increased the speed of this change in the late 1990s. The new system created fields where the public employment model became subordinate to the requirements of capital accumulation (Aslan, 2012). The health sector is one of these fields.

4.4.2 Performance-Based Revolving Fund Premiums and Wage Flexibility

Performance-based revolving fund premiums are a glaring effect of neoliberal policies in the healthcare system in Turkey. These funds were first established in 1961 by Law 209 and have undergone changes in 1975, 1983 and 2001 (Pala, 2005). Revolving fund premiums were transformed into performance-based revolving funds in hospitals affiliated with the Turkish Ministry of Health in 2004 (Aka et al., 2012). Performance-based pricing reflects an understanding that considers both patients, who receive the services, and physicians, who provide the services, as *homo economicus*. To maximise their own interests, physicians perform as much work as they can in a short time, extend their workdays and reduce the time they spend with patients (Ulutaş-Ünlütürk, 2011). In fact, performance-based revolving fund premiums are a wage flexibility model. Those working in this system are encouraged and obliged to follow this practice because performance-based revolving fund premiums are the only way to increase rates that are actually low. A low wage policy permits the state to allocate less public finance to employees. Instead, government agencies are expected to create revolving funds, and public employees work more because this is almost the only way to increase their wages (Kablay, 2014a).

Performance-based revolving fund premiums, the commodification of health services, differentiated wage systems, and time-based salaries are replaced by performance-based salaries, or more precisely, piece work (Kablay, 2011). At first, this system used indications such as seniority, title, but in later years, criteria such as personal transaction scores, internal and external customer satisfaction and the fulfilment of criteria by hospitals were considered. High scores are also given in the calculation of the premiums of those who work in special areas such as operating rooms, intensive care units, etc. However, the system is fundamentally based on the performance scores of physicians who can set them, and interventional transactions, in particular, lead to higher scores and increased pay (Kablay, 2011, 2014b). This led to a more technology-based service mentality and increased the number of examinations and interventions. However, the case is different in surgical indications, where high-score transactions are preferred, and low-score transactions are not (Kablay, 2014b, 2017). Kablay's study on healthcare professionals (2014b) found that 60 per cent of them considered performance-based revolving fund premiums inconvenient and detrimental both to society and healthcare workers due to their effect particularly on indication decisions.

Along with patient rights, performance-based revolving fund premiums have a negative effect on the interventional transactions of the patients at risk. Healthcare professionals think that they commercialise health. Kablay's study also notes other negative effects of performance-based revolving fund premiums such as employees' unwillingness to take leave and report sick except for compulsory leave (for radiation exposure) because their income will be reduced. The funds also increase competition among employees (particularly physicians), which leads to strife in the workplace. Physicians' efforts to increase their performance cause tension in their relationships with other healthcare professionals because the system is based on physicians, and other employees cannot exceed a certain premium rate. This is because increasing physician premiums raises the unpaid workload of other employees. Physicians, particularly those with specialised training, cannot spend much time on their studies and education, and they turn into workers of the specialists. Healthcare professionals say that the system particularly favours the surgical sciences, and that more time should be allocated to patients in some special areas such as oncology, but the system does not allow it or these areas receive low scores, and thus, low rates in performance evaluation, and therefore the system is not working well (Kablay, 2014b, 2017).

4.4.3 Patient Rights and Violence Against Health Workers

With the transformation of health programmes, citizen-based healthcare was replaced by customer-oriented healthcare. Customer-based requests and complaints have increased because healthcare is now a service that can be bought and sold on the market in this system. This increases both the supervision of and the pressure on the healthcare professionals. Patients even intervene in the area of indication, a concept that is quite important in the health sector and under the responsibility of physicians. Although the regulations on patient rights are a significant means of protecting patients, they are now used to control healthcare professionals and commit violence against them. Current practices require more active participation from patients and their relatives, and changes the course of their relationships with healthcare professionals (Kablay, 2017). Patient requests come to the fore in physicians' decisions. This is ensured by the complaint mechanism. The requirement of increasing performance due to market pressure creates psychological pressure. Kablay's (2017) study of healthcare professionals found that patient rights regarding procedures have a negative effect on risky procedures. In the case where the patient's relatives are prone to violence and the interventions are too risky, no assertive behaviour is exhibited as in the past because of this risk. The Turkish Penal Code and patient rights were apparently affecting this issue. The same study reported that 62.5 per cent of healthcare professionals had been considering quitting their profession in the last five years, which reveals their level of discontent.

Cases of physical violence against healthcare professionals have increased in Turkey in recent years, and code white was put into effect to protect them. However, code white cannot prevent healthcare professionals from being exposed to violence or even being killed. Healthcare has become a commodity in the market, which requires meeting customer demands. Patient rights ensure that the active use of the right to well-being is turning into a way to commit violence against healthcare workers. For example, waiting in line for examination, refusing to write a prescription or unnecessary medication without seeing the patient in person, and restricting a patient's relatives entry to the intensive care units to visiting hours are the main reasons for the violence against healthcare professionals. However, patients and their relatives think that these are the rights of the patients.

4.4.4 Family Practice

Primary healthcare is one of the most important areas of the transformation in healthcare. In the new system, primary healthcare centres were replaced by family practice. A pilot implementation started in 2005 with reinforced basic health services, and effective and staged referral chains. It was intended to provide widespread, accessible and friendly healthcare announced by the HTP in 2003, and it was put into practice throughout Turkey in 2010. However, the new system abolished a society-oriented, holistic primary care health service financed by the public and based on primary healthcare centres, and introduced a clinic-like, pricing-based, profit-driven and personalised approach (Ataay, 2006; Aka et al., 2012). The family practice system's most important effect on the labour force is that family physicians are exposed to market pressure and forced to prioritise profit as they have to finance their services as well. In this system, higher numbers of patients and examinations indicate better results. The rent of the institution and wages of employees are paid by family practitioners. This results in a business relationship between family practitioners and other employees which is similar to an employee-employer relationship except for the team mentality. Since other healthcare personnel work on contract, the satisfaction of physicians and patients becomes more important.

Physicians' freedom of choice is misused for patients in some respects (for example, unnecessary prescriptions of medicines and examinations, pressure regarding health certificates, etc.). This is unfavourable and not good for medical ethics. Prioritising therapeutic services over preventive health services is the most significant weakness of the system. However, preventive healthcare should always be the preferred option for a country because it is both more cost-effective and easier. It is also more useful for the entire community's health. On the other hand, treating is more challenging and expensive, more individual-focused and has fewer social benefits.

With family practice, therapeutic medical practices have become widespread instead of preventive medicine in primary healthcare. Communication among professionals in the health labour force has changed because the business relationship is based on contracts with family practitioners. People who were teammates in the previous system have become employees and employers. Family practitioners are exposed to the pressure of the market, and to a financial pressure to pay rent, general expenses and wages.

4.5 CONCLUSION

The health sector is one of the most tempting areas for neoliberal policies. Medical and technological advances in the field, increased life expectancy, and therefore increased chronic diseases are increasing the need for health services day by day along with changes in cosmetic trends. New transformation programmes are commercialising the healthcare sector as well. These programmes affect many areas from the organisation of health services to their financing and the health labour force. They affect employees and, indirectly, people who receive health service. Changes in employment models, performance-based revolving fund premiums, abuse of patient rights, increased violence against healthcare professionals and family practice affect the health labour force most by making flexibility and precarity widespread in the health service. Changes in employment models have made many workers non-essential, reduced the health labour force's job security and exposed them to the pressure of the market.

Performance-based revolving fund premiums are a wage flexibility model that produces competition among employees. Keeping the fixed fees low and providing an opportunity to increase the fees with performance-based revolving fund premiums puts pressure on employees to increase the number of their operations. This specialist physician-based system increases the workload of other employees and resident physicians, which leads to strife in the workplace.

Patient rights also put pressure on employees. For example, if the patient dies due to a risky operation, the patient's family may file a lawsuit. Or if the patient's condition worsens or the patient dies, the patient's relatives may use violence against healthcare workers. Such events make it difficult for physicians to make decisions about risky operations. However, such a tendency, particularly in university and research hospitals, negatively affects the patients who are referred to these centres especially because their treatment is risky. Customer-based healthcare service increases violence against employees to the extent that it even affects physicians' specialisation preferences. Fields that do not require direct, face-to-face communication with the patients are preferred and risky fields are avoided.

Family practice is particularly unfavourable for primary care preventive medicine. Regarding the health labour force, this practice has damaged the work environment because it has transformed physicians into employers, left them with financial problems, and other healthcare professionals have become their employees.

Every change in health policies directly affects the health labour force. In particular, the commodification of healthcare by neoliberal policies has subjected the health labour force to market conditions. Therefore, the health labour force should remember that it is not made up of competitors, but teammates, and it should struggle for unity and solidarity.

4.6 POSTSCRIPT: HEALTH WORKERS AND THE COVID-19 PANDEMIC IN TURKEY

The Covid-19 pandemic made health workers' already unfavourable conditions worse in Turkey.[6] As observed throughout the world, health workers are at biggest risk during the pandemic. As early as April 2020, the Turkish Health Minister announced that 7428 health workers were infected with Covid-19 which amounts to 6.5 per cent of all patients. This situation did not improve much in the following months as the measures were relaxed in the beginning of June, mainly for economic reasons. As such, in July 2020 the Ankara Chamber of Medicine declared that 449 health workers were infected by the virus in Ankara (ATO, 2020); and in Diyarbakır this number was 218 (Bianet, 2020). Actual numbers are perhaps higher, as the criteria for tests changed which would affect the real figures. Up to 22 May 2021, 156 physicians and 417 healthcare workers in total died due to Covid-19 (ATO, 2021).

As Amnesty International (2020) revealed in its report on the pandemic, health workers were not sufficiently protected by the governments in most of the world. Especially in the early days of the pandemic, in many countries including Turkey, health workers had difficulties in accessing Personal Protective Equipment (PPE). The organisation also documents the injustices and persecutions (arrests, detainment, abuse, threats, suspending from duty, etc.) that health workers faced throughout the world. Turkey was no exception; since March 2020 the Turkish authorities have targeted doctors in senior positions in professional bodies; started criminal investigations against the doctors and furthermore detained the leaders of medical chambers in cities such as Şanlıurfa, simply because of their comments related to the pandemic in media interviews and on social media posts (Human Rights Watch, 2020).

Despite calls from international organisations such as Amnesty International and local unions to recognise Covid-19 as an occupational disease, the Turkish authorities recognised it as an ordinary disease in the early period. This meant that health workers affected by the virus would not be receiving any compensation or specific aid related to an occupational disease. However, the death of an ambulance driver in the 112 Emergency Health Services due to Covid-19 was considered an occupational disease by Social Security Institution High Health Board. The Board stated that Covid-19 should be included among communicable diseases in the regulation determining occupational diseases. The authority to make this decision rests with the Social Security Board (Birgün, 2020). In another recent incident, an occupational physician died due to Covid-19, and the Social Security Board did not consider the incident an occupational disease. The event was later accepted as an occupational disease with a decision of the Social Security Institution High Health Board (Sansür, 2021). The authorities introduced some additional payment scheme for three months for health workers in March; but this scheme was discriminatory against the medical workers working in private hospitals and support workers in public hospitals, which was protested by the unions (Tez-Koop-İş, 2020).

The AKP government has praised its handling of the pandemic and presents it as a 'success story', although as of 4 June 2021 more than 47,768 people lost their lives with almost 5.5 million declared cases in total.[7] If there has been any success and the health system was able to function, this was due to the enormous efforts of Turkey's health workers who have been working under severe conditions for a long time. However, if the pandemic continues and the conditions are not improved, this resilience of the health workers could collapse.

BIBLIOGRAPHY

Aka, A., Kablay, S. and Demir, M.C. (2012) Neoliberal *Politikalar ve Sağlık Çalışanları*, Ankara: Nobel Publications.

Akdur, R. (2018) 'Cumhuriyet'ten Günümüze Sağlık İnsan Gücü Politikaları', https://tinyurl.com/y4vjjla8 (accessed 9 December 2018).

Amnesty International (2020) 'Exposed, Silenced, Attacked: Failures to Protect Health and Essential Workers during the Covid-19 Pandemic', https://tinyurl.com/y3lnewb8, 13 July 2020 (accessed 14 July 2020).

Aslan, O.E. (2012) *Devlet Bürokrasisi ve Kamu Personel Rejimi*, Ankara: İmge Publications.

Ataay, F. (2006) *Neoliberalizm ve Devletin Yeniden Yapılandırılması*, Ankara: De Ki Publications.

Atalay, A.S. (2015) 'Sağlıkta Piyasalaşma ve Kamu Özel Ortaklığı', in Yenimahalleli-Yaşar, G., Göksel, A. and Birler, Ö. (eds), *Türkiye'de Sağlık Siyaset Piyasa*, Ankara: NotaBene, 57–83.

ATO (Ankara Chamber of Medicine) (2020) 'Ankara'da Covid-19 Tanısı Alan Sağlık Çalışanlarının Sayısı 469'a Yükseldi', https://tinyurl.com/y4zyffqy (accessed 12 July 2020).

—— (2021) 'Kaybettiğimiz Sağlık Çalışanlarına Saygıyla', https://koronavirus.ato.org.tr/saygiyla/27-kaybettigimiz-saglik-calisanlarina-saygiyla.html (accessed 29 May 2021).

Birgün (2020) 'Emsal Karar: SGK Yüksek Sağlık Kurulu, Covid-19'u Meslek Hastalıkları Arasına Aldı', www.birgun.net/haber/emsal-karar-sgk-yuk-sek-saglik-kurulu-covid-19-u-meslek-hastaliklari-arasina-aldi-328613 (accessed 29 May 2021).

Bianet (2020) 'Diyarbakır'da 218 Sağlık Çalışanına Covid-19 Tanısı Konuldu', https://tinyurl.com/y2blrl8m (accessed 12 June 2020).

Fişek, N. (1982) 'Sağlık Hizmetleri ve İşçi Sağlığı Ailelerinin Sağlık Sorunları', *Prof. Dr. Nusret Fişek'in Kitaplaşmamış Yazıları-I Sağlık Yönetimi, Modern Yönetim Semineri*, Türk-İş Yayınları No. 144, www.ttb.org.tr/n.fisek/kitap_1/33,html (accessed 9 December 2018).

—— (1992) '506 Yerine 224', Çalışma Ortamı Dergisi, November, No. 5, 9–10.

Görmüş, A. (2013) *Sağlık Sisteminde Dönüşüm ve Sağlık İnsan Gücü Üzerindeki Etkileri*, Ankara: Siyasal Publications.

Hamzaoğlu, O. (2007) 'Yeni Liberal Politikalar ve Türkiye'de Sağlıkta Reform-Dönüşüm', *Toplum ve Hekim*, 22 (6), 418–31.

Human Rights Watch (2020) 'Turkey: Probes over Doctors' Covid-19 Comments', https://tinyurl.com/y7f5xdss (accessed June 2020).

Kablay, S. (2002) 'Sağlık Bakanlığı'nın Hastaneleri Özerkleştirme Politikasına Eleştirel Bir Bakış', *Kamu Yönetimi Dünyası Dergisi*, 3 (11–12), 36–41.

—— (2011) 'Sağlık Alanında Uygulanan Ücret Politikalarının Bir Aracı Olarak Döner Sermaye Primi Uygulamaları', in Birler, Ö., Coşar, S., Mıhcı, H. and Yücesan-Özdemir, G., *2000'li Yıllarda Türkiye'de İktisat ve Siyaset Rüzgarları*, Ankara: Efil Publications, 49–67.

—— (2012) 'Teacher Employment Under Neoliberalism', in Ginsburg, M. (ed.), *Preparation, Practice, and Politics of Teachers*, Rotterdam/Boston/Taipei: Sense Publishers, 161–73.

—— (2014a) 'Kamu İstihdamındaki Esnekleşmeye 4B Örneğinden Bakış', in Müftüoğlu, Ö. and Koşar, A. (eds), *Türkiye'de Esnek Çalışma*, İstanbul: Evrensel, 158–84.

—— (2014b) 'Performansa Dayalı Döner Sermaye Primi Uygulaması ve Sağlık Çalışanlarına Etkisi', *ISGUC The Journal of Industrial Relations and Human Resources*, 16 (4), 82–110.

—— (2017) 'The Practice of Patient Rights in the Eyes of Health Workers', *Turkish Yearbook of Human Rights*, Vol. 35–36, 49–70.

Karasu, K. (2011) 'Sağlık Hizmetlerinin Örgütlenmesinde Kamu-Özel Ortaklığı', *Sağlık Alanında Kamu-Özel Ortaklığı Sempozyumu*, Ankara.

MY (Mevzuatın Yeri) (2017) 'Kamu Hastaneleri Genel Sekreterlikleri Kapatılıyor', https://tinyurl.com/y7a37vas (accessed 12 May 2018).

Pala, K. (2005) 'Sağlık Hizmetlerinde Döner Sermaye Uygulaması', *Toplum ve Hekim*, 2 (1), 72–4.

Sansür, L. (2021) 'Covid-19 Meslek Hastalığı Olarak Kabul Edildi', Sözcü. www.sozcu.com.tr/2021/saglik/saglik-calisanlari-icin-emsal-karar-6425466/ (accessed 29 May 2021).

Tez-Koop-İş (2020) 'Sağlık Çalışanlarının Tamamı Ek Ödemeden Eşit Biçimde Yararlanmalıdır', https://tinyurl.com/yyp4p9sk (accessed 22 May 2020).

TOBB (The Union of Chambers and Commodity Exchanges of Turkey) (2017) 'Türkiye'de Sağlık Sektörüne Genel Bakış', https://tinyurl.com/y4hl6tdm (accessed 15 November 2018).

Tortop, N. (1992) *Personel Yönetimi*, Ankara: Türkiye ve Orta Doğu Amme İdaresi Enstitüsü.

The Turkish Medical Association (2008) 'Füsun Sayek TTB Raporları-2008 Sağlık Emek Gücü: Sayılar ve Gerçekler', TTB Yayınları, Ankara, https://tinyurl.com/y2vee2vz (accessed 15 November 2018).

Turkish Ministry of Health (2007) 'Transformation in Health', https://tinyurl.com/ya8san5c (accessed 15 November 2018).

Ulutaş-Ünlütürk, Ç. (2011) *Proleterleşme ve Profesyonelleşme Işığında Türkiye'de Sağlık Emek Sürecinin Dönüşümü*, Ankara: Nota Bene.

WHO (2006). *World Health Report 2006 Working Together for Health*, Geneva.

Yavuz, C.I. (2018) 'Şehir Hastanelerinde Çalışanların İstihdam Koşulları ve Özlük Hakları', in Pala K. (edt), *Türkiye' de Sağlıkta Kamu-Özel Ortaklığı Şehir Hastaneleri*, İstanbul: İletişim Publications, 227–47.

Yazıcı, E. (2018) 'Sağlık Politikalarındaki Değişim ve İstihdam Biçimine Etkisi', *'Is, Guc' Industrial Relations and Human Resources Journal*, 20 (3), 121–46.

Yenimahalleli-Yaşar, G. (2011) 'Health Transformation Programme in Turkey: An Assessment', *International Journal of Health Planning and Management*, 26 (2), 110–33.

Yılmaz, V. (2017) *The Politics of Healthcare Reform in Turkey*, Switzerland: Springer Nature.

Gender, Migration and Rural Aspects
of Neoliberal Restructuring

5

Between Neoliberalism and Conservatism: Recent Developments and New Agendas in Female Labour Policies in Turkey

Demet Özmen-Yilmaz

5.1 INTRODUCTION

Based on the gender relationships governing the division of labour, men are primarily assigned to areas of production and tend to acquire jobs that are more valuable (political, religious, military, etc.) while women to areas of reproduction. As stated by Kergoat (2009: 95), the principle of separation that defines the work of men and women and the hierarchical principle asserting that men's work is worth more than the work of women are two of the standing main principles that have remained throughout history. Through the development of kinship-based property and the social relationships that it represents, it has been recognised that the gender-based division of labour has been transformed into the exploitation of women's labour (Coontz and Henderson, 2008: 37). Gender-based division of labour is both a concrete expression of gender relationships and a dynamic of genderisation, or the patriarchal reproduction of gender relationships. Based on Hartman's definition, it is possible to define patriarchy as a system that functionalises, legitimises, naturalises and reproduces the dominance of men over women in all areas of social production and reproduction (Hartman, 1979). Within the framework of the concept of 'patriarchal capitalism' defined by Hartman as a historically specific articulation style of production and gender relations system, Hartman explains the mutually reinforcing position of women in production and reproduction areas. Thus, it is not possible to understand the secondary position of women in the labour market without considering their unpaid domestic labour, their obligation to marriage and therefore to domestic labour (Acar-Savran, 2004: 45).

In this chapter, based on the aforementioned perspective, the meaning of recent female labour policies in Turkey under the AKP (Justice and Development Party) rule will be discussed in the context of the paid and unpaid labour. Following the presentation of the general condition of female labour in Turkey, we will address these recent policies in three steps: (1) flexible employment and informality, (2) demographic opportunity and protection of family, and (3) poverty and social policies.

5.2 RECENT POLICIES AND TENDENCIES IN WOMEN'S EMPLOYMENT

The neoliberal transformation has directly affected production and reproduction areas in Turkey. In the pursuit to decrease costs in globally competitive circumstances as part of the neoliberal transformation process, labour markets were made flexible as much as possible, with working hours getting longer, and elements like work security, work safety and social security being gradually removed. The area of social policy and services also underwent a radical transformation because of marketisation, and areas never subjected to market relation have been rapidly commodified. The redundancy of employees become more prevalent through privatisations, and within the framework of the downsizing of the state, fundamental areas like education, health and infrastructure have been left to market relations as the new accumulation areas of capital.

This period caused negative results both for the paid and unpaid labour of women. In contemporary Turkey, women's labour force participation and employment are significantly lower than those of men's. The main reasons for this situation are the dominant patriarchal structure and the gender-based division of labour. In relation with this dominant structure, women are considered responsible for housework and care. Hence, this understanding restricts women's access to opportunities for education and employment. Therefore, the demand for female labour has remained limited in Turkey. Various regimes of capital accumulation, such as export-oriented growth and policies in the 1980s and the import-substitution industrialisation process beforehand, did not help this situation and female employment continued to decrease until the 2000s. Although it started to look like this tendency would be reversed with the policies supporting women's labour force participation in the 2000s, a careful analysis of these policies and practices indicates the existence of significant problems. The following three sections will critically evaluate the policies and plans aiming to increase women's employment and to reconcile work and family life.

5.3 FLEXIBLE EMPLOYMENT AND INFORMALITY

In Turkey, the aim of regulation of a secure and flexible labour market compatible with the fundamental framework of the European Social Model (ESM) came into prominence in the Seventh Development Plan (1996–2000) (MOD, 1995). One of the most concrete manifestations of this transformation was the new Labour Law No. 4857 that came into effect in 2003; one of the first acts of the incoming AKP government. With this law whose primary aim was flexibilisation of the labour market, open-ended (indefinite) employment contracts were abandoned to a large extent, new flexible forms of employment were arranged and based on the freedom of contract. The law also introduced important regulations regarding working time, and most of the labour force was left unprotected against employers' demands and choices. The emphasis on increasing the non-agricultural employment of women started in the 1990s, and with the EU accordance process this increase gained momentum in the 2000s. With the flexibility of the labour market, it is argued that women's employment would increase in Turkey, which is low compared to the EU and OECD countries. For instance, in the plans and programmes developed in 2007, policymakers placed greater emphasis and importance on extending flexible forms of employment. The aim was to make entry to the labour market easier; and in the plans and programmes that follow, the labour market was expected to gain an even more flexible and mobile structure. The major changes were the 'secure' flexibility and entrepreneurship approach, and increasing the rate of women's employment would continue to be an important focus (MOD, 2006, 2008).

In the 10th Development Plan (2014–18), the flexibility and family-based infrastructure continued to gain strength. The plan emphasises that in the current state of the global economy, Turkey cannot maintain a cheap labour-based development strategy any longer and therefore the quality of the labour force should be improved. The plan further states that under the demands of the labour market, the education level and status of the quality of the labour market will be increased, work and family life will be better adapted to each other, informal employment will be curbed, and temporary work applications will be managed by private employment agencies through active labour market policies, professional education and life-long learning activities (MOD, 2014).

In the employment vision of Turkey for the year 2023, in accordance with the National Employment Strategy Document (NES) (MOLSS, 2017), concrete strategies will be followed to restructure labour markets. The main policy lines are ensuring security and flexibility in the labour market, strengthening links between education, employment and social protection, and increasing the employment of vulnerable groups (MOLSS, 2017). The strategy has particularly emphasised the necessity of the creation of special employment conditions for vulnerable groups of the labour market, especially women, youth and the disabled; and it also aims to increase temporary and part-time employment via private employment agencies (Ciğerci-Ulukan, 2014; Erdoğdu, 2018).

Flexibility and women's employment function as a gender-based mutually reinforcing process. The proliferation of atypical employment forms defined as 'women's work' in labour markets would increase women's employment, and this increase in women's employment and employment forms defined as women's work would make labour force markets more flexible, not only for women but for men as well (Standing, 2011). It is possible to increase women's employment through the proliferation of employment forms provided for women, with flexibility, whereby it can be made into the dominant employment form. This process is realised by recognising previously illegal unregistered and flexible forms of employment through new legal arrangements. The establishment of a temporary work regime with Private Employment Agencies (PEA) was entered into force with Omnibus Law No. 6715 issued in May 2016. According to this regulation, businesses can employ workers in periods when there is an increase in their production and service capacities, and these workers can be dismissed from their jobs when the businesses no longer need them (Ciğerci-Ulukan, 2014). Thus, the 'secure' flexibility that has been provided to increase women's employment has been transformed into one of the chief causes of unemployment by extending temporary forms of employment rather than providing job security (Ulukan, 2014). It is important to highlight that this flexibility, which is presented as good news for women because it creates the perception that women can work at their will or to spend time at home, includes no special provisions for women. Despite all the negativities related to employment as subcontractors, particularly in the public sector, this work, compared to the previously mentioned employment forms, has been in greater demand by women because of factors such as receiving a relatively regular salary and social security (Ciğerci-Ulukan and Özmen-Yılmaz, 2016).

5.4 DEMOGRAPHIC OPPORTUNITY, PROTECTION OF FAMILY

Both the 10th Plan and the NES mentioned the fact that Turkey's 24.3 per cent youth population gives the country a global competitive advantage (MOLSS, 2017). Turkey is a country which tries to benefit from a 'Demographic Window of Opportunity'. It is expected that this opportunity will continue to the year 2050. The aim is to increase the fertility rate to maintain the share of the working age population in Turkey (15–64 years old) at a high level. The conservative emphasis of the AKP governments on strengthening the family and increasing the fertility rate has been part of the discourse on 'increasing women's participation in the economy', as seen in policy papers like the 'National Action Plan on Gender Equality 2008–2013' and 'the Action Plan on Women's Employment 2016–2018' (KEİG,

2014). The same perspective is included in the 'Action Plan for Protection of Family and Dynamic Population Structure', which aims to increase the fertility rate, considering the future prediction that the share of the old population and the non-active population will increase in line with the increase in divorce rates, the prevalence of single-parent families and the decrease in fertility rate (MOD, 2015; TAYA, 2016). For instance, with the Omnibus Law No. 6637 dated 2015, a marriage benefit is paid in cases of opening a dowry account for first time marriages before the age of 27, and birth benefits of 300 Turkish lira (TL) are paid for the first-born child, 400TL for the second child, and 600TL for the third and subsequent children. In the same year, the Constitutional Court annulled a law that criminalised performing religious marriages without civil marriages. Through a regulation made in 2017, religious officials (Muftis) gained the right to perform civil marriages, a move which women organisations were against on account that it would make child marriages easier. The measures enacted to prevent divorces, such as conciliation, family counselling and religious guidance, serve as examples of the initiatives offered to protect and 'bless' the family. Under the ruling AKP's mantra of 'at least three children', C-section operations are restricted because they prevent the birth of more than three children. Instead, among the current objectives of the Ministry of Family and Social Policies (MFSP), vaginal birth is encouraged, and abortion is considered to be equivalent to 'murder' and therefore heavily restricted.

Within this framework, policies directed at the 'reconciliation of work and family life' have been brought to the agenda. With the discourses on the continuation of the family and increasing women's employment, the goal is to remove the contradiction between the objectives of increasing women's employment and fertility by institutionalising 'flexible forms of employment' (Ünlütürk-Ulutaş, 2015, Gün, 2016). The reconciliation of work and family life policies that have been a focus of European countries since the 1970s are expected to offer support to women with children to participate in work life and also aim to provide an equal division of domestic responsibilities for spouses/partners and gender equality of employment opportunity. Thus, employment-based measures, such as those involving working hours and allowances, service-based measures, especially child care opportunities, and financial measures, such as child allowances and tax discounts, should be determined together. However, the direction and extent of these aforementioned policies differ from the dominant welfare regimes, employment policies, gender regimes, and population and body politics (Ünlütürk-Ulutaş, 2015: 727).

In Turkey, given that women are seen to be responsible for domestic works and care in the family, it is observed in the labour laws that women are the ones expected to provide the related reconciliation. Maternity leave for women stands at eight weeks before and eight weeks after giving birth (16 weeks in total). Paternity leave is 10 days, and it is optional and only pertains to civil servants. The Omnibus Law No. 6663 legislated in January 2016 gave the right of part-time work to mothers of children until the children reached the age of compulsory primary education and after completion of the maternity leave and the half-time work period, which proportionally increases with the number of children, in line with the child allowance. It was further mentioned in the law that the insurance premiums and wages corresponding to the hours worked would be paid by the employer, and that the state would cover insurance premiums and wages for off-hours through the Unemployment Insurance Fund (UIF). However, as this right is subject to the condition of a minimum of 600 days of unemployment insurance premiums, notified to the employee within the last three years prior to childbirth, its scope is limited. Yet, with transferring the employee from half-time work to part-time work, the labour contract of an employee who is temporarily employed by a person – probably another woman – is cancelled (Resmi Gazete, 2016). Considering that maternity leaves are not designed as parental leaves, there are discriminatory implementations of employers against women, and as part-time work leads to the loss of rights for women, in terms of their salaries and retirement in the long run, it is clear that women will pay the price of this reconciliation (KEİG, 2017). Therefore, perhaps the Turkish implementation of these policies does not aim to establish gender equality at home and at work, but is focused on ensuring female labour force participation by offering flexible working conditions that allow for increasing fertility rates and do not jeopardise the existing family structure (Dedeoğlu and Şahankaya 2015; Ünlütürk-Ulutaş, 2015).

5.5 POVERTY AND SOCIAL POLICIES

The neoliberal transformation characterised by the downsizing of the state, privatisation, marketisation, and frequently recurring crises at the macro level, generates income destabilisation and an increase in indebtedness and poverty at the household level. This process leads to income generating and expense reducing measures to facilitate the social reproduction of the family (Dedeoğlu, 2004: 105). To stave off poverty, women cut down on the consumption of products and services and manage the 'poverty of resources' they face by producing certain products with their own labour force inside the house (Güneş, 2014). Performing domestic works, such as shopping, cooking, washing up, laundry, cleaning and keeping the home heated at lower costs is only possible through an increase in women's domestic labour. Therefore, this scenario translates into an increase in the domestic workload of women and higher amounts of labour and time spent for reproduction (Dedeoğlu, 2004). Certain policies that have been brought to the agenda have led to an increase in the domestic workloads of women. For instance, in the 'Energy Lady Project' prepared cooperatively by the Ministry of Energy and Natural Resources (MOENR) and the Ministry of Family and Social Policy (MFSP), several recommendations have been presented to housewives to provide energy savings. As in-house works are counted as part of women's duty, the savings are expected to be provided by women. A similar framework is dominant in the family education programmes started in 2013, which were created to strengthen and protect the family. As part of the education provided to families, it is emphasised that women in particular should refrain from waste in care and house works, should focus on saving, and should use whatever small savings there are to benefit from micro-credit applications for entrepreneurship (Özmen-Yılmaz, 2013).

Apart from the increase in the domestic workload, women also pursue income-generating activities to meet more expensive needs, particularly ones that are required to be supplied from the market. These activities are entered into when there is no male presence at home, the male at home does not have a job, or loses their job, high debts or insufficient male income to earn a living for the family. As stated above, low education status and lack of work experience direct many women to unskilled, low-paying and insecure jobs, such as caring for babies, children, elderly, sick or disabled, day labour and cleaning. The domestic work and care services demanded by relatively highly educated women who are employed in high-skilled professions functions as another dynamic of this process. However, as flexible forms of employment are also insecure, this increases the women's dependency on social security through the working man-father/husband, which therefore increases their dependency on the male (Ergüneş, 2015).

With the Social Insurance and General Health Insurance Law No. 5510 entered into force in 2008, large sections of society were made vulnerable to social risks. Through the premium payment-based insurance system, the retirement age increased, and the right to retirement became more difficult. Especially for women who are employed in the private sector, it appears impossible for them to engage in paid out-of-home working life because of the burden of having to work both at home and at work, or to take maternal leave off work (Osmanağaoğlu, 2013). Based on gender inequality in registered, formal employment in Turkey, the secondary position of women in the social security area and the weakening of their social security right, women are forced to meet the most essential requirements through their status as a wife, a daughter or a mother who is bound to the male worker in the house – with certain criteria – rather than through the use of their citizen rights (Şahin, 2012: 232, KEİG, 2015). This situation reinforces the family rhetoric, eliminates the conditions of women's existence without a family, and imposes marriage and motherhood as a 'career' for women.

It is important to note that women constitute 70 per cent of the beneficiaries of social aid, such as poverty aid (which functions as one of the survival strategies of families), healthcare aid and education aid. As stated in the 10th Development Plan, in the provision of social aids and services on a family basis, women, who are defined based on their maternity and wifehood duties, have become the fundamental actors responsible for reducing the public burden of social services and aid (Urhan and Urhan, 2015: 253). Özateş-Gelmez (2018) points out that aid provided to women with children as part of the conditional education and health aids and social-economic support bring the mother's role to the forefront in child care, the results of which contribute to the failure seen in the transformation of the traditional gendered division of labour. Urhan states that the social aids, besides strengthening women's in-house responsibilities, cause women to withdraw from the labour market or become a cheap source of labour (Urhan, 2016). Thus, a conservative approach which limits the women's role to the family penetrates into social service and social aid implementations and addresses the woman only in terms of her position within the family. This, and the instrumentalisation of the female body that it speaks to, deepens the paid and unpaid gender-based division of labour.

One of the most significant obstacles faced by women in acquiring a paid job is the care work. It should also be approached in the context of the transformation of the social-political system. Care services for children, the elderly and the disabled are not sufficient in Turkey. For instance, among the potential users of daily care and early childhood education services, only 54,232 or just 2 per cent of the 22.5 million children can receive these services (Atasü-Topçuğlu, 2013). The capacity, quality of service, distance to the place of work and expensiveness of existing kindergartens are among the most significant problems. It has been argued that because of the regulation in 2008, kindergartens and nurseries in public institutions were regarded in terms of their social facility and were required to meet their own expenses, which led to a decrease in the number of kindergartens in the public area from 492 in 2007–08 to 109 in 2013–14 (Soyseçkin, 2015). Under Labour Law No. 4857, a lactation room must be provided by employers who employ between 100 and 150 women, and for companies with over 150 women workers, it is mandatory that the employer establish a day care centre for the 0–6 age group or contract out the service; however, it is well known that there is no supervision of this regulation and no implication of penal sanctions for companies that do not establish a day care centre.

The 13-item Prime Ministerial circular titled 'Increasing the Employment of Women and Ensuring Equality of Opportunity' was released in 2010. The circular aimed to provide a series of regulations and supervisions to increase women's employment and ensure gender equality. It included important regulations, such as the opening of kindergartens and day care centres in public and private workplaces, the promotion of gender equality in working life, and the collection of statistics based on gender. However, it was 'updated' in 2017 under the 'country conditions and current needs'. In this 'updating', the circular was rewritten based on a perspective that seemed to ignore women almost completely. Indeed, the items related to the equal pay for equal work were removed, and there was no mention of the supervision of this through the reports, nor of determining and taking action on whether the public and private companies complied with gender equality or not. There was not any mechanism to monitor whether proper procedures were followed for equality of opportunities in the recruitment, education and promotions, and if the priority for the projects prepared was being given to the women who are victims of domestic violence or who are widows. Furthermore, there was no check on whether the gender-based statistics were kept, on whether nurseries and day care centres had been established in the private and public companies, nor on the supervision of them if they were established (Akgökçe, 2017).

Reflecting the neoliberal logic, public institutions, professional chambers and NGOs have adopted the view that the increase in women's employment is only possible with their participation in employment through the entrepreneurship channel, a view derived from the difficulty in addressing the low demand of female employment. Being unable to create paid, regular and secure employment opportunities for women contributed to introducing the 'entrepreneurship route', as it aims to give women every opportunity to become producers (Buğra, 2010: 16). As stated by Toksöz (2007), the building block of the European Employment Strategy (EES) regarding the support of entrepreneurship has been adopted, with supporting activities for women's employment being almost transformed into support of entrepreneurship. Presenting entrepreneurship as a solution to women's employment is based on the articulation of women's work at home, through the supply of jobs similar to the work they do at home. It should be stated that although entrepreneurship 'liberalises' women, it causes the informalisation of female labour and strengthens the domestic gender division of labour (Ergüneş,

2015; Özmen-Yılmaz, 2015). It has been observed that micro-credit practices for low-income women, particularly those living in rural areas of Turkey, function as a way of compensating their debts or to manage their poverty rather than to establish a business (Toksöz, 2007). Women are directed to entrepreneurship through active employment policies, such as entrepreneurship trainings, vocational education courses or micro-credit applications, so the solution to women's employment problem is assigned to the women.

These flexibility-based, family-based and market-based legal transformations promote the idea of women participating in the labour market through flexible employment and entrepreneurship models without disturbing their domestic reproduction activities. It also assigns the public care burden to the family, which is placed on women's shoulders. These types of employment, which do 'not ignore the family', are in line with the conservative/Islamist neoliberal approach. Therefore, the exploitation of female labour, which is considered as an unused potential of the economy, gradually increases under the mutual interests of capitalism and patriarchy.

5.6 CONCLUSION

In Turkey, although policies aimed at providing gender equality and increasing women's employment have gained importance in the development plans and other policy texts, particularly after the 2000s, these have been non-functional and have had extremely limited positive effects on the paid and unpaid labour of women. In fact, we can state that in contemporary Turkey under the AKP governments, where capitalism has been restructured along the lines of neoliberal and conservative policies, all the regulations have led to an increase in the exploitation of labour (Erol, 2019). Yet, the situation is much worse for women. The number of women who have become unemployed increased by 5.5 times compared to that of men. The areas with the highest informal employment are those in which the highest concentration of women can be found. Besides this, the ratio of self-employed women has increased with the incentives offered as part of the entrepreneurship path, the result of which is the increase in informal employment among women, as almost all self-employed women are informal. In this sense, it can be argued that the temporary employment provided as a solution for unemployment and to prevent informality of the labour market reproduces informality.

Unemployment, particularly youth unemployment is very high, but the unemployment of young women is even higher and continues to rise (27.4 per cent as of April 2020). Not only are the institutional care services provided by the state for children, elderly and disabled citizens insufficient, but also are efforts to increase the number of nurseries and kindergartens. The shortage of these has been the biggest obstacle to women's employment, but they are not even on the government's agenda. Although it is mandatory for the local governments to open nurseries, there are no mechanisms to control if they are opened. It has been observed that even half-hearted regulations of this aspect have been removed through the now defunct Prime Ministry circular under the name of 'updating'. There has been no new plan prepared regarding gender equality since 2013, which reveals that objectives related to gender equality on paper have been totally off the government's agenda. The conservative/Islamist discourse on the importance of women for the continuation of the family increased especially with the slowdown in the EU negotiations after 2006–07, which had a neoliberal but 'egalitarian' discourse (see Toksöz, 2016). In this context, in 2011, the Ministry of State Responsible for Women and Family Affairs was replaced by the Ministry of Family and Social Policies. After the July 2018 elections, this ministry was merged with the Ministry of Labour and Social Security to form a new ministry called the 'Ministry of Family, Labour and Social Services' (with the Presidential Decree published in Official Journal on 21 April 2021 The Ministry of Family, Labour and Social Services divided into two). Considered with recent debates on withdrawing from the 'Istanbul Convention'[1] – which promotes women's rights and aims to prevent violence against women – and other related Islamist discourses, this orientation reiterates the attempts to restrain women within their family status, and to demolish women's social security through flexible work and social aids at the institutional level.

I contend that the problem is the framework itself rather than any obstacles in its implementation. Is increasing women's employment a neoliberal strategy, a tool of flexibilisation of labour markets, and an objective of population policies and conservative family policies, or is women's employment primarily a women's issue? The provision of gender equality is related to the removal of extremely interrelated inequalities in many economic and social areas. Employment is one of these areas. In fact, a realist policy for women's employment requires an organisation that includes coordinated policies in areas such as women's education, pre-school education and care for children, elderly, disabled, unpaid domestic labour, unpaid family labour; and these policies should involve the effective participation of women in the policy-making and implementation process. To achieve this, it requires a strong will to improve the status of women in every sense. However, it has been clearly observed that this is not the perspective of the AKP governments; as the common core of these policies and papers focuses on the reconciliation of work and family life through protecting the family and dynamic population structure for competitiveness, extending the flexible forms of employment by not disturbing the 'fundamental duty' of women, such as giving birth, providing care and doing housework, and highlighting entrepreneurship opportunities.

The policies enacted based on gender equality and women's employment that focus on population, family and economic growth have become a tool for embedding women into a conservative family structure and for including them in the Turkish labour market unequally. As remarked at the beginning of this chapter, this situation once again reveals the necessity to consider women's paid and unpaid labour in an interrelated manner.

BIBLIOGRAPHY

Acar-Savran, G. (2004) *Beden Emek Tarih*, İstanbul: Kanat.
Akgökçe, N. (2017) 'Kadınlara Güvencesiz İstihdam Genelgesi', *BirGün*, https://tinyurl.com/y3lv4arg (accessed 1 July 2019).
Atasü-Topçupoğlu, R. (2013) 'Sosyal Haklar Piyasalaşır mı? Çocuk Hakları ve Kadın Emeğinin Kesişiminde Türkiye'de Kreşler', *V. Sosyal Haklar Uluslararası Sempozyumu*.
Buğra, A. (2010) 'Toplumsal Cinsiyet, İşgücü ve Refah Rejimleri: Türkiye'de Kadın İstihdamı', *TÜBİTAK Project Report*, İstanbul.

Ciğerci-Ulukan, N. (2014) 'İşsizlik Versus Geçici Çalışma: Özel İstihdam Bürolarının Kiralık İşçileri', in Müftüoğlu, Ö. and Koşar, A. (eds), *Kapitalist Üretim İlişkilerinde Yeniden Esneklik, Türkiye'de Esnek* Çalışma, İstanbul: Evrensel, 143–57.

Ciğerci-Ulukan, N. and Özmen-Yılmaz, D. (2016) 'Kamu Sağlık Sektöründe Çalışan Taşeron Kadın İşçiler: Samsun ve Ordu İli Örneği', *Çalışma ve Toplum*, 48, 87–114.

Dedeoğlu, S. (2004) 'Dünya Ekonomisi ve Hayatta Kalmanın Feminizasyonu, Toplumsal Cinsiyet, Kalkınma ve Küreselleşme', in Dedeoğlu, S. and Subaşat, T. (eds), *Kalkınma ve Küreselleşme*, İstanbul: Bağlam, 87–111.

Dedeoğlu, S. and Şahankaya, A. (2015) 'Türkiye'de İş ve Aile Yaşamını Uyumlaştırma Politikaları', in Dedeoğlu, S. and Elveren, A.Y. (eds), *2000'ler Türkiye'sinde Sosyal Politika ve Toplumsal Cinsiyet*, Ankara: İmge, 93–121.

Erdoğdu, S. (2018) 'Özel İstihdam Büroları Aracılığıyla Geçici İşçilik: Padrone'ler ve Kelly Kızı'ndan Küresel İstihdam Şirketlerine', in Ünlütürk-Ulutaş, Ç. (ed.), *Feminist Sosyal Politika Bakım-Emek-Göç, Gülay Toksöz'e Armağan*, Ankara: Nota Bene, 141–71.

Ergüneş, N. (2012) 'Sosyal Politikada Dönüşümüm Etkilerini Biz Kadınlar Nasıl Yaşıyoruz?', Karaburun Bilim Kongresi, Bildiri Metni.

—— (2015) 'Kadın İstihdamı, Evet Ama Nasıl?' *TTB Mesleki Sağlık ve Güvenlik Dergisi*, 56, 30–6.

Erol, M.E. (2019) 'State and Labour under AKP Rule in Turkey: An Appraisal', *Journal of Balkan and Near Eastern Studies*, 21 (6), 633–77.

Gün, S. (2016) 'Neoliberal Muhafazakarlığın İş ve Aile Yaşamını Uzlaştırma Yaklaşımı', *Mülkiye*, 40 (3), 35–54.

Güneş F. (2014) 'Yoksullukla Başa Çıkma Stratejileri, Kaynakların Yoksulluğu mu? Kadın Emeği Merkezli Eleştirel Bir Analiz', in Topçuoğlu, A., Aksan, G. and Alptekin, D. et al. (eds), *Yoksulluk ve Kadın*, İstanbul: Ayrıntı, 89–128.

Hartman, H. (1979) 'The Unhappy Marriage of Marxism and Feminism: Towards a More Progressive Union', *Capital & Class*, 3 (2), 1–3.

KEİG (2014) *Esnekleşme ve Enformelleşme Kıskacında Türkiye'de Kadın Emeği ve İstihdamı, Politika Metinleri Çerçevesinde Bir Analiz*, https://tinyurl.com/y2gyqy3v (accessed 7 July 2018).

—— (2015) *Türkiye'de Kadınlar Sosyal Güvenliğin Neresinde? 5510 Sayılı Sosyal Sigortalar ve Genel Sağlık Sigortası Kanununun Toplumsal Cinsiyet Açısından Analizi*, https://tinyurl.com/y46hear2 (accessed 7 July 2018).

—— (2017) 'İşgücü Piyasasında Gelişmeler: 2014–2016 Döneminde Kadınlar ve Erkeklerin İstihdamı ve İşsizliği Ne Yönde Değişti?' https://tinyurl.com/yxesffhn (accessed 7 July 2018).

Kergoat, D. (2009) 'Cinsiyete Dayalı İşbölümü ve Toplumsal Cinsiyet İlişkileri', in Hırata, H., Laborie, F., Le Doare H. and Senotier D. (eds), Acar Savran G. (trans.), *Eleştirel Feminizm Sözlüğü*, Kanat, İstanbul, 94–105.

MOD (Ministry of Development) (1995) *Yedinci Beş Yıllık Kalkınma Planı (1996–2000)*, https://tinyurl.com/yyvflvnm (accessed 3 March 2017).

—— (2006) *Dokuzuncu Kalkınma Planı (2007–2013)*, https://tinyurl.com/y3oc9vv2 (accessed 8 April 2018).

——(2008) *2008 Annual Programme*.

—— (2014) *Onuncu Kalkınma Planı (2014–2018)*, https://tinyurl.com/y5l45tzu (accessed 8 April 2018).

—— (2015) *Ailenin ve Dinamik Nüfus Yapısının Korunması Eylem Planı, Onuncu Kalkınma Planı Öncelikli Dönüşüm Programları*, 22, https://tinyurl.com/yxr6kzjm (accessed 8 April 2018).

MOLSS (Ministry of Labour and Social Security) (2017) *National Employment Strategy*, www.uis.gov.tr/uis/EylemPlanlariEN (accessed 12 April 2020).

Osmanağaoğlu, H. (2013) 'AKP Kadınları Eve Kapatmıyor, Aileye Zincirliyor', *Perspectives*, 5, 13, Heinrich Böll Stiftung Derneği, 40–3, https://tinyurl.com/yygmnt5g (accessed 12 April 2017).

Özateş-Gelmez, S. (2018) 'Sosyal Yardımların Toplumsal Cinsiyetli Doğası: Cinsiyetçi İşbölümünün Yeniden Üretimi', in Kutlu, D. (ed.), *Sosyal Yardım Alanları, Emek, Geçim Siyaset ve Toplumsal Cinsiyet*, İletişim, İstanbul, 193–206.

Özmen-Yılmaz, D. (2013) 'Kalkınma ve Kadın İlişkisi Bağlamında Aile Eğitim Programının Eleştirel Bir Değerlendirmesi', *Praksis*, 33, 111–28.

——(2015) 'Beyond Neoliberal Development: Socialist Feminist Alternatives from Turkey', in Marois, T. and Pradella, L. (eds), *Polarizing Development, Alternatives to Neoliberalizm and the Crisis*, London: Pluto, 237–47.

Republic of Turkey, Prime Ministry Directorate General on the Status of Women (2008) 'National Action Plan on Gender Equality 2008–2013', https://tinyurl.com/y57lud9r (accessed 17 April 2018).

Resmi Gazete (2016), Sayı 29620, www.resmigazete.gov.tr/eskiler/2016/02/20160210.pdf (accessed 12 April 2020).

Soyseçkin, İ.S. (2015) 'Türkiye'de Kadın İstihdamı ve Sosyal Refah Uygulamaları', *Mülkiye*, 39 (3), 245–70.

Standing, G. (2011) *Precariat: The New Dangerous Class*, London: Bloomsbury.

Şahin, M. (2012) 'Türkiye'de Sosyal Güvenlik Reformu ve Kadınlar Üzerine Etkisi', in Dedeoğlu, S. and Elveren, A.Y. (eds), *Türkiye'de Refah Devleti ve Kadın*, İletişim, İstanbul, 231–49.

TAYA (2016) 'Türkiye Aile Yapısı Araştırması, Tespitler Öneriler', Aile ve Sosyal Politikalar Bakanlığı, İstanbul, https://tinyurl.com/y4mhapoa (accessed 20 November 2018).

Toksöz, G. (2007) *Türkiye'de Kadın* İstihdamı, Ankara: ILO Publications.

——(2016) 'Kadın'dan Aile'ye Geçiş AKP Döneminin İstihdam Politikalarının Toplumsal Cinsiyet Açısından Analizi', *VIII. Sosyal* İnsan *Hakları Ulusal Sempozyumu*.

Ulukan, U. (2014) 'Esneklik ve Güvence Arasında Bir Denge Mümkün Mü? Avrupa ve Türkiye'den 'Güvenceli' Esneklik Pratikleri', in Müftüoğlu, Ö. and Koşar, A. (eds), *Kapitalist* Üretim İlişkilerinde *Yeniden Esneklik, Türkiye'de Esnek* Çalışma, Evrensel, İstanbul, 68–87.

Urhan, B. (2016) 'Kadın Emeği ve Toplumsal Cinsiyet', in Saygılıgil, F. (ed.), *Toplumsal Cinsiyet Tartışmaları*, Dipnot, Ankara, 119–49.

Urhan, G. and Urhan, B. (2015) 'AKP Döneminde Sosyal Yardım', in Koray, M. and Çelik, A. (eds), *Himmet, Fıtrat, Piyasa, AKP Döneminde Sosyal Politika*, Ankara: İletişim, 229–58.

Ünlütürk-Ulutaş, Ç. (2015) 'İş ve Aile Yaşamını Uzlaştırma Politikaları Türkiye'de Yeni Politika Arayışları', *Ankara* Üniversitesi *SBF Dergisi*, 70 (3), 723–50.

6

The Making of the Rural Proletariat in Neoliberal Turkey

Coşku Çelik

6.1 INTRODUCTION

Deepening of neoliberalism in the countryside of Turkey corresponds to the aftermath of the 2000–01 financial crises and the consecutive AKP (Justice and Development Party) governments. The impact of neoliberalism in the countryside of Turkey has been impoverishment, dispossession and therefore proletarianisation of the small-scale agricultural producers. As a result of the neoliberal transformation of agriculture, input prices have continuously risen whereas prices of products have fallen. This has increased the market dependency of agricultural producers and their reproduction has become more cash-dependent. Within this 'reproduction squeeze' (Bernstein, 1979), rural households started to develop certain survival strategies. The most common strategy has been migration to the urban centres for wage work. The majority of the rural population has migrated to city centres and constituted the most precarious segment of the urban labour force. However, the agrarian change of the AKP period cannot be analysed as a simple process of de-agrarianisation and urbanisation. The main transformation has been the elimination of the former smallholder-based to an agribusiness-based agrarian structure (Gürel et al., 2019: 465). Therefore, class relations in the countryside is still a significant issue to understand the authoritarian neoliberalism of the AKP. This study aims to analyse the formation of the rural proletariat in neoliberal Turkey whose protagonists are the 'classes of labour' – conceptualised by Henri Bernstein as a component of the proletariat neither dispossessed of all means of reproducing itself nor possessing sufficient means to reproduce itself – and the completely dispossessed seasonal migrant workers.

Despite the massive urbanisation which started in the 1980s and accelerated from the early 2000s onwards, around a quarter of Turkey's population (20,331,797 in 2019) is still rural (World Bank, 2019). As a result of the neoliberal transformation of agriculture, small-scale producers have been developing various survival strategies in the countryside by diversifying their means of income in wage work in agriculture and off-farm employments such as tourism, construction or mining. In addition, the composition of the rural labour markets is determined by gender and ethnicity. Firstly, proletarianisation of the peasantry is a gendered process as diversification of the means of income indicates various forms of use of labour power potential within rural households. Mostly, male members of these households start working in rural industries such as mining, construction or tourism whereas female members continue farm work in several ways such as petty commodity production, agricultural wage work and subsistence production. Therefore, proletarianisation of the rural households in Turkey has indicated further[1] feminisation of agricultural labour. Secondly, the ethnic structure in Turkey is reproduced in the rural labour markets. Two turning points determined the ethnic structure of the rural labour markets in Turkey: the forced migration of the Kurdish peasants in the late 1980s and migration of the Syrian refugees in the early 2010s. On the one hand, these two groups have constituted the cheap labour force for the Turkish farmers, whereas on the other hand ethnic discrimination has constituted a moment of intra-class conflict for the rural proletariat in Turkey.

This chapter consists of four main sections. The first section presents the theoretical foundations of my analysis. The second section summarises the neoliberal transformation of agriculture in Turkey. In the third section, class relations in the countryside of Turkey is examined with reference to proletarianisation of the petty commodity producers, and feminisation and ethnicisation of the agricultural labour. The last section discusses the rural politics and moments of resistance in the countryside with specific reference to the factors preventing the formation of organised resistance against policies that have led to the massive dispossession.

6.2 FORMATION OF THE RURAL PROLETARIAT
UNDER NEOLIBERALISM

In the context of neoliberalism, the global wave of proletarianisation and the class formation process of the recently dispossessed population has taken a peculiar form. One of the most important strategies of neoliberalism has been expropriating the commons and the small individual property for capital accumulation. The impact of this strategy in the countryside has been subjection of the small-scale agricultural producers to the imperatives of the market. Therefore, they have adopted a variety of survival strategies to cope with the uncertain market conditions (Aydın, 2001). These strategies may either be migration to the cities and quitting agricultural production or diversification of the income sources in the countryside (Keyder and Yenal, 2011; Çelik, 2017, 2019). From the 1970s onwards, proletarianisation of the peasantry in the Global South has accelerated in parallel with the neoliberal transformation of the world economy. This is a clear indicator of the structural adjustment programmes and economic liberalisation, both of which resulted in the subsistence crisis (Johnson, 2004: 56). Just like Kautsky (1899 [1988]) and Lenin (1899 [1974]) underlined with reference to the emergence of capitalist relations in agriculture, in the context of neoliberalism as well there is no uniform or linear path of proletarianisation of the peasantry. Instead, it is a complicated process constantly subject to contradictory tendencies. The main transformation for the peasantry under neoliberalism has been the commodification of the production and reproduction processes that direct producers' access to the means of production, and means of subsistence have increasingly been mediated by the market (Wood, 2009: 38).

Contemporary Marxist literature on proletarianisation of the peasantry links the commodification of means of subsistence to the dissolution of the peasantry, and analyses proletarianisation in the countryside as the diversification of rural means of livelihood (cf. Bernstein, 1979, 2001; Bryceson, 1999; Johnson, 2004). For Bernstein (2004), neoliberalism in agriculture has changed the social composition in the countryside and transformed peasantry into petty commodity producers. Meanwhile, prices of the products produced for the market have fallen, whereas the input prices (cost of production) have risen. This resulted in a subsistence crisis, defined by Bernstein (1979) as 'simple reproduction squeeze' (1979: 427). Small-scale producers have become unable to reproduce themselves and have had no option but to sell their labour power.

Bernstein's analysis of the rural proletariat follows the definition of Lenin that it is composed of 'completely landless; but most typically ... the allotment-holding farm labourer, day labourer, unskilled labourer, building worker or other allotment holding worker' (1899 [1974]: 173) whose defining feature is inability to survive without the sale of the labour power (1974: 177). Following this definition and Lenin's (1899 [1974]) critique of the stereotyped understanding of capitalism that it requires completely dispossessed, free workers, Bernstein argues that the rural population who sell their labour power while having access to a certain plot of land is a part of the rural proletariat. In other words, loss of the non-market access to means of production and subsistence resulted in increasing cash dependency and therefore the necessity for regular income for the rural population to finance both costs of agricultural production and daily consumption. Thereby petty producers cultivating a plot of land, together with the landless rural population or seasonal migrant workers swelled the ranks of the rural proletariat. For Bernstein, this process has resulted in the formation of the 'classes of labour', 'a component that is neither dispossessed of all means of reproducing itself nor in possession of sufficient means to reproduce itself' (2010: 73).

Classes of labour comprise the 'growing numbers ... who now depend – directly and indirectly – on the sale of their labour power for their daily reproduction' (Panitch et al. 2001: ix). Bernstein uses the term classes of labour over semi-proletarian by arguing that this term is 'less encumbered with problematic assumptions and associations in both political economy (e.g. functionalist readings of Marx's reserve army of labour) and political theory and ideology (e.g. constructions of an idealised (Hegelian) collective class subjects' (Bernstein, 2010: 73). Accordingly, proletarianisation of the peasantry indicates a class formation in the countryside. As stated by Araghi (2009: 138), proletarianisation of the peasantry 'is not a completed or self-completing process leading to death of the peasantry.

Social classes do not simply end or die; they live and are transformed through social struggles.' Instead, it is 'an ongoing process "a happening" in Thompson's words' (Araghi, 1995: 359).[2] Furthermore, based on Shanin's (1986) argument that rural relations must be understood in terms of the capital-labour relation beyond agriculture, Bernstein conceptualises the classes of labour side of this relation as 'labour beyond the farm' (Bernstein, 2010: 110). Accordingly, he claims that neoliberal transformation also generates increasing fragmentation of the rural proletariat in the countryside (Bernstein, 2004: 204–5). The combination of growing land shortage, economic crises and unfavourable policies for domestic agriculture under neoliberalism has indicated that rural households can no longer sustain themselves on the basis of agriculture alone. This led to the increase in the number of rural household members pursuing off-farm activities (Deere, 2005: 1).

In defining the rural proletariat in Turkey, I follow the definitions of Lenin and Bernstein. Accordingly, in neoliberal Turkey, the rural proletariat includes petty commodity producers in the process of dispossession, workers of the rural industries, landless agricultural workers and seasonal migrant workers.

6.3 NEOLIBERAL TRANSFORMATION OF AGRICULTURE IN TURKEY

Before the 1980s – particularly after the late 1940s – Turkey's countryside made significant gains from the state subsidies and the provision of infrastructure, education and health services. In the context of the Marshall Plan, during the late 1940s and early 1950s, the role attributed to Turkey in the international division of labour was providing agricultural products to Europe especially for grain production (Gürel, 2011: 202). The Marshall Plan enabled mechanisation of agricultural production and expansion of the cultivated areas. More significantly, it encouraged the intensification of state support for agriculture in the forms of development of infrastructure and transportation, input provisioning and guarantee of state purchase of main crops (Aydın, 2010: 153). In the 1950s, agricultural production rose significantly. From the 1960s onwards, until the 1980s, policies supporting agriculture were maintained and even expanded (Oyan, 2015: 113). Also, during this period, large-scale State Economic Enterprises (SEEs) were effective. SEEs were operating as monopolies in the corresponding product and were encouraging the expansion of agricultural production through the provision of cheap inputs and purchase guarantee to the producers. In this period, small-scale and independent producers were dominant in agricultural production (Keyder and Yenal, 2013: 108). Between 1948 and1980, the number of harvesters rose from 1000 to more than 13,000 (Gürel, 2011: 203). This significant increase in the number of harvesters clearly shows the considerable state support for small-scale agricultural producers.

Since the early 1980s, neoliberal policies have had an inevitable impact on agriculture. In the Global South, Structural Adjustment Programmes were imposing reforms such as withdrawal of the state's protectionist role in input subsidies, implementation of the minimum price, removal of guarantee of purchase, and reconstruction of agricultural policies in accordance with the free-market logic. Until the 1980s, market dependency in agricultural production was limited to the input and product markets and farmers as commodity producers were able to control the production process. The most significant transformation in Turkey within this process was that agribusiness capital started to control producers from the production process to the marketing of the food (Bor, 2014: 104–5). On the other hand, implementation of neoliberalism in agriculture in Turkey has not been a smooth process. Especially in the second half of the 1980s and during the 1990s when the number of parties contesting in the elections was quite high, government interventions in the price formation or reintroduction of certain subsidies and supports could be on the agenda despite the irritation of the IMF and World Bank. A significant turning point for the restructuring of agricultural policies in Turkey was the 5 April stabilisation programme under the control of the IMF in the aftermath of the 1994 crisis. From 1994 onwards, the transformation of agriculture as envisaged in the 24 January decisions has accelerated. In the context of the 5 April programme, the number of guaranteed procurements of crops was limited, the power of the Union and Agricultural Sales Cooperatives was weakened, and input supports were diminished. However, again, implementation of the programme in agriculture was not smooth due to political expediency, electoral concerns and change of governments (Aydın, 2010: 158).

Deepening of neoliberalism in agriculture or 'great neoliberal transformation' (İslamoğlu, 2017: 75) in the countryside of Turkey corresponds to the aftermath of 2000–01 crises and the AKP governments. Determinants of the agricultural policies of this period have been IMF and World Bank agreements, letters of intentions, and the initiation of Agricultural Reform Implementation Project (ARIP) that resulted in a significant reconstruction of the state-countryside relations. The main transformations in this context have been (Günaydın, 2009: 178; BSB, 2015: 96–7):

1. Withdrawal of the former support system and initiation of Direct Income Support.
2. Withdrawal of subsidised agricultural credit system of the Agricultural Bank.
3. Determination of the prices by the world stock prices.
4. Restructuring of the Union and Agricultural Sales Cooperatives.
5. Privatisation of agricultural State Economic Enterprises such as Turkish Sugar Factories Corporation, General Directorate of Tea Enterprises (Çaykur) and the State Monopoly of Tobacco and Alcoholic Beverages (Tekel).

As a result of these transformations in agricultural policies starting from the 1980s and accelerating from the 2000s onwards, Turkey's total agricultural production fell drastically. The share of agriculture in GDP fell from 23.8 per cent in 1978 to 18.9 per cent in 1988, and 9.1 per cent in 2010. On the other hand, the value of total agricultural production rose from 17 billion in 2000 to 79 billion in 2009 (Gürel, 2014: 352). Also, the average annual growth rate of the value-added per worker in agriculture rose from 4 per cent between 1991 and 2002 to 4.9 per cent between 2003 and 2016 (Gürel et al., 2019: 465). Therefore, despite the dramatic fall of the share of agriculture in GDP, it would be wrong to claim that this process has indicated the elimination of agrarian relations (or de-agrarianisation) in the countryside. Instead, the former agricultural structure dominated by small-scale farming has transformed and agriculture has become a more profitable sector in accordance with the interests of national and international agribusiness capital.

The neoliberal transformation of agriculture in collaboration among the state, international organisations and agribusiness firms indicates a process of 'modern enclosures' (Aysu and Kayalıoğlu, 2014: 11). This modern enclosure has been targeting not only the expropriation of land but also expropriation of the subsistence production or family farming. This enclosure has been manifested in the countryside in the form of impoverishment, dispossession and therefore proletarianisation of the small-scale agricultural producers.

6.4 FORMATION OF THE RURAL PROLETARIAT: PROLETARIANISATION, FEMINISATION AND ETHNICISATION

The rural proletariat in neoliberal Turkey is composed of petty commodity producers in the process of dispossession, workers of the rural industries, landless agricultural workers and seasonal migrant workers. Therefore, the agricultural workforce in the countryside cannot be defined as limited to paid labour. It includes agricultural wage workers (local and migrant), petty commodity producers (or family farmers) and unpaid subsistence producers. As a matter of fact, these groups mostly are not mutually exclusive. For example, it is quite common for a petty commodity producer to work as a wage worker in other farms after completing work on her own farm. Three factors have determined the composition of the rural labour markets in neoliberal Turkey, which are proletarianisation of small-scale agricultural producers, feminisation of agricultural work and ethnicisation of the agricultural workforce.

Firstly, to grasp the transformation of the rural class relations, analysis of proletarianisation is essential given that family farming and petty commodity production had been the prevalent form of agricultural production in the countryside of Turkey. From the early 2000s onwards, the number of small-scale agricultural producers fell drastically and there has been a limited possibility for the population detached from the land to be absorbed in urban employment.

Despite the massive wave of proletarianisation from the early 2000s onwards, the rural population constitutes around one quarter of the population. Small-scale agricultural producers who developed specific survival strategies in the countryside constitute the majority of the rural proletariat. Therefore, reliance on supplementary sources of income and off-farm employment does not necessarily result in migration to the larger cities. Instead, it is quite common to continue to reside in the villages and commute to daily work in nearby cities or in the rural industries such as mining, tourism or construction (Keyder and Yenal, 2011; Çelik, 2017). The relation of the peasant household to wage labour is related to the household labour reserve, use of this reserve in the production and reproduction processes of the household, the sexual division of labour within the family, and the relation between productive and reproductive labour (Özuğurlu, 2011; Çelik, 2019).

Another form of survival strategy of this population in the country-side is contract farming. In contract farming, farmers transfer control over the production process to agribusiness firms and maintain the production by using their family labour and means of production. In the absence of the former state subsidies, farmers may prefer contract farming due to the purchase guarantee and, in this way, agribusiness firms or supermarkets exploit the agricultural producers as 'hidden proletarians' on their own land. On the other hand, agribusiness firms prefer contract farming because by avoiding direct control of production, they get rid of the cost of the social wage necessary for the survival of the whole family (Aydın, 2015: 313). Therefore, contract farming equates to the implementation of subcontracting in agriculture and transforms the family farmers into subcontracted workers. The direct producers lose control over the production and solely possess simple property rights (Bor, 2014: 116–17).

The second determinant of the composition of rural labour markets is the feminisation of agricultural work. Proletarianisation of the rural population under neoliberalism generates significant changes in the sexual division of labour within rural households and in the rural economy as a whole (Katz, 2003: 32). Proletarianisation of the rural population is mostly associated with male proletarianisation, especially in the extractive regions. But as the classes of labour are employed in precarious, informal and low wage jobs, income generated by the wages mostly is not sufficient for the survival of the whole family. Therefore, the wave of proletarianisation under neoliberalism has mostly been in the form of men moving out of agriculture and women remaining at the farm or moving out much slower. According to the 2017 data of the Food and Agricultural Organization of the United Nations (FAO), the share of women in agriculture has been growing in almost all developing countries in the twenty-first century (FAO, 2017: 88).

In Turkey, women are employed in agriculture mostly in temporary, seasonal and informal ways. On the other hand, diversification of the rural income generating strategy and the search for off-farm employment resulted in women's increasing participation in agriculture not only as wage workers but also on their own account and for subsistence production. Therefore, women's work in the countryside mostly includes at least one of the following forms: subsistence production, petty commodity production, (daily) wage work in agriculture and reproductive work within the family. These forms do not exclude each other as they are mostly done simultaneously. For example, for mobile agricultural workers who live in the tent shelters during the harvest season, agricultural work and reproductive work of women such as cleaning the tent shelter and preparing the meal are intertwined. On the other hand, women who live in their villages mostly continue petty commodity production on their own land; after the harvest season they work as agricultural wage labourers at big capitalist farms and while doing this, they continue producing fruits, vegetables or raising animals for their own consumption. Therefore, for the analysis of women's work in the countryside, there is a need to consider the internal relationship between social relations of production and reproduction as they are mostly intertwined (see: Çelik and Balta, 2017; Çelik 2019).

Women also constitute the majority of agricultural wage labourers in capitalist farms. The work arrangements in agriculture are far from being formal and legal. It is a personalised labour arrangement based on the exploitation of the cheapest and weakest labour force (Pelek, 2010: 23). Female members of the petty agricultural commodity producer families experiencing the process of dispossession is the relatively cheaper and weaker component of the rural house-holds' labour reserve and they are employed in the capitalist farms as informal and unregistered workers. Also, according to several studies (cf: Çınar, 2014; Çelik, 2019; Pelek, 2019; also see chapter 5) women work in agriculture informally, for low wages, long hours and under extremely arduous conditions. According to the data of Health and Safety Labour Watch, in Turkey between 2013 and 2019, at least 817 women died at the workplace and 51 per cent (419) of them were working in agriculture (Figure 6.1). As almost all women work infor-mally and without social insurance, this number is limited to the observed cases. Also, even for these confirmed ones there is no liabil-ity of the farmers or labour intermediaries because their work is not registered.

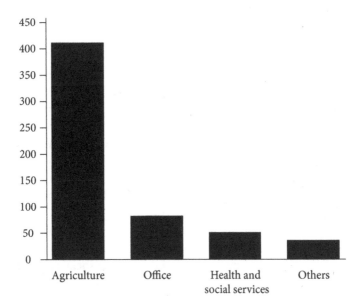

Figure 6.1   Workplace Deaths of Women in Turkey 2013–19
Source: ISIG (2020).

The third factor determining the composition of rural labour markets is the ethnicisation of agricultural work. In her extensive research, Dedeoğlu (2018: 40) argues that structural transformation of agriculture resulted in the need for a cheap labour force and the mobile seasonal agricultural workers are from the poorest segments of the society. As in most parts of the world, in Turkey as well, migrant workers constitute the cheapest group in the labour markets. Two main turning points determined the ethnic structure of the rural labour markets in Turkey. The first one is the forced migration policy of the 1990s which quickly displaced and urbanised the Kurdish peasants.[3] Families who have social networks in the metropolis migrated to these places with the support of their relatives. The rest of them migrated to city centres in the east and southeast region and few job opportunities force them to work as migrant farm workers seasonally (Pelek, 2010: 51). The second turning point is the Syrian war. Since 2011 Turkey has been the preferred migration destination for Syrian refugees; there are around 3.5 million Syrian refugees in Turkey who escaped the civil war in Syria. These refugees constitute the new precarious labour force in the countryside of Turkey (Kavak, 2016; Pelek, 2019). Due to their fragile legal status, Syrian refugees constitute the cheapest and most disciplined labour force for the Turkish farmers.

6.5 RURAL CLASS STRUGGLE AND MOMENTS OF RESISTANCE IN THE COUNTRYSIDE

Despite the immense wave of dispossession and terrible conditions of the agricultural workers in Turkey, there has not been any massive resistance against the agricultural policies of the neoliberal governments. Although there have been moments of resistance in the countryside since the mid-2000s, they have largely not targeted the agricultural policies that led to the impoverishment and dispossession of the rural population. Instead, they were against the construction of fossil fuel and hydroelectricity plants in the Black Sea region (such as Gerze, Cerrattepe, Fındıklı), Aegean Region (such as Bergama and Yırca) and in the Marmara Region (Ira Mountains). However, these struggles have been place-based, short-term protests focusing on particular investments and have not turned into stable broad-based alliances. Therefore, they have not been reflected in the political dispositions of the rural population (Avcı, 2018: 76; Gürel et al., 2019:

472). Indeed, the AKP received significant political support from the rural population from the beginning. I argue that there are two significant reasons behind the consent of the rural population to the neoliberalism of the AKP: (1) employment generation capacity of the extractive investments in the countryside and (2) intra-class conflict within the rural proletariat.

Firstly, the extractive investments' function as a consent making mechanism for the AKP has been much more effective than the struggles against their environmental impact. Despite small-scale and short-term moments of resistance, extractive investments in the countryside received popular support as the AKP governments presented its construction and extraction boom as a manifestation of successful economic development. Developmentalism of the AKP based on construction, energy and transportation is presented as a symbol of national power and independence trivialising socio-economic inequalities. More significantly, employment creation potential of the extractive industries has been especially significant for the state-countryside relations under the AKP rule as these investments coincided with dispossession of the small-scale agricultural producers. Therefore, these investments have been regarded as an employment opportunity in their villages by the rural population (see Çelik, 2017). Even though they have been private sector investments, the successive AKP governments have assumed a pivotal role in these investments and transformed its top-down developmentalism into the base support (Erensü, 2018; Akbulut, 2019; Adaman and Akbulut, 2020). The discourse of employment generation in the countryside seemingly promised prosperity for all segments of the society. Instead of organising broad-based political alliances targeting the neoliberal agricultural policies of the AKP, the rural population has supported the AKP for providing employment in the countryside.

Secondly, despite the terrible working conditions of the agricultural wage workers, it would appear that they do not form an organised class movement. The most significant reason behind this is their works being unregistered. Therefore, it is not likely for such a disintegrated workforce to identify their collective interests. On the other hand, ethnic differentials between migrant, non-migrant, emigrant and refugee statuses generate intra-class conflict within the agricultural workers in Turkey. As exemplified by several studies, ethnic structure in the society in general is reproduced in the structure of the agricultural labour force, and this directly affects rural class relations (cf. Duruiz, 2015; Dedeoğlu, 2018; Pelek, 2018, 2019). Duruiz (2015: 291–2) analyses the significance of ethnic differences in the country-side in her field research in western Turkey. Accordingly, there is a spatial difference between the local (Turkish) and migrant Kurdish or Romany gypsy workers. Whereas local workers who work in the big capitalist farms reside in their village houses, migrant workers stay in tents close to the fields that they work. These tents are pitched in places away from the city centres because Romany and Kurdish workers are considered dangerous. Romany workers are regarded as potential robbers whereas Kurdish are regarded as terrorists. Also, local workers who are in the process of dispossession mostly work for higher wages whereas migrant workers supply cheap labour for farmers (see Dedeoğlu, 2018). Pelek (2018, 2019) exemplifies ethnic discrimination in the rural labour markets with reference to the condition of Syrian refugees. Accordingly, factors such as complete dispossession, fear of deportation, dependency on labour interme-diaries, language problems, conflict with other worker groups and fear of death and violence determine the working conditions of the Syrian workers (2018: 616). Mainly due to their fragile legal status, Syrians constitute the cheapest group of workers in agriculture and they mostly earn less than two thirds of the other workers (Dedeoğlu, 2018: 57–8). Indeed, Syrian workers are blamed by Turkish and Kurdish workers for the dropping income level and causing unem-ployment (see Pelek, 2018).

One of the most significant differences between local and migrant workers – which is not specific to Turkey – is the reproduction of labour power. Accordingly, migrant workers' reproduction and renewal processes are more dependent on income generated by the wage work (Burawoy, 1976; Ferguson and McNally, 2015) whereas local workers' reproduction is less cash-dependent and they may be able to develop certain survival strategies such as subsistence produc-tion on their own land. Migrant workers' relatively high dependence on wage income makes them more obedient and weakens the bar-gaining power of the labour power as a whole (see Çelik, 2017; 2019).

6.6 CONCLUSION

In this chapter, I have analysed the formation of the rural proletariat in neoliberal Turkey through proletarianisation of the small-scale agricultural producers; feminisation of agricultural labour; and reproduction of the ethnic structure of the country in the rural labour markets. I first underline that despite the widespread argument in the mainstream literature (and even in the critical literature to a certain extent) on rural change, neoliberal transformation in the countryside of Turkey does not merely indicate de-agrarianisation. The main transformation has been the elimination of the smallholder-based agrarian structure, and increasing dominance of agribusiness firms. Therefore, besides massive rural-urban migration, the neoliberal transformation of agriculture resulted in the formation of the classes of labour in the countryside of Turkey whose survival strategy has been diversification of the income resources in agricultural and off-farm works. Together with the landless rural population and completely dispossessed seasonal migrant workers, they constitute the rural proletariat in neoliberal Turkey.

The composition of rural labour markets and rural proletariat is characterised by a sexual division of labour and ethnic differences. Firstly, as long as diversification of the rural means of livelihood indicates the use of labour power potential of the household in various forms, the proletarianisation of the peasantry is characterised by a sexual division of labour. In the countryside of Turkey, this process indicated men's move out of agriculture and further feminisation of agricultural labour. As male members of rural households start working in off-farm works, female members maintain the agricultural production in several forms such as petty commodity production (in their own account or as contract farmers), subsistence production and agricultural wage work. Secondly, the general ethnic structure in the society is reproduced in the countryside through labour migration. As a result of the forced migration of the Kurdish peasants in the late 1980s and migration of Syrian refugees in the 2010s, ethnic discrimination has constituted a significant dimension of rural class relations.

All in all, there has not been a massive struggle against agricultural policies of the AKP governments in Turkey. On the one hand, increasing energy and construction investments in the country-side have been regarded as an 'employment opportunity' for the recently dispossessed rural population. Instead of developing a political movement against the agricultural policies that resulted in their impoverishment and dispossession, the rural population, in general, has supported extractivism of the AKP for its employment generation potential in the countryside. This is directly reflected in the electoral support for the AKP. On the other hand, reproduction of ethnic struggle in the countryside has resulted in intra-class conflict within the rural proletariat and this has been a significant impediment for the development of collective class interest.

BIBLIOGRAPHY

Adaman F. and Akbulut B. (2020) 'Erdoğan's Three-pillared Neoliberalism: Authoritarianism Populism and Developmentalism', *Geoforum*. https://doi.org/10.1016/j.geoforum.2019.12.013.

Akbulut B. (2019) 'The "State" of Degrowth: Economic Growth and the Making of State Hegemony in Turkey', *Nature and Space*, 2 (3), 513–27.

Araghi, F. (1995) 'Global Depeasantization, 1945–1990', *Sociological Quarterly*, 36 (2), 337–68.

—— (2000) 'The Great Global Enclosure of Our Times: Peasants and the Agrarian Question at the Beginning of the Twenty-first Century', in Magdoff, F., Foster, J.B. and Buttel, F.H. (eds), *Hungry for Profit: The Agribusiness Threat to Farmers, Food, and the Environment*, New York: Monthly Review Press, 145–60.

—— (2009) 'The Invisible Hand and the Invisible Foot: Peasants, Dispossession, and Globalisation', in Akram-Lodhi, H.A. and Kay, C. (eds), *Peasants and Globalisation: Political Economy, Rural Transformation and the Agrarian Question*, New York: Routledge, 111–47.

Avcı, D. (2018) *Transformative Politics in Environmental Struggles: A Comparative Analysis of the Mining Conflicts in Intag, Ecuador and Mount Ida, Turkey*, PhD Thesis, International Institute of Social Studies at Erasmus University.

Aydın, Z. (2001) 'Yapısal Uyum Politikaları ve Kırsal Alanda Beka Stratejilerinin Özelleştirilmesi: Söke'nin Tuzburgazı ve Sivrihisar'ın Kınık Köyleri Örneği', *Toplum ve Bilim*, 88, 11–31.

—— (2010) 'Neoliberal Transformation of Turkish Agriculture'. *Journal of Agrarian Change*, 10 (2), 149–87.

Aysu, A. and Kayalıoğlu, M.S. (2014) 'Sunuş', in Aysu, A. and Kayalıoğlu, M.S. (eds), *Köylülükten Sonra Tarım: Osmanlı'dan Günümüze Çiftçinin Ilgası ve Şirketleşme,* Ankara: Epos Yayınları, 11–16.

—— (2015) 'Neoliberal Transformation of Turkish Agriculture: Internationalisation and Financialisation', Fessud Working Paper.

Bernstein, H. (1979) 'African Peasantries: A Theoretical Framework', *The Journal of Peasant Studies,* 6 (4), 421–43.

—— (2001) 'The Peasantry' in Global Capitalism: Who, Where, and Why', in Panitch, L. and Leys, C. (eds), *Socialist Register 2001: Working Classes Global Realities,* 37, 25–51.

—— (2004) ''Changing Before Our Very Eyes': Agrarian Questions and the Politics of Land in Capitalism Today' *Journal of Agrarian Change,* 4 (1–2), 190–225.

—— (2010) *Class Dynamics of Agrarian Change,* Halifax: Fernwood Publishing.

Bor, Ö. (2014) 'Yeni Tarım Düzeni', in Aysu, A. and Kayalıoğlu, M.S. (eds), *Köylülükten Sonra Tarım: Osmanlı'dan Günümüze Çiftçinin Ilgası ve Şirketleşme,* Ankara: Epos Yayınları, 82–121.

Bryceson, D.F. (1999) 'African Rural Labour, Income Diversification & Livelihood Approaches: A Long-term Development Perspective', *Review of African Political Economy,* 26 (80), 171–89.

BSB (2015) *AKP'li Yıllarda Emeğin Durumu,* İstanbul: Yordam.

Burawoy, M. (1976) 'The Functions and Reproduction of Migrant Labor: Comparative Material from Southern Africa and the United States', *American Journal of Sociology,* 81 (5), 1050–87.

Çelik, C. (2017) 'Kırsal Dönüşüm ve Metalaşan Yaşamlar: Soma Havzasında İşçileşme Süreçleri ve Sınıf İlişkileri', *Praksis,* 43, 785–810.

—— (2019) *Extractive Industries and Changing Means of Rural Livelihood: Patterns of Proletarianization and Labour Processes in Soma Coal Basin.* PhD Thesis, Middle East Technical University.

Çelik, C. and Balta E. (2017) 'Soma Maden Havzasında Görünmeyen Emek: Kadın', *Ayrıntı Dergi,* 20, 71–9.

Çınar, S. (2014) Öteki Proletarya: De-Proletarizasyon ve Mevsimlik Tarım İşçileri, Ankara: Notabane.

Dedeoğlu, S. (2018) 'Tarımsal Üretimde Göçmen İşçiler: Yoksulluk Nöbetinden Yoksulların Nöbetine', *Çalışma ve Toplum,* 56, 37–67.

Deere, C.D. (2005) 'The Feminisation of Agriculture? Economic Restructuring in Rural Latin America', Occasional Paper No. 1, Geneva: United Nation Research Institute for Social Development, https://tinyurl.com/y34dbjcz (accessed 28 March 2020).

Duruiz, D. (2015) 'Embodiment of Space and Labour: Kurdish Migrant Workers in Turkish Agriculture', in Gambetti, Z. and Jongerden, J. (eds), *The Kurdish Issue in Turkey: A Spatial Perspective*, London and New York: Routledge, 289–308.

Erensü S. (2018) 'Powering Neoliberalization: Energy and Politics in the Making of a New Turkey'. *Energy Research and Social Science*, 41, 148–57.

FAO (Food and Agricultural Organization of the United Nations) (2017) The State of Food and Agriculture, www.fao.org/3/a-i7658e.pdf (accessed 11 June 2020).

Ferguson S. and McNally D. (2015) 'Precarious Migrants: Gender, Race and the Social Reproduction of a Global Working Class', in Panitch, L. and Albo, G. (eds), *Socialist Register: Transforming Classes*, 51, 1–23.

Günaydın, G. (2009) 'Türkiye Tarım Politikalarında 'Yapısal Uyum': 2000'li Yıllar', *Mülkiye Dergisi*, 33 (162), 175–221.

Gürel, B. (2011) 'Agrarian Change and Labour Supply in Turkey, 1950–1980', *Journal of Agrarian Change*, 11 (2), 195–219.

—— (2014) 'Türkiye'de Kırda Sınıf Mücadelelerinin Tarihsel Gelişimi', in Savran, S., Tanyılmaz, K. and Tonak, E.A. (eds), *Marksizm ve Sınıflar: Dünyada ve Türkiye'de Sınıflar ve Mücadeleleri*, İstanbul: Yordam, 303–85.

Gürel B., Küçük, B. and Taş, S. (2019) 'The Rural Roots of the Rise of the Justice and Development Party in Turkey', *The Journal of Peasant Studies*, 46 (3), 457–79.

ISIG (2020) 'Son Yedi Yılda En Az 817 Kadın İşçi İş Cinayetlerinde Yaşamını Yitirdi', https://tinyurl.com/y3e7qrkf (accessed 11 July 2020).

İslamoğlu, H. (2017) 'The Politics of Agricultural Production in Turkey', in Adaman, F., Akbulut, B. and Arsel, M. (eds), *Neoliberal Turkey and Its Discontents: Economic Policy and the Environment under Erdoğan*, London and New York: I.B.Tauris, 75–102.

Johnson, H. (2004) 'Subsistence and Control: The Persistence of the Peasantry in the Developing World', *Undercurrent*, 1 (1), 54–65.

Katz, E. (2003) 'The Changing Role of Women in the Rural Economies of Latin America', in Davis, B. (ed.), *Food Agriculture and Rural Development: Current and Emerging Issues for Economic Analysis and Policy Research Volume I* (Latin America and Caribbean), Rome: Food and Agriculture Organization of the United Nations (FAO).

Kautsky, K. (1988) [1899] *The Agrarian Question*, London: Zwen.

Kavak, S. (2016) 'Syrian Refugees in Seasonal Agricultural Work: A Case of Adverse Incorporation in Turkey', *New Perspectives on Turkey*, 54, 33–53.

Keyder, Ç. and Yenal, Z. (2011) 'Agrarian Change under Globalisation: Markets and Insecurity in Turkish Agriculture', *Journal of Agrarian Change*, 11 (1), 60–86.

—— (2013) *Bildiğimiz Tarımın Sonu: Küresel İktidar ve Köylülük*, İstanbul: İletişim.

Lenin, V.I. (1974) [1899] *The Development of Capitalism in Russia*, Moskow: Progress Publishers.

Oyan, O. (2015) 'Tarımda IMF-DB Gözetiminde 2000'li Yıllar', in Oral, N. (ed.), *Türkiye'de Tarımın Ekonomi Politiği: 1923–2013*, Ankara: Notabene, 111–30.

Özuğurlu, M. (2011) *Küçük Köylülüğe Sermaye Kapanı*, Ankara: Notabene Yayınları.

Panitch L., Leys C., Albo, G. and Coates, D. (2001) 'Preface', in Panitch, L. and Leys, C. (eds), *Socialist Register 2001: Working Classes Global Realities*, 37, vii–xi.

Pelek, D. (2010) *Seasonal Migrant Workers in Agriculture: The Case of Ordu and Polatlı*, MSc Dissertation Boğaziçi University, Atatürk Institute for Modern Turkish History.

—— (2018) 'Syrian Refugees as Seasonal Migrant Workers: Reconstruction of Unequal Power Relations in Turkish Agriculture', *Journal of Refugee Studies*, 32 (4), 605–29.

—— (2019) *Migrant Workers in Turkish Agriculture: Patterns of Mobility and Dispossession (1990–2018)*, PhD Thesis, Boğaziçi University, Atatürk Institute for Modern Turkish History.

Shanin, T. (1986) 'Chayanov's Message: Illuminations, Miscomprehensions, and the Contemporary 'Development Theory', in Chayanov, A.V., Thorner, D., Kerblay, B. and Smith, R.E.F. (eds), *The Theory of Peasant Economy*, Madison: University of Wisconsin Press.

Thompson, E.P. (1963) *The Making of the English Working Class*, London: Penguin Press.

—— (1978) 'Eighteenth-century English Society Class Struggle Without Class?' *Social History*, 3, 133–65.

Wood, E.M. (1995) *Democracy Against Capitalism*, Cambridge: Cambridge University Press.

—— (2009). 'Peasants and the Market Imperative', in Akram-Lodhi, H.A. and Kay, C. (eds), *Peasants and Globalisation: Political Economy, Rural Transformation and the Agrarian Question*, New York: Routledge, 37–56.

World Bank (2019) World Bank Open Data, https://tinyurl.com/yya4m2va (accessed 15 July 2020).

Yüksel, A.S. (2015). 'Rescaled Localities and Redefined Class Relations: Neoliberal Experience in the Southeast Turkey', in Gambetti, Z. and Jongerden, J. (eds), *The Kurdish Issue in Turkey: A Spatial Perspective*, London and New York: Routledge, 289–308.

7

Burden or a Saviour at a Time of Economic Crisis? AKP's 'Open-Door Migration Policy' and its Impact on Labour Market Restructuring in Turkey

Ertan Erol

7.1 INTRODUCTION

When the first followers of the Islamic prophet Muhammad faced a series of threats and offences in Mecca, they were forced to leave the city and emigrated to the city of Yathrib – later called Medina, 'the City'. The citizens of Yathrib earned the title of '*ansar*', which means 'the helpers', as they opened their houses and helped those newcomers who were called *muhajirun* (migrants in Arabic), fleeing from the oppression and death. As the large volume of Syrian migrant inflow to Turkey became a very visible reality following the intensification of the Syrian civil war, this seventh-century identification of 'migrants and helpers' was frequently employed as a relationship model by the ruling political-Islamist AKP government; though even the AKP supporters did not adopt it neither rhetorically nor practically.

Nevertheless, the AKP government continued to utilise religious references alongside regular accusations towards the indifference of the international community and European states to this humanitarian crisis. Furthermore, besides hosting the largest volume of Syrian refugees, Turkey claims to have spent $40 billion since 2011 for these refugees. These claims further consolidate the negative public opinion towards the Syrians in the country, which perceives the Syrians as an economic burden that has led to the recent deterioration of the country's economy.

It is correct that after a decade of economic growth Turkey finds itself in a full-fledged economic crisis. A significant contraction of economic growth, increasing unemployment, widening budgetary deficit, exchange rate instability and the constant depreciation of the Turkish lira as well as an explosion of non-financial and household indebtedness appear as the main manifestations of this current economic crisis. And it is not uncommon that many attribute the recent crisis to the AKP government's authoritarian 'turn' in recent years – that weakened the institutional framework of the country – coupled with its betrayal to the neoliberal orthodoxy in its economic policies. This chapter claims both explanations need to be taken with a grain of salt. The AKP still represents and follows the neoliberal orthodoxy which no other political actor in the Turkish political spectrum was able to adhere to and implement in the last four decades. Meanwhile, the repressive and undemocratic policies were not only present from the very beginning of AKP rule but in fact played a central aspect of the wider neoliberal framework.

Integration with the world markets 'as an end in itself' emerged as an important milestone of the neoliberal transformation of the Turkish economy since the 1980s which had been relentlessly promoting a rapid trade liberalisation and deregulation of capital markets as the new mode of integration (Yalman, 2016: 255). Even though the premature liberalisation of the capital accounts was the main cause of the financial crises of 1994, 1998–99 and 2000–01 through increasing the exposure of the fragile Turkish economy and financialising the productive capital, the coalition governments were the weakest links and held responsible for the economic mismanagement (Yalman, 2018: 72). In fact, the policies followed in the late 1990s and post-2001 eras had a similar direction, but now under the aegis of the IMF. Turkey substantially increased interest rates, followed a strict fiscal austerity and a contractionary monetary policy to control inflation in this period. The existence of the IMF was not only a factor that increased the creditworthiness of the economy, it was also a tool to depoliticise the bitter structural adjustment policies (Erol, 2016: 302). Meanwhile, the Turkish economy once again entered into a phase determined by increasing foreign capital inflow which made the Turkish lira overvalued, thus paving the way for an expansion of imports both in consumer goods and investments. Therefore, the success of the post-2001 IMF programme was based on a speculative capital-led and jobless growth model (Yeldan, 2007: 4–5).

This pattern of growth had direct impacts on the organic composition of capital. While small and medium-sized enterprises (SMEs) benefited from the capital inflows, low-value-added sectors like textile integrated into the world markets as labour-intensive subcontractors, and inevitably traditional Turkish exports started to lose their global competitiveness as the new heavily export-dependent areas emerged (Yeldan, 2007: 14; Bekmen, 2014). In that sense, particularly small and medium capital increasingly resorted to the exploitation of labour through intensification of work in an increasingly flexible labour market where the wages were continuously suppressed (Bozkurt-Güngen, 2018: 227). Thus, Turkish capital was able to compensate its losses in global competitiveness without increasing its organic composition. SMEs have also been subject to additional financial support since 2008 via creation of several projects or credit guarantee mechanisms which aimed for a constant cash flow to these sectors through credit expansion (Topal, 2018: 231; Orhangazi and Yeldan, 2020: 22). Furthermore, high interest rates and the overvaluation of the Turkish lira led an expansion of domestic consumption for the commodities produced by those SMEs while at the same time cheapening the imports of intermediate goods. Meanwhile, major public construction projects and urban reconstruction boom became another area of capital accumulation process and generation of employment.

Nevertheless, the fragility of the Turkish economy that mainly depended on foreign capital flows manifested itself in many fronts particularly after the currency crisis of August 2018 during the 'Pastor Brunson' dispute with the US. Orhangazi and Yeldan (2020) argue that the contemporary crisis was in fact conditioned by the intrinsic contradiction of the existing economic model. The AKP did indeed excel with the neoliberal economic model, and thus was praised by the IMF, national and international capital and the financial markets for a long time. However, it was this economic model, dependent on constant foreign capital inflow, centred on a credit boom and construction bonanza that brought premature de-industrialisation of the Turkish economy which at the same time led to a massive de-population of the agricultural production (Orhangazi and Yeldan, 2020: 13). The deceleration of labour productivity further suppressed real wages from 2016 (Orhangazi and Yeldan, 2020: 18). The deterioration of the price stability and suppression of wages led to a substantial increase in households' indebtedness particularly among low-income people and wage-earners like never before in order to cover the daily consumption needs (Karaçimen, 2014: 174).

In this context of deepening economic crisis, it is more crucial to question the role of the refugees and other irregular migrants on the economy as a whole. Even though the refugees are an important part of the Turkish economy, both in demand and supply sides and in the creation and the distribution of income, they are often not even included in the macroeconomic data sets, thus appearing as the silent participants of the economy. With its open-door migration policy, there are around 4 million registered migrants in Turkey particularly from Syria (3.6 million), Afghanistan, Pakistan, Iran, Iraq and North African countries, which comprise 5 per cent of the country's population (UNHCR, 2020). Considering that only in 2020 the number of unregistered refugees apprehended by the Turkish authorities was 455,000 – half of them were Afghan refugees – it is possible to predict the actual numbers of irregular migrants in Turkey to be higher (GİGM, 2020). Even these figures would exclude the people who enter the country with tourist or student visas and work in temporal or seasonal jobs such as Georgians, Armenians, Azerbaijanis, Turkmens and Uzbeks. Therefore, it is a grave mistake to neglect a section of the society that amounts to 5–6 per cent of the total population that actively participates in the economy.

In this vein, this chapter aims to point out the need for inclusion of the refugees and migrants in the general evaluation of Turkish capitalism. More specifically, it will argue that the integration of the migrants into the country had a 'positive' effect in alleviating and holding off the inevitable disruption of the AKP's speculative capital-led jobless growth economic model. The impact of the migrants on the economy should be further analysed in three main areas: labour market, capital accumulation and consumption. Nevertheless, there are political repercussions that need to be taken into account as well.

7.2 THE EFFECTS OF THE INCORPORATION OF FOREIGN-BORN WORKERS INTO THE TURKISH LABOUR MARKET

It has been well discussed that the labour market regime that was adopted after the 1980s in Turkey has created significant institutional and legal obstacles that progressively diminished the bargaining power of labour. As a result, the increases in the GDP or productivity hardly created any upward trend on real wages and on the minimum wage since the link between those are pretty much broken (Yildirim, 2015: 100; Koç, 2016: 1404). Wages in the Turkish labour market seem to be more sensitive to the foreign capital influx rather than the changes in the productivity or real GDP, since the major hikes in the minimum wages occurred during the global foreign exchange inflow experienced by the emerging markets during the 2000s (Koç, 2016: 1403; see also Chapter 2).

This phenomenon manifested itself in the changes of global competitiveness of the Turkish economy which was stagnant in the first decade of the 2000s and deteriorating in the second. This downward trend was largely attributed to the structure of the labour market and macroeconomic environment (Schwab, 2019: 20). Supressing the wages through increasing informality and easing the integration of the foreign workers into the labour market – as the aforementioned World Economic Forum report praised – emerged as the main forms of maintaining the competitiveness of the traditional Turkish export goods such as garment products (Bozkurt-Güngen, 2018: 227).

Since the start of the civil war in Syria in 2011, Turkey had been following an open-door policy to the Syrian refugees and has overlooked the informal employment of the Syrians in the labour market. In fact, this policy is a continuum of the existing attitude towards the informal employment of the foreign-born workers in various sectors. In this vein, two main outcomes from the integration of a migrant workforce into the Turkish labour market could be expected. First of all, the SMEs particularly benefited from the flexibility of this informal workforce by lowering the wages considerably. Even though Turkey eased the conditions to obtain work permits for foreign-born workers, the number of Syrian immigrants holding a work permit only reached 34.375 in 2018, comprising 29.84 per cent of the total number of foreigners who currently receive a work permit (AÇSHB, 2018: 10). Considering the fact that the foreign-born participants in the workforce in Turkey reach 53.9 per cent, it is possible to estimate that only 3–4 percent of the Syrian immigrants would be working with a permit and only in the formal sector (OECD, 2020).

The logic behind the persistent exclusion of the migrant labour from the formal workforce is hidden in the costs of wages; while a Syrian male worker in the garment industry earns a third less than a Turkish male worker, a Syrian female worker only receives around half of a Turkish male worker's wage (Erol et al., 2017: 53). Migrant workers' wages are further cheapened with informality, since the additional fees and taxes cost the employer almost half of the net wage received by the worker. Therefore, sectors like the garment industry that employs a significant part of the informal workforce benefits from the integration of a new army of workers that accepts to work under informal and flexible conditions (Erol et al., 2017: 59, Mutlu et al., 2018: 82–3). The wage difference between Syrian and local workers, underpayment or sometimes no payment for the job, and illegal practices like the employment of underage children is almost undetectable in those informal sectors. It has been observed that the majority of the working children are significantly underpaid, not able to continue their education and work 12 to 14 hours a day (Lordoğlu and Aslan, 2018: 727). Child labour is mostly found in the seasonal agricultural production and informal sector, but it can also penetrate the formal sections within the garment industry, since the subcontractors that produces commodities to the global commodity chains also further subcontract to the local sweatshops that have no official registration and formal existence.[1]

Construction and agriculture are two other sectors where the constant demand for low-skilled, low-wage and flexible labour has led to the widespread integration of the Syrian workforce. It has been observed that the Syrian migrants who work in low-skilled and low-wage work receive almost half of the wages obtained by the local workers (Lordoğlu and Aslan, 2016: 793). Nevertheless, wages would tend to converge if the type of work necessitates more skilled labour, though usually immigrants would not be able to work in the sectors where they can use their skills and qualifications (Lordoğlu and Aslan, 2016: 802, 806).

The second expected outcome of the integration of the migrant workforce is the expansion of the native reserve army of labour in the formal sector as well. Migrant labour would push the native labour out of the informal sector and low-skill jobs to the formal labour market, thus inevitably increasing the pressure on real wages in general by expanding the native reserve army of labour. In other words, Syrian and the other foreign-born workers in fact are replacing the native labour from the most precarious, insecure and irregular jobs (Şahankaya Adar, 2018: 24–5). Considering that native workers are more likely to compensate unemployment via credit or social and family networks, migrant workers have no option but to work which gives the employer the absolute upper hand on the wage and work relations. Other research shows that while the replacement of the native workers by the Syrian workers mainly occurs in the informal sector, the native workers – female workers earning higher rates of pay – who lost their jobs usually left the workforce or remained unemployed (Ceritoğlu et al., 2017: 3). Del Carpio and Wagner (2015) reach a similar conclusion pointing out that female workers are the most vulnerable to being replaced, and noted that the unemployment rates also initially fell since some of the workers chose to continue their education when facing difficulties in the labour market. Therefore, integration of Syrian and other foreign-born workers into the labour force becomes critical in order to ensure the Turkish industries remain competitive and even profitable, and at the same time to keep the general wages under pressure in the rest of the labour market through increasing the reserve army of labour.

The existence of the migrant labour has been mostly neglected in the assessment of the employment and unemployment trends in the Turkish labour market. In the last decade, it is possible to observe that there is a substantial expansion of the rate of unemployment even during the years of substantial GDP growth (Table 7.1). This is mostly related to the capital accumulation regime adopted by the

AKP government, previously identified as the speculative capital-led jobless growth model. However, it is impossible to underestimate the relationship between the integration of foreign-born workers into the labour market and the increasing rates of unemployment among native workers.

Table 7.1   Employment and Growth

Year	Labour force (thousand)	Employed (thousand)	Unemployed (thousand)	Unemploy-ment rate (%)	Unemployment rate excluding agricultural employment (%)	Growth GDP (%)
2007	22 253	20 209	2044	9.2	11.2	5.0
2008	22 899	20 604	2295	10.0	12.3	0.8
2009	23 710	20 615	3095	13.1	16.0	−4.7
2010	24 594	21 858	2737	11.1	13.7	8.5
2011	25 594	23 266	2328	9.1	11.3	11.1
2012	26 141	23 937	2204	8.4	10.3	4.8
2013	27 047	24 601	2445	9.0	10.9	8.5
2014	28 786	25 933	2853	9.9	12.0	5.2
2015	29 678	26 621	3057	10.3	12.4	6.1
2016	30 535	27 205	3330	10.9	13.0	3.2
2017	31 643	28 189	3454	10.9	13.0	7.5
2018	32 275	28 738	3537	12.3	12.9	2.8
2019	32 549	28 080	4469	13.7	16.0	0.5

Note: Based on the data presented in the DİSK-AR employment reports (2018, 2019, 2020) and Turkish Statistical Institution (TurkStat).

According to DİSK-AR employment report (2020) the scale of unemployment in Turkey is even underestimated due to the narrow definition of unemployment by the TurkStat. According to the broader definition of employment, the number of unemployed increased to 7.22 million in 2019 from 6.26, thus placing the unemployment rate at 20.7 per cent (DİSK-AR, 2020: 3). In that sense, the substantial and continuous expansion of the reserve army of labour due to the AKP's growth strategy and the steady integration of foreign-born workers enabled the capital to supress wages to be able to maintain global competitiveness and profitability.

7.3 MIGRANT LABOUR AND TURKISH CAPITAL

The inclusion of foreign-born labour in the workforce presents various advantages for capital that varies from lowering the cost of wages to being able to control labour relations. In addition to low wages, the fact that the migrant workers could be 'disciplined' much more easily than the local workers, that they cannot join trade unions and are not protected by laws and regulations in the informal sector makes the migrant labour much more attractive for employers (Toksöz et al., 2012: 23). As Rittersberger-Tılıç argued (2015), incorporation of the migrant labour into the local labour markets is part of the global stratification of the labour force, inevitably related to the neoliberal restructuring of the labour markets and its further flexibilisation under informality. There are a significant amount of case studies establishing valuable data sets on the integration of the migrants into the workforce in Istanbul and other major Anatolian cities where Syrian and foreign-born labour emerged as a significant part of the reserve army of labour (Özkarslı, 2015; Çetin, 2016; Lordoğlu and Aslan, 2016; Erol et al., 2017; Akbaş and Ünlütürk-Ulutaş, 2018; Çınar, 2018).

All of these case studies agree that Syrian and the other foreign-born migrant labour has been preferred and welcomed by employers due to its low cost, flexibility and unprotected nature. An interesting case study conducted to analyse the employers' perspective on the Syrian migrant labour in the border city of Şanlıurfa shows that 88 per cent of employers want Syrians to return to Syria and 68 per cent believe that hiring Syrian workers creates risks for security (Pınar et al., 2016: 22). However, the same study points out that while 67 per cent of employers in the city believe the language barrier is a serious problem for employment and 63 per cent claim that Syrians are not sufficiently equipped to be employed, only 32 per cent appear to be unwilling to employ any Syrian under any circumstances (Pınar et al., 2016: 22). While the local employers generally look down upon the Syrian workforce and undervalue their qualifications, they are overwhelmingly eager and ready to employ the migrants when and if it is possible. Some of the employers' associations like MÜSİAD openly demanded more flexible labour relations and state support for the employment of the Syrian migrant labour, mostly relating to social security contributions and lower minimum wages (Çetin, 2016: 1005).

A report called *Syria Within: Gaziantep Common Mind Report II* was published by Gaziantep Chamber of Commerce in 2015, analysing the impact of Syrian migrants in this and other border cities on various matters like security, economy, health system and tourism. The report singles out Gaziantep, likewise the other border cities, due to the fact that these cities had also been affected by the severed economic relations with Syria and further Levant region since the beginning of the war (GTO, 2015: 7–9). The same report calls for 'an only temporary work permit' that would not affect the 'work peace' and special regulations:

> The only method that should be followed in the temporary work permit is that our state should meet the social security (health services) expenses of the Syrian workers. The temporary work permit should be ceased as soon as the war ends, and there should be a system created – taking the international law into consideration – that will ensure while Syrians are returning to their home the rights acquired by them and the indemnity demands will not be met. (GTO, 2015: 11)

Another report concerning the employers' views and suggestions on the Syrian migrant labour force emphasizes and somehow links the lack of apprentices and middle-strata semi-skilled young workers in the labour market with the incorporation of the Syrian migrants into the workforce (Erdoğan and Ünver, 2015: 61). In that sense, according to the report, a general positivity is observed among the employers towards Syrians to meet these needs but with the condition of being registered, oriented with vocational training, planning and under formal work relations (Erdoğan and Ünver, 2015: 63). It has been noted that only tourism sector representatives do not share this 'positive view', since 'tourism is an industry of aesthetics, peace and confidence' and therefore Syrians need to be kept away from the sector and touristic cities such as İstanbul, İzmir, Antalya and Muğla (Erdoğan and Ünver, 2015: 64).

It is possible to argue that since the Turkish economy entered a new and prolonged phase of economic crisis, the employment of Syrian and other migrant labour also provided a quick-fix for the local capital, particularly for the subcontractors and SMEs in textile and construction to balance the increasing costs. As mentioned, Turkish exports are very much import dependent, thus quite vulnerable to the foreign exchange hikes which had become more frequent since 2016. In that sense, the informal integration of Syrian and other foreign-born irregular workforce into the labour market helped particularly the SMEs to compensate for the eroding global competitiveness and increasing costs of raw material and intermediate goods. The other two solutions for maintaining the SMEs' profitability was firstly the continuous expansion of credit via public banks and credit guarantee mechanisms, and secondly, periodic tax exemptions or relief packages towards SMEs. Therefore, the integration of irregular migrant labour into the informal labour market fits perfectly with the AKP's strategy of 'keeping the SMEs afloat', particularly during periods of deepening economic crisis.

Nevertheless, there would be short-term and long-term effects of the irregular migrants' integration into the informal labour force. First of all, particularly SMEs would benefit from the absolute surplus value exploitation of labour as the major source of profit generation, since the migrant labour inflow significantly enlarges the unskilled and low-cost reserve army of labour (Koç et al., 2015: 88). Secondly, it reinforces the process of premature de-industrialisation by keeping afloat, and even expanding the industries operating within the informal sector which had been incorporated into the global commodity chains as subcontractors. The very detailed research concludes that the integration of the Syrian workforce caused a decrease in capital intensity and investment – particularly in small-size firms – while pushing the native workers out from manually intensive jobs (Akgündüz and Torun, 2019: 20–1). At the same time, sectors such as construction would also benefit from this labour force, further consolidating the processes of de-industrialisation and decrease in the organic composition of capital.

Following Rittersberger-Tılıç (2015), incorporation of the irregular migrant labour with great enthusiasm is part of the global restructuring of labour markets towards flexibility and insecurity, while establishing a stratified global labour market. In that sense, Turkey's open-door policy under AKP rule presents a continuum of the policies that were implemented during the 1980s. Nevertheless, this open-door policy never played such a substantial role before, particularly to maintain profitability of SMEs and the construction sector that could be closely associated with the AKP era capitalist accumulation model. It is possible to expect that during a deepening economic crisis the importance of irregular migrant labour will become even more critical for SMEs and the construction sector, as well as the AKP regime that owes significant electoral support to the 'success' in those two sectors.

7.4 IRREGULAR MIGRANT LABOUR AND CONSUMPTION

It would be an extremely inadequate explanation to reduce the impact of the migrants on the economy to the incorporation of the migrant workforce into the labour market. In very detailed research on the impact of Latino migrants on the economy of Memphis USA, Mendoza et al. (2000) pointed out that from the $570.8 million of earnings of Latino migrants in the city, only $125.6 million were sent to origin country as remittances. Meanwhile, $85.6 million had been collected as tax, $359.6 million of earnings of the migrants had been spent in the local economy, mostly in accommodation, transportation, supermarkets, domestic appliances and restaurants (Mendoza et al., 2000). Other research estimated that the Mexican-born and Mexican descendants made an 8 per cent contribution to the GDP growth of the US economy between 1994 and 2010 (Delgado Wise and Gaspar Olvera, 2012: 6).

Nevertheless, the role of irregular migrants as a factor that contributes to the expansion in the aggregate demand has generally been overlooked. Furthermore, the impact of the Syrian migrants has mostly been viewed negatively and attributed to increasing prices and inflation. However, it is indispensable to take migrant consumption into consideration particularly during the economic crisis and with a special emphasis on sectors such as consumer goods production and real estate. First of all, it has been observed that the substitution of the native workers with the low-cost Syrian workers – and other irregular migrant labour – led to a reduction of the prices of goods by 2.7 per cent – commodities particularly produced by informal and small-size firms – and to a reduction of the prices of services by 2.2 per cent (Balkan and Tümen, 2016: 15; Tümen, 2016: 458). In other words, the incorporation of a large volume of migrant labour particularly into the small-size firms had a positive effect on consumer prices.

Meanwhile, since almost all of the Syrian migrants live outside the refugee camps, a substantial 5.5 per cent increase in housing rents has been observed (Tümen, 2016: 459). In terms of house prices and rents, two trends can be identified. Firstly, the instant demand of a large volume of immigrants for accommodation increases house prices and rents in the host cities. Secondly, there is a trend of internal migration from the cities and districts that receive the most Syrian migrants, which causes house prices to increase in other cities and districts as well (Akgündüz et al., 2015: 12–13). In that sense, the increase in rents for high quality rental units in low migrant hosting neighbourhoods are much higher (11.1 per cent) than the lower quality housing (1.1 per cent) in the poorer neighbourhoods (Tümen, 2016: 459). Therefore, it is possible to predict that the Syrian migrants and other foreign-born workers directly and indirectly boosted demand in the Turkish real estate and construction sectors.

The economic boost generated by migrants through consumption is manifested most concretely in the current increases in the growth of the agricultural sector, which is the highest in the last decade (Kuyumcu and Kösematoğlu 2017: 79). Through employing an input-output approach to evaluate the economic stimulus generated by the Syrian refugees, Mahia et al. (2019) estimated that the direct demand generated by the Syrian migrants' consumption was 0.3 per cent of Turkey's GDP in 2017, while the indirect demand effect stands at 0.12 per cent for the same year. The same research concludes that the overall impact of the Syrian workforce is 1.96 per cent of the total Turkish GDP with the sectors benefiting the most from the Syrian immigrants' demand/consumption appearing to be the wholesale and retail trade, real estate activities, manufacturing and energy (Mahia et al., 2019: 16). Since the Syrian immigrant population is quite young, the production effects are expected to be higher in the very near future, possibly reaching 4.05 per cent in 2028 (Mahia et al., 2019: 16).

One of the limitations of these assessments is calculating the income of Syrian immigrants through their incorporation into the labour market and, thus, excluding other substantial resources provided by the European Union (EU) and international aid organisations. According to the EU Facility for Refugees in Turkey report, between 2016 and 2019 4.7 billion euros were contracted and 3.4 billion euros were disbursed via several funding instruments. The majority of this fund was distributed through 'Emergency Social Safety Net – ESSN', which is a regular monthly cash transfer mechanism reaching 1.75 million people in 2019, while 714,000 Syrian immigrants also received irregular aid comprising one-off or seasonal food and non-food items (EC, 2020: 25). Therefore, the impact of Syrian immigrants' consumption on the aggregate demand should be expected to be higher than the salaries that they obtain from the local workforce.

Lastly, it should be noted that the Syrian migrants also generate employment with increasing numbers of investments, and thus, had a positive impact on the consumption/demand via creation of employment as well as through utilisation of local goods and services. While the number of investments owned by Syrians in Turkey was 157 in 2012, this number mounted to 1599 in 2015 (Esen and Binatlı, 2017). According to the Ministry of Commerce the number of companies owned by at least one Syrian citizen reached 15,159 in 2019 (Mülteciler Derneği, 2020). Therefore, Syrians are also contributing to the demand growth through capital investments and job creation.

7.5 CONCLUSION

The integration of the Syrian refugees and other foreign-born irregular migrants into the labour market in Turkey has received a very negative reaction from the general public, and the recent deterioration of the Turkish economy has been frequently attributed to the migrants and refugees. This chapter claims the opposite; the migrants and refugees in fact alleviated and impeded the deepening economic crisis. The economic crisis was not conditioned by the institutional weaknesses or democratic deficits inflicted during the AKP rule, but in fact the very structural reforms implemented during the 'golden years of the AKP' paved the way for the transformation of the economy towards a foreign capital-inflow addicted jobless-growth accumulation model.

Migrants and refugee workers who now comprise at least 4 per cent of Turkey's population (1) lowered the production costs of the SMEs and thus helped to compensate eroding global competitiveness; (2) pushed the natives out of the informal sector and thus increased the reserve army of labour in the formal sectors leading to a further suppression of wages in other sectors; (3) enabled the SMEs and informal small-sized firms to maintain profitability via the expanding exploitation of absolute surplus value; (4) generated a downward effect on the prices of consumer goods; (5) boosted the aggregate demand, particularly in the sectors of consumer good production and real estate; and (6) created employment and further demand through the investments and capital that they move from their origin countries.

In that sense, Turkey's open-door policy should not be seen as an ideological choice or a rupture from the previous policies, but a perfect fit to the existing accumulation model and a quick – but critical and temporal – fix to the deepening economic crisis. Only from this standpoint is it possible to understand why the neoliberal AKP government cannot give up on the open-door migration policy even though it generates substantial electoral opposition and discontent.

BIBLIOGRAPHY

AÇSHB (Aile, Çalışma ve Sosyal Hizmetler Bakanlığı) (2018) Yabancıların Çalışma İzinleri İstatistikleri, www.ailevecalisma.gov.tr/media/31746/yabanciizin2018.pdf (accessed 20 March 2020).

Akbaş, S. and Ünlütürk-Ulutaş, Ç. (2018) 'Küresel Fabrika Kentinin Görünmeyen İşçileri: Denizli İşgücü Piyasasında Suriyeli Göçmenler', *Çalışma ve Toplum*, 56 (1),167–92.

Akgündüz, Y.E. and Torun, H. (2019) 'Two and a Half Syrian Refugees, Tasks and Capital Intensity', Central Bank of the Republic of Turkey, Working Paper No. 19/23.

Akgündüz, Y., Van den Berg, M. and W.H.J. Hassink. (2015) 'The Impact of Refugee Crises on Host Labor Markets: The Case of the Syrian Refugee Crisis in Turkey', IZA Discussion Papers, No. 8841.

Balkan Konuk, B. and Tümen, S. (2016) 'Immigration and Prices: Quasi-experimental Evidence from Syrian Refugees in Turkey', Central Bank of the Republic of Turkey, Working Paper No. 16/01.

Bekmen, A. (2014) 'State and Capital in Turkey During the Neoliberal Era', in Akça, İ., Bekmen, A. And Özden, B.A (eds), *Turkey Reframed: Constituting Neoliberal Hegemony*, London: Pluto Press, 47–74.

Bozkurt-Güngen, S. (2018) 'Labour and Authoritarian Neoliberalism: Changes and Continuities under the AKP Governments in Turkey', *South European Society and Politics*, 23 (2), 219–38.

Ceritoglu, E., Yunculer, H.B.G., Torun, H., and Tumen, S. (2017) 'The Impact of Syrian Refugees on Natives' Labor Market Outcomes in Turkey: Evidence from a Quasi-experimental Design', *IZA Journal of Labor Policy*, 6 (1), 1–28.

Çetin, İ. (2016) 'Suriyeli Mültecilerin İşgücüne Katılımları ve Entegrasyon: Adana-Mersin Örneği', *Gaziantep University Journal of Social Sciences*, 15 (4), 1001–16.

Çınar, S. (2018) 'İnşaat İşgücü Piyasasında Yeni Aktörler ve Yeni Çatışmalar: Türkiyeli İşçilerin Gözünden Suriyeli İnşaat İşçileri', *Çalısma ve Toplum*, 56 (1), 121–38.

Del Carpio, X.V. and Wagner, M. (2015) *The Impact of Syrians Refugees on the Turkish Labor Market*, Washington, DC: The World Bank.

Delgado Wise, R. and Gaspar Olvera. S. (2012) 'Quién Subsidia a Quién? Contribución de los Migrantes Mexicanos a la Economía de Estados Unidos', *Observatorio del Desarrollo*, 1 (2), 4–9.

DİSK-AR (2018) 'İşsizlik Azalmıyor, Artıyor', https://tinyurl.com/y2es25r2 (accessed 21 June 2020).

—— (2019) *İşsizlik ve İstihdam Raporu*, https://tinyurl.com/yxt2jlgp (accessed 21 June 2020).

—— (2020) *İşsizlik ve İstihdamın Görümü Raporu: 2019 Yıllık Rapor*, https://tinyurl.com/y626tl6a (accessed 21 June 2020).

EC (European Commission, The Facility for Refugees in Turkey) (2020) 'The Facility Results Framework Monitoring Report: Output Achievement Progress as of December 2019', https://tinyurl.com/y2ma3x38 (accessed 26 June 2020).

Erdoğan, M.M. and Ünver, C. (2015) *Türk İş Dünyasının Türkiye'deki Suriyeliler Konusundaki Görüşleri, Beklenti ve Önerileri*, Türkiye İşveren Sendikaları Konfederasyonu.

Erol, E. Akyol, A.E., Salman, C. Et al. (2017) 'Suriyeli Sığınmacıların Türkiye'de Emek Piyasasına Dahil Olma Süreçleri ve Etkileri: İstanbul Tekstil Sektörü Örneği', *İstanbul: Birleşik Metal-İş Yayınları*.

Erol, M.E. (2016) 'Adalet ve Kalkınma Partisi (AKP) Döneminde İktisadi Politika Yapımının Siyaseti: Süreklilik ve Kopuş Bağlamında Bir Tartışma', in Tören, T. and Kutun, M. (eds), *Yeni Türkiye? Kapitalizm, Devlet, Sınıflar,* İstanbul: Sosyal Araştırmalar Vakfı, 280–329.

Esen, O. and Oğuş Binatlı, A. (2017) 'The Impact of Syrian Refugees on the Turkish Economy: Regional Labour Market Effects', *Social Sciences,* 6 (4), 129, 1–12.

GTO (Gaziantep Ticaret Odası) (2015) 'İçimizdeki Suriye: Gaziantep Ortak Akıl Raporu-2', https://tinyurl.com/y6thaqyn (accessed 4 September 2019).

GİGM (Göç İdaresi Genel Müdürlüğü) 'İstatistikler, Düzensiz Göç', www.goc.gov.tr/duzensiz-goc-istatistikler# (accessed 15 April 2020).

Karaçimen, E. (2014) 'Financialization in Turkey: The Case of Consumer Debt', *Journal of Balkan and Near Eastern Studies,* 16 (2), 161–80.

Koç, A. (2016) 'Türkiye'de 1980 Sonrasının Politik İktisadı Bağlamında Asgari Ücret Analizi', *Çalışma ve Toplum,* 50 (3), 1387–408.

Koç, M., Görücü, İ. and Akbıyık, N. (2015) 'Suriyeli Sığınmacılar ve İstihdam Problemleri', *Birey ve Toplum Sosyal Bilimler Dergisi,* 5 (1), 63–94.

Kuyumcu, M.İ. and Kösematoğlu, H. (2017) 'The Impacts of the Syrian Refugees on Turkey's Economy', *Journal of Turkish Social Sciences Research,* 2 (1), 77–93.

Lordoğlu, K. and Aslan, M. (2016) 'En Fazla Suriyeli Göçmen Alan Beş Kentin Emek Piyasalarında Değişimi: 2011–2014', *Çalışma ve Toplum,* 49 (2), 789–808.

—— (2018) 'Görünmeyen Göçmen Çocukların İşçiliği: Türkiye'deki Suriye'li Çocuklar', *Çalışma ve Toplum,* 57 (2), 715–32.

Mahia, R., de ARCE, R., Koç, A.A. and Bölük, G. (2019) 'The Short and Long-term Impact of Syrian Refugees on the Turkish Economy: A Simulation Approach', *Turkish Studies,* 1–23.

Mendoza, M., Ciscel, D.H. and Smith. B.E. (2000) 'El Impacto de los Inmigrantes Latinos en la Economía de Memphis, Tennessee', *Revista de Estudios Migratorios Latinoamericanos,* 46, 659–75.

Mülteciler Derneği (2020) 'Türkiye'de Suriyeli Sayısı', https://multeciler.org.tr/turkiyedeki-suriyeli-sayisi/ (accessed 01 July 2020).

Mutlu, P., Mısırlı, K.Y., Kahveci, M. et al. (2018) 'Suriyeli Göçmen İşçilerin İstanbul Ölçeğinde Tekstil Sektörü Emek Piyasasına Eklemlenmeleri ve Etkileri', *Çalışma ve Toplum,* 56 (1), 69–92.

OECD Data (2020) 'Foreign Born Participation Rates', https://tinyurl.com/y64w4fb8 (accessed 28 March 2020).

Orhangazi, Ö. and Yeldan, E. (2020) 'Re-making of the Turkish Crisis', *PERI Working Papers*, 504.

Özkarslı, F. (2015). Mardin'de enformel istihdamda çalışan Suriyeli Göçmenler. *Birey ve Toplum Sosyal Bilimler Dergisi*, 5(1), 175–92.

Pınar, A., Siverekli, E. and Demir, M. (2016) *Şanlıurfa'da İşverenlerin ve İşçilerin Suriyeli İstihdamına Bakışı*, ILO-Türkiye Ofisi.

Rittersberger-Tılıç, H. (2015) 'Managing Irregular Labor Migrants in Turkey', *Göç Araştırmaları Dergisi*, 1 (1), 80–107.

Şahankaya Adar, A. (2018) 'Türkiye'de Yeni Prekarya Suriyeli İşgücü Mü?', *Çalışma ve Toplum*, 56 (1), 13–36.

Schwab, K. (2019) *The Global Competitiveness Report 2019*, Geneva: World Economic Forum.

Toksöz, D., Erdoğdu, S. and Kaşka, S. (2012) *Türkiye'ye Düzensiz Emek Göçü ve Göçmenlerin İşgücü Piyasasındaki Durumları*, International Organisation for Migration.

Topal, A. (2018) 'The State, Crisis and Transformation of Small and Medium-sized Enterprise Finance in Turkey', in Yalman, G.L., Morais, T. and Güngen, A.R. (eds), *The Political Economy of Financial Transformation in Turkey*, Oxon: Routledge, 221–42.

Tümen, S. (2016) 'The Economic Impact of Syrian Refugees on Host Countries: Quasi-experimental Evidence from Turkey', *American Economic Review*, 106 (5), 456–60.

UNHCR 'Operational Update: Turkey' (2020) https://tinyurl.com/y2s7ezbx (accessed 3 February 2020).

Yalman, G.L. (2016) 'Crises as Driving Forces of Neoliberal "Trasformismo": The Contours of the Turkish Political Economy since the 2000s', in Cafruny, A., Talani, L.S. and Martin, G.P. (eds), *The Palgrave Handbook of Critical International Political Economy*, London: Palgrave Macmillan, 239–66.

—— (2018) 'The Neoliberal Transformation of State and Market in Turkey', in Yalman, G.L., Morais, T. and Güngen, A.R. (eds), *The Political Economy of Financial Transformation in Turkey*, Oxon: Routledge, 51–87.

Yeldan, E. (2007) 'Patterns of Adjustment under the Age of Finance: The Case of Turkey as a Peripheral Agent of Neoliberal Globalization', *PERI Working Papers*, 86.

Yildirim, Z. (2015) 'Relationships among Labour Productivity, Real Wages and Inflation in Turkey', *Economic Research-Ekonomska Istraživanja*, 28 (1), 85–103.

PART II

Containment

8

Social Assistance as a Non-Wage Income for the Poor in Turkey: Work and Subsistence Patterns of Social Assistance Recipient Households

Denizcan Kutlu

8.1 INTRODUCTION

There have been comprehensive neoliberal transformations in the regulations pertaining to the establishment of welfare and social policies in Turkey. A social policy programme in which social assistance stands out as a basic social security technique accompanies this transition process, which can be evaluated within the transformation of the traditional welfare regime. However, it can be asserted that social assistance programmes can only promise a compensatory and minimal welfare status to the poor or to large masses with a risk of impoverishment. It can be observed that an increasingly large section of the population has been strongly linked to the social assistance in terms of working and subsistence patterns in Turkey. This segment of the society, which can be defined as the social assistance recipients, was formed during the process of their exclusion from secure employment, regular income, minimum subsistence level and impoverishment of the several layers of the working class and more precisely the reserve army of labour.

There has been an increasing attempt to manage the cash deficiency of the households through non-wage means of support, especially in the 2000s under the Justice and Development Party (Adalet ve Kalkınma Partisi – AKP) governments. The social and economic programme compatible with the adjustment of wages as a kind of laissez-faire area can be said to depend on social benefits. Indeed, during the 2000s, social assistance programmes in Turkey become varied, the number of recipients increased, the number of beneficiary households increased faster than the total number of households, and expenditures have also risen (Buğra and Keyder, 2006: 222–6; Kutlu, 2015; Erdoğdu and Kutlu, 2017; Yentürk, 2018: 49–70).

Also, social assistance is established as a political tool in order to manage the extensive sections of urban working and unemployed poor. This political tool has some critical functions for households to tolerate the destruction of neoliberalism, and was added to the new political power relations of the 2000s. Social benefits are offered as a favour and charitable activity distributed by the government, not as a vested social right of the poor in need of social assistance. The goal of strengthening political power relations through social assistance has an important role in such a tendency. Also, there was almost an absolute overlap between the poor, women, children, disabled, elderly, martyrs sections – identified as the subject of social policy and social assistance in the 2000s – and the AKP which had a direct relationship with these groups in the society through a new inclusive and appeasing discourse. The subjects of social policy were built as the main target population segments in the AKP's organisation of clientelist relations. Ultimately, social assistance could be presented to society as a common social service and activity of the state, government and party. The fact that a semi-statist and paternalist, semi-philanthropist and conservative ideology could be created around this political action was one of the important facts that completed this process. In this process, social assistance was politicised in presentation of the whole party and power together with central and local administrators to society. These facts should be counted among the unique and distinctive aspects of social assistance during the AKP period.

The realisation of this kind of clientelism has some technical and institutional reasons. These include lack of an explicit provision in the Constitution regarding the right to social assistance; the absence of a separate and single law governing social assistance schemes; regulation of some programmes by law, some by circulars or guidelines, etc; the lack of judicial decisions; and discretionary power of the

Board of Trustees of Social Mutualisation and Solidarity Foundations (institutions which implement central social assistance schemes of the Ministry in localities). Such a vague structure in decisions regarding the eligibility makes the process open to the personal initiative of the professional staff working in the foundations. In addition, the anxiety of beneficiaries about the continuity of the cash or in-kind assistance of central or local administrations is still widespread. All those sets of relations create a sense of gratitude and indebtedness in social assistance recipients and produce consent that strengthens political power relations.

In such an economic, social and political environment, social assistance has served as a kind of non-wage income and means of support. It takes on a new meaning as an economic and social protection related to subsistence issues occurring because of low-paid work and inadequate income of poor working-class households or others who are a part of the reserve army of labour. This chapter thus focuses on putting social assistance in its place as a permanent social policy tool of the AKP, located in the gap between needs and subsistence level, yet not able to fill the gap completely. As a tool, social assistance is connected with the phenomena that create the poverty, wage labour, subsistence and poverty patterns of social assistance recipients.

8.2 NEOLIBERALISM, WORK/WAGE-POVERTY LINK AND CASH DEFICIT

The effects of neoliberal transformations that took place in the labour markets, demographics and welfare policies led to poverty conditions in work and unemployment. It can be argued that wages acquire a bonding character between the transformations that take place in the capital accumulation process and the aforementioned forms of new capitalism. This phenomenon is particularly valid in terms of the proletarianisation process that occurs in today's capitalism, as well as the connection between capitalism and wages, and the historicity of the social outcomes of this connection. In contemporary capitalism, it is observed that wages are desired to be adjusted as a kind of laissez-faire area under a flexible and low-wage system without collective bargaining processes, related to the transformations in relations of production around the determining requirements of capital accumulation, and restructuring of the labour markets around neoliberal principles (Jessop, 1994: 259–67; Peck, 1996: 195–6; Standing, 1999: 88–97).

This process also has the characteristics of the historical link between poverty and work, which is strongly re-established today (Erdoğdu and Kutlu, 2017: 71–3). In this context, it is necessary to share an observation regarding the material life conditions of the working and unemployed poor, and segments that are candidates to impoverishment: these groups are pushed into a cash need based on being wage labourers. Precarious forms of employment that disrupt regular cash supply have diversified and become widespread in the labour markets, which are the only way of obtaining cash (Özuğurlu, 2005: 91). Poverty, unemployment and insecurity have surrounded the material conditions of the poor and impoverished households by forcing them to adopt contemporary neoliberal forms.

A similar process is experienced in Turkey (Yücesan-Özdemir and Özdemir, 2008: 163). It can be observed that, in Turkey, working-poor and unemployed-poor households are trying to manage their lives under a cash need which occurs as a kind of market pressure. This cash need increases in terms of maintenance of daily life and reproduction of labour power and household. It is also based on pricing and commodification (Özuğurlu, 2005: 91; Yücesan-Özdemir and Özdemir, 2008: 159–218; Topak, 2012: 271–304); dispossession, dissolution of subsistence spheres and proletarianisation (Bağımsız Sosyal Bilimciler, 2011: 99–101, 151–82; Bahçe et al., 2011a; Bahçe and Köse, 2017); precarious, irregular, low-paid labour and unemployment (Yücesan-Özdemir and Özdemir, 2008: 69–156; Hacısalihoğlu, 2014). It can be seen that working conditions and wage levels of a certain group of the working population are far from providing the individual and household welfare (Erdoğdu and Kutlu, 2017: 93–4).

Minimum wage earners are so pervasive in the labour market in Turkey; however, that minimum wage does not save the workers from poverty. The net minimum wage level that is determined by the Minimum Wage Determination Commission for one single worker has always fallen short of the minimum subsistence level amount calculated for one worker by the Turkish Statistical Institute (TurkStat). On average, net minimum wages cover only 75.4 percent of the minimum subsistence level since 2000. Minimum wage is determined without the family/household being taken into account; and thus, it could be named as 'poverty wage'. Bahçe and Köse (2018: 47–8) calculated the average monthly wages of the poor and non-poor labourers as a ratio of the net monthly minimum wage. They state that poor labourers have an income structure that is very close to the minimum wage. Thus, in terms of a wage level around the net minimum wage and minimum subsistence wage levels, it can be seen that poor labourers barely have the minimum subsistence and living conditions.

Based on the Household Budget Surveys, between the years 2002 and 2009, TurkStat has established the ratio of poverty of the household individuals according to their status at work, in the context of poverty statistics based on expenditures. It is possible to argue that working poverty had a tendency to decline between the years 2002 and 2009. TurkStat also established the individual poverty rates of the same period and up to 2016, according to poverty-level methods. The downward trend seen in these statistics seems to be connected to the relative and fluctuating upward trend in the coverage ratio of the net minimum wages to the minimum subsistence for a worker, and the increase in social assistance expenditures. On the other hand, while the number of working poor seems to decrease, according to Bahçe and Köse's calculations (2018: 46), it can be observed that the share of labourers, propertyless labourers and the urban unemployed have been increasing in poor households.

The proletarianisation process in Turkey has been integrated with a jobless growth and employment structure that does not eradicate poverty. Along with the neoliberal transformation, market dependence of larger population sections has increased, and this process reinforced the relationship between the need for cash and wages. Households have been experiencing the wage bond that occurs based on market dependency, need for cash, and the tendency of wages being rearranged as a non-invasive area as cash deficiency. It can also be observed that cash deficiency, which cannot be fully compensated, is being managed with non-wage subsistence tools. Non-wage subsistence tools are defined as social assistance in this chapter.

8.3 SOCIAL ASSISTANCE AND SOCIAL ASSISTANCE PROGRAMMES IN TURKEY

Social assistance in Turkey – as a part of a global tendency (see Ditch, 1999: 119; Barrientos and Hulme, 2008; Leisering and Barrientos, 2013) – has become prominent in social policy both as a paradigm and practice in the 2000s, as a part of the minimum welfare regime. It has grown in terms of amount, coverage of population, number of recipients and programmes. In this process, while public social assistance providers consisting of central government and municipalities gained importance, the activities of faith-based 'charities' in terms of private social assistance also showed a remarkable development.[1]

Table 8.1   Social Assistance Programmes

Regular Social Benefits (Except for the Universal Health Insurance Premium Support)	Periodical (Temporary) Social Benefits
Conditional Education Assistance	Food
Conditional Health Assistance	Coal
Conditional Pregnancy Assistance	Housing Assistance
Widowed Women	Education Assistance
Assistance for Needy Soldier Families	Health Assistance
Assistance within the Law No. 2022 (Old-Aged, Disabled, Disabled's relative, Silicosis)	Disabled Need Assistance
Home Care Assistance	Assistance for Private Purposes
Assistance for the Needy Children of Soldiers	Clothing and Other Family Assistance
Assistance for Orphaned Children	Employment Assistance
	One-off Assistance
	Maternity Assistance

Source: T.R. Ministry of Family and Social Policies (2016: 118).

There are a number of social assistance programmes carried out by different public institutions in Turkey. The Ministry of Family and Social Services categorises social benefits into regular and periodical social benefits, except premium grants within the scope of Universal Health Insurance.

Individuals and households that benefit from social assistance in Turkey are determined by needs assessment criteria that change according to different types of social assistance (Table 8.1). Needs assessment criteria are shaped according to income and social security assessment,[2] which can be applied separately or together according to the social assistance programme. Needs assessment criteria and social assistance programmes are constituted in accordance with consolidating the participation of households in the labour market.

As observed in Table 8.2, social assistance programmes can be classified according to participation in employment, and income and social insurance assessment. Social assistance programmes and needs assessment criteria are classified based on participation in employment. Beneficiary households are subject to labour market participation and employment assessment through the insurance and income assessment. When criteria are evaluated, it can be noted that: (1) registered and unregistered working poor and unemployed households receive such social benefits that are determined without the social security assessment criteria; (2) unregistered working poor and unemployed households receive such social benefits that are determined according to the social security assessment criteria; (3) when there is only one person in the household who is within the scope of social security, registered and unregistered working poor and unemployed households whose per capita income of the household is below the indigence criteria receive such social benefits determined according to the income assessment criteria.

In this process, first of all, the share of social assistance expenses has an increasingly fluctuating trend in GDP through the years (Figure 8.1). This ratio increased from 5 per thousand to 1.40 per cent starting from 2005.

Also, the number of social assistance recipient households has increased and social assistance has become a part of the subsistence pattern for more households gradually.

Table 8.2 Classification of Social Assistance Programmes Based on Social Security, Employment and Income Test

Social Assistance Programmes	Needs Test Criteria Based on Social Security, Employment, Income and Other Payments (Receiving Monthly Pay and Income from Social Security Institution, Unemployment Insurance, Alimony: those who receive alimony or are able to receive, Allowance: those who receive an allowance according to the Social Services Law No. 2828)	Beneficiary Households
Food (package or check), Coal, Educational Materials Assistance, Home Care Assistance, Assistance for Tuberculosis and Subacute Sclerosing Panencephalitis (SSPE) Patients	Income test	Registered and unregistered working poor and unemployed poor households
Conditional Education and Health Assistance, Regular Cash Benefits for Women Whose Spouse Has Passed Away, Regular Cash Benefits for Needy Soldier Families, Silicosis Assistance, Assistance for the Children of Soldiers, Assistance for Orphaned Children, Disabled's Relative Pension (Disabled under 18 years old), Electricity Support Assistance	Social security, other payment and income test	Out of social security coverage and unregistered working poor and unemployed poor households
Disabled Assistance (Adults aged 18 and older)	If the disabled person is not covered by social security and the other payments, income test is made even if there is a person under social security in the household	Registered and unregistered poor and unemployed poor households whose level of income per capita is below the income-based needs test, even if there is a person under social security in the household
Old-Age Assistance	If the old-aged person is not covered by social security and the other payments, income test is made even if there is a person under social security in the household	Registered and unregistered poor and unemployed poor households whose total income for himself/herself and his/her spouse is below the income-based needs test, even if there is a person under social security in the household

Source: Updated and arranged based on Erdoğdu and Kutlu (2017: 99).

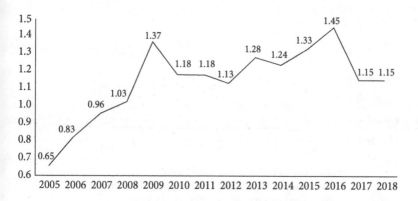

Figure 8.1 Share of Social Assistance Expenses in GDP by Years

Source: Annual Programmes of Ministry of Development for 2005–14 data; 2015 and 2016 data are from Administrative Activity Reports of Abrogated Ministry of Family and Social Policies; 2018 data are from Ministry of Family, Labour and Social Services 2018 Activity Report; 2019 and 2020 data are from Ministry of Family, Labour and Social Services 2019 and 2020 Years Activity Reports.

Figures 8.2 and 8.3 reveal that there is an increase in social assistance recipient population in Turkey. The upward trend, which seemed to accelerate in 2017 and 2018, can be explained by the reflections of the economic woes following 2016, which ended up with a currency crisis in 2018. In Figure 8.2, the increase in the number of households receiving regular and temporary benefits draws attention. In Figure 8.3, it is seen that this group has the fastest rate of increase. Based on these data, it is safe to argue that the unregistered working poor and unemployed poor people have a strong tendency to receive both types of social assistance. On the other hand, there is an increase in beneficiaries of regular social assistance programmes received by unregistered working poor and unemployed poor people. According to Figure 8.3, the rate of increase in households receiving social assistance is above the rate of increase in total households. All these data reveal that working poor and unemployed poor households tend to compensate their cash deficit through a non-wage subsistence tool such as social assistance. In the next sections of this chapter, the results of the field research that I conducted on social assistance are discussed.

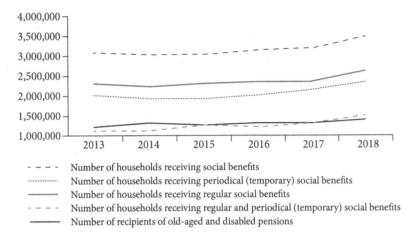

Number of households receiving social benefits
Number of households receiving periodical (temporary) social benefits
Number of households receiving regular social benefits
Number of households receiving regular and periodical (temporary) social benefits
Number of recipients of old-aged and disabled pensions

Figure 8.2   Increase in Number of Social Assistance Recipient Households

Note: The Abrogated Ministry of Family, Labour and Social Services announced the total number of social assistance recipient households for 2020 as 6,630,682 by adding the additional population because of the cash transfers during the pandemic. Here, on the other hand, the total number of social assistance recipient households was determined by using the calculation method used in previous years based on subtracting the number of households receiving both benefits from the total number of households receiving temporary and regular benefits in order to create data continuity.

Source: Abrogated Ministry of Family and Social Policies Activity Reports, Ministry of Family, Labour and Social Services Activity Reports.

8.4 METHODOLOGY AND DATA COLLECTION TECHNIQUES

Qualitative research methods were used in this study. The data were interpreted with an inductive logic within a design from codes to concepts. The aim of the study was to determine common experiences and collect extensive information by including more than one neighbourhood and institution, and to get information from people who work in specified institutions who were knowledgeable with the subject to observe specific dynamics and developments in the field on the basis of maximum variety sampling. The data in the study were obtained using face-to-face, in-depth interviews and participant observation techniques in terms of typical case sampling.

The research was carried out in Ankara, within the context of a completed (2014) and published (2015) PhD thesis; and includes

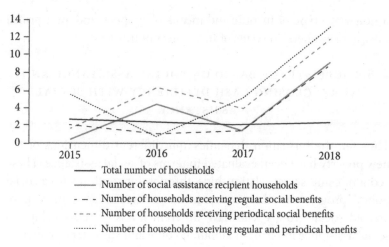

Total number of households
Number of social assistance recipient households
- — - Number of households receiving regular social benefits
- - - - Number of households receiving periodical social benefits
·········· Number of households receiving regular and periodical benefits

Figure 8.3 Rate of Increase in Total Number of Households and Social Assistance Recipient Households (%)

Source: Abrogated Ministry of Family and Social Policies Activity Reports, Ministry of Family, Labour and Social Services Activity Reports and TurkStat, Address Based Population Registration Statistics.

semi-structured, in-depth interviews with social assistance recipients (54), and institution representatives; ministry (5), Social Assistance and Assistance Foundations (10), municipalities (10), neighbourhood mukhtars (17), and private social assistance institutions (2), as well as participant observations during the needs test processes in houses (40) and also social assistance distributions in districts (3).

Moreover, another field research was conducted which includes semi-structured, in-depth interviews with 33 beneficiaries and 66 institution representatives in 2017. Therefore, we were able to observe the subsistence and living conditions of households consisting of 450–500 people in their own neighbourhood and home environment. The data based on qualitative research design have been interpreted with an approach that uses qualitative codes and associates these codes with concepts. Data analysis has been concluded with a number of generated concepts that include patterns in order to thoroughly examine the world of facts of the social assistance recipients and social assistance. These concepts can be stated as 'a non-wage type of income and means of support' and 'non-priced subsistence sphere' in terms of the subject of this study.

8.5 SUBSISTENCE BASED ON SOCIAL ASSISTANCE AND WORK: CLOSING CASH DEFICIENCY WITH SOCIAL ASSISTANCE

Thus far, the formation dynamics and different dimensions of the new poverty have been evaluated in terms of social assistance. These economic and social relationships, through integration with a social policy programme that concentrates on social assistance, have created social groups who have different levels of relationships to social assistance in terms of labour, income and subsistence patterns. It is possible to determine this group as social assistance recipients. In the following, the subsistence patterns of the social assistance recipient working and unemployed poor are analysed.

8.5.1 Main Features of Working Patterns

The key features of the working patterns of social assistance recipients can be examined under the titles of 'refraining from employment and unemployment trap', 'precarity, unregistered employment, and unemployment', and 'gender norms and the child'.

8.5.1.1 Refraining from Employment and Unemployment Trap? It is an object of interest whether beneficiaries participate in employment processes or abstain from work because of social benefits. Our research shows that, as a general tendency, social benefits do not lead households to refrain from participating in the labour market, prevent them from working, or cause the beneficiaries to lose their discipline or work habit. Again, as a general tendency, the 'unemployment trap' which would occur as a result of receiving social assistance has not been observed yet. Non-wage income and means of support obtained in the form of social benefits would not make households refrain from selling their labour power.[3]

When appropriate my spouse worked in car-wash, now he will become unemployed. He went and talked to the car-wash whether he could work again. He does not have insurance, think how much money he could get in the car-wash in this weather [it was winter]. He will work if he gets a job. (Interview No. 1)

A working life and subsistence experience based on an obligation of selling the labour power, combined with market pressure, is the dominant tendency among social assistance recipients. Selling the labour power, to compensate the cash deficiency and to satisfy the needs that cannot be compensated with in-kind or cash social assistance show that the social assistance do not possess the character of bargaining vis-à-vis the employer. In this context, it can be observed that social benefits do not reduce the market dependency or eliminate the household subsistence structure based on work. Therefore, it is safe to argue that the decommodifying characteristic of social benefits is not strong enough.

Another fact that can be analysed in this context is related to the social assistance recipients' working experience and perceptions. Some social assistance recipients, in a way that could be defined as an intra-class disintegration, expressed the existence of such a phenomenon based on the observations of their environment. It can be seen that the ones who express such a thought exclude themselves from this behaviour. The predominant group of beneficiaries reject the claims about being lazy and state that refraining from employment takes its source from the general features of working life, not from social benefits:

It is not about disliking the job, they offer the worst conditions. Can you work under the worst conditions? Nobody wants to work under such conditions, and that is it. (Interview No. 2)

There is no 'disliking the job', it is hard to like the job. Working is hard. (Interview No. 3)

I do not agree with this. Let me start with myself. If they have not dismissed me, why am I leaving the job? I will fall out of work for 4–5 months until April. Why would I be idle? What will my home [family] eat? I don't dislike the salary, I do not say that it is not worth working for this money. I earn 800 TL, I was working. I was supplying the needs of my home, I was feeling at peace with my family. (Interview No. 4)

8.5.1.2 Precarity, Unregistered Employment and Unemployment
Social assistance recipient households can only sustain their existence in the labour market in such a precarious working structure in the form of irregular and temporary jobs, and unregistered work. It is a basic finding that social assistance recipients can only participate in the labour market with precarious forms of employment and remain in working life with such forms of employment. This struggle for existence in the labour market forms a common typology for social assistance recipients that can be described as working poor and unemployed poor in terms of their working and subsistence characteristics. In this typology, households' dependency on social assistance appear or disappear according to their participation in employment relations. There is a strong connection between the reasons and processes why the poor receive social assistance and their types of participation in the labour market. Households' dependency on social assistance emerges at the heart of their labour market experience. This common tendency reveals the dependent structure of household poverty on the features of the work. This fact also shows that labour and wage can be the source of poverty as well as welfare. As Buğra-Kavala and Keyder (2008: 27) stated, the reason for poverty is implicit in the precarious characteristics of the jobs, rather than unemployment.

There is too much unemployment. For example, he is not unemployed; but he constantly quits jobs and gets jobs. I say, for example, how many months will you work here? And he says, I suppose I will work for six months. (Interview No. 5)

The dependency on social assistance is based on the grounds of precarity experience. Some of the beneficiaries, who are able to participate in the labour market in registered and unregistered ways, have an interwoven experience of mostly job and wage insecurity.

Unregistered work, which is one of the main features of the labour market together with unemployment, is extremely common among beneficiaries. A beneficiary, while telling of her spouse's work experience, states this fact as 'He even had insurance for a while.' The long period of time between the start of work and the attachment date (the date the insurance starts) is an important finding. This brings about a working environment in which the connection between work and insurance is broken. In such an environment without this connection, unregistered work could be experienced for many years. Getting involved in a working life with unregistered jobs brings about a continuity for informality. Thus, accepting unregistered work transforms into strategies of participating and surviving in working life.

> My father died when I was seven. I did not go to school, I grew up in orphanages. My mother married here, with someone from Ankara. I have been working since that day. There is no job [I have not done], I worked in Siteler [production and sales zone in Ankara full of furniture business], well I mean that, I worked as a porter, I worked in construction, in factories, I worked in all kinds of jobs. But for more than half of them, I had to worked without any insurance; permanently uninsured, permanently uninsured. (Interview No. 4)

Based on these facts, it is safe to claim that the main factor that prevents beneficiary households participating in the labour market is irregular and precarious labour relations.

8.5.1.3 Gender Norms and Child Care While refraining from working life because of social benefits appears to be a weak tendency, as a finding, it becomes predominantly valid for women, considered with a gender-based division of labour. Included in this pattern, the number of children, as well as the men's permission and presence, is one of the factors which prevents women from employment. Receiving social assistance experience coincides with the dominant gender-based division of labour norms. Women are mostly responsible for the process and for paperwork[4] about social assistance. This practice is realised as a house-based gender-related division of labour, and child and elderly care is experienced as an additional phenomenon that prevents women from employment processes together with practices related to the reproduction of labour power and household.[5]

8.5.2 Main Features of Subsistence Patterns

Households' coping capacity and compensation level of cash deficiency gradually comes to a state of dependency on the wage income and participation in wage labour. It can be revealed that this structure is supported with active labour market policies. It can also be argued that social benefits, sometimes by going beyond coping with poverty, reach significant levels as a kind of survival strategy for poor households. Social benefits are experienced as an additional income and function as a means of support which creates an unpriced subsistence sphere. Based on social assistance, this is the main character that forms the subsistence pattern of beneficiary working poor and unemployed poor households.

8.5.2.1 Social Assistance and Cash Deficiency (1): Additional Income – a Non-Wage Type of Income and Means of Support   Social assistance recipients are in a subsistence level that does not meet their needs. Social benefits are placed in this gap between the need and subsistence level, occurring due to a cash deficiency. They are experienced as a kind of additional income by households.

> It is important for my subsistence. A ton of coal is 575 liras. It makes 40 bags of coal, if I give 575 liras for coal, my spouse earns 960 liras. What do I get with 400 liras? There is the electricity, the water, food for children and so on ... When the child is having breakfast, he asks for eggs. When he says he wants pastry for dinner, I need to get that assistance to buy it. Because I do not have the luxury to pay 575 liras for the coal. (Interview No. 1)

> For example, I received my assistance, I felt a bit relieved, at least my budget got better. (Interview No. 6)

> The district governorship [refers to Social Assistance and Solidarity Foundation that was established under district governorship]

gives my coal. I do not spend money for coal. I think the money for the coal remains in my pocket. I get a 100 liras cheque but it is not enough; but in the end, I get the assistance. It salves as it was. Maybe I do not have any money in my pocket that day, I need it. Then it salves beside it. When necessary it compensates, why do I lie, sometimes I do not have two nickels to rub together, I think about what I am going to do, what the hell I am going to do. They say the district governorship's cheque is ready, come and take it, then I go and take it. (Interview No. 7)

Social assistance is experienced as an additional income that closes the cash deficiency of households. So, it has a characteristic which contributes to the reproduction of labour power and the household, and is incorporated into the wage as a non-wage type of income and means of support. It can be argued that social assistance, in this manner, is a compensatory subsistence and coping strategy which is incorporated into the wage for closing cash deficiency.

8.5.2.2 Social Assistance and Cash Deficiency (2): An Unpriced Subsistence Sphere   Social benefits reach significant levels as a means of support to compensate cash deficiency and surpass the pricing and commodification pressure for households. It also needs to be highlighted that contributions in-kind such as food, basic consumption goods and coal have also such complementary effects on market and general consumption tendencies of social assistance recipient working and unemployed households:

Yesterday I went and bought my needs for 100 liras. Oil, sugar, tomato paste, breakfast food, meals and drinks with bits and pieces for our children. I spent 100 liras yesterday. Maybe if the food [she refers to contributions in-kind] was distributed, then I would have kept 100 liras. (Interview No. 8)

Why would I spend 600 liras and buy coal? It would be difficult for us. One [bottle] of oil is 20 liras, for example. Why would it be an out-of-pocket expense? I used it for example, I used it for three months, it just finished, I just bought the oil. I would buy something else for my child rather than it [oil], I would buy clothes. (Interview No. 5)

It can be argued that the contributions in-kind have created an unpriced subsistence area for households.

8.6 CONCLUSION

Based on the findings, it is safe to argue that the social assistance recipients survive on an increasing need for cash based on the dispossession and proletarianisation processes that separate them from their subsistence tools. The predominant subject in terms of households' relationship to work, social assistance and subsistence is the obligation to participate in employment and a market dependency that does not exclude them from general commodification processes. The subsistence patterns of social assistance recipient households have acquired a character that is more open to the types of employment participation due to cash need. In other words, the subsistence patterns of those households come into existence under the pressure of participation in the labour market as a wage labourer. It was found that households' need for social assistance emerged on the basis of labour market dynamics. Social assistance becoming prominent as a basic social policy tool is compatible both with the dominance of the wage relation within historical functioning tendencies of capitalism and tendencies to make the wage relation laissez-faire in the neoliberal phase. The neoliberal capital accumulation strategy which is formed as the reconstruction of wages as a laissez-faire area also created objective conditions for households to compensate this situation reflected as cash deficiency with social assistance.

Households' need for and dependency on social benefits become more and more important in such a structure. It can be observed that households, by overcoming market pressure and dependency created by commodification and pricing strategies, aim to loosen the cash link, and social assistance is a developing and expanding subsistence strategy on this basis. Social assistance is a coping and even a survival strategy for some households that has become increasingly widespread during the deepening neoliberal transformation process in the 2000s. It can be observed that social assistance recipients are in a subsistence level that does not meet their needs. They cut down on expenses in terms of their own basic needs. In such living conditions, social benefits are located in the gap between the need and subsistence level as an additional income. It can be contended that social assistance, as a non-wage income, has an important role in the toleration of poor households and in closing the gap in their cash needs. Social assistance has turned into a permanent social policy tool to close the revenue gap of working poor and unemployed poor households in terms of subsistence level. In such a structure, it can be observed that households which are embedded to low-wage working relations aim to overcome the cash need through receiving social assistance. However, the very same social assistance structure strengthens the dependency of the recipient households on the political institutions which deliver this assistance.

In any case, social assistance recipients experience a cash deficiency that it is not possible to fully compensate with social benefits. It has been observed that instead of social assistance alleviating poverty, social assistance recipients continue to maintain their lives under an elevated poverty level. In the case of subsistence, social assistance also does not eliminate poverty. Based on the findings of the research I conducted, the unpriced means of support keeps the households in a level of poverty; a continuous cash deficiency between need and subsistence, and experienced as an additional income.

Social assistance as a form of cash is associated with wages and thus tolerates the low-paying jobs and reproduces them in the labour market. This phenomenon turns social assistance into a type of labour market tool and wage relation category in terms of the deprivatisation of the reproduction of labour power cost. This type of relationship, on the one hand, equips social assistance with a labour market character and tells us that the social assistance recipient households have a working-class character. Social assistance recipients cannot give up participating in the labour market, even if they receive social assistance. Social assistance programmes are also regulated in such a form that they cannot enable households to make ends meet without working and being subject to cash need. It was not seen as a general unemployment trap due to receiving social assistance. It has been observed that an unemployment trap may be valid for women on the basis of gender norms. Our findings show that the social benefits do not possess the quality of discouraging households from participating in the labour market, prevent them from working, or diminish their work discipline and habits. The main factor that removes social assistance recipient households from the labour market is irregular and precarious employment relations. Social benefits have functioned as a non-wage type of income and means of support to close the cash deficiency on the basis of this employment relationship. To the degree that social assistance is experienced as an additional income, it makes precarious and low-paid working relations tolerable, which constantly creates a cash deficiency for households and therefore reproduces such practices and this employment structure in the Turkish labour market.

BIBLIOGRAPHY

Bağımsız Sosyal Bilimciler (2011) *Ücretli Emek ve Sermaye Derinleşen Kriz ve Türkiye'ye Yansımaları*, İstanbul: Yordam Kitap.

Bahçe, S. and Köse, A.H. (2017) 'Social Classes and Neo-liberal Poverty Regime in Turkey, 2002–2011', *Journal of Contemporary Asia*, 47 (4), 575–95.

—— (2018) 'Kapitalizmin Yoksulluğu: Vatandaş ya da Toplumsal Sınıf Olarak Yoksullar', in Kutlu, D (ed.), *Sosyal Yardım Alanlar Emek, Geçim, Siyaset ve Toplumsal Cinsiyet*, İstanbul: İletişim Yayınları, 41–57.

Bahçe, S., Günaydın, F.Y. and Köse, A.H. (2011a) 'Türkiye'de Toplumsal Sınıf Haritaları: Sınıf Oluşumları ve Sınıf Hareketliliği Üzerine Karşılaştırmalı Bir Çalışma', in Şahinkaya, S. and Ertuğrul, İ. (eds), *Bilsay Kuruç'a Armağan*, Ankara: Mülkiyeliler Birliği, 359–92.

Barrientos, A. and Hulme, D. (2008) 'Social Protection for the Poor and Poorest in Developing Countries: Reflections on a Quiet Revolution', *Brooks World Poverty Institute Working Paper 30*.

Buğra-Kavala, A. and Keyder, Ç. (2006) 'The Turkish Welfare Regime in Transformation', *Journal of European Social Policy*, 16, 211–28.

—— (2008) 'Kent Nüfusunun En Yoksul Kesiminin İstihdam Yapısı ve Geçinme Yöntemleri', https://tinyurl.com/ydechbo5 (accessed 4 February 2018).

Ditch, J. (1999) 'Full Circle: A Second Coming for Social Assistance', in Clasen, J. (ed.), *Comparative Social Policy Concepts, Theories and Method*, Oxford and Malden, MA: Blackwell, 114–35.

Erdoğdu, S. and Kutlu, D. (2017) 'Çalışan Yoksulluğu: Türkiye İçin Sosyal Politikalar Bağlamında Bir Değerlendirme', in Makal, A. and Çelik, A. (eds), *Zor Zamanlarda Emek Türkiye'de Çalışma Yaşamının Güncel Sorunları*, Ankara: İmge Kitabevi, 65–112.

Göçmen, İ. (2014) 'Religion, Politics and Social Assistance in Turkey: The Rise of Religiously Motivated Associations', *Journal of European Social Policy*, 24 (1), 92–103.

—— (2018) 'Non-public Welfare in Turkey: New and Old Forms of Religiously Motivated Associations', *Research and Policy on Turkey*, 3 (2), 187–200.

Hacısalihoğlu, E. (2014) *Türkiye İşçi Sınıfı Haritasında Güvencesizlik Deneyimleri*, PhD Thesis, Ankara Üniversitesi, Ankara.

Jessop, B. (1994) 'Post-Fordism and the State', in Amin, A. (ed.), *Post-Fordism A Reader*, Oxford and Malden, MA: Blackwell, 251–79.

Kutlu, D. (2015) *Türkiye'de Sosyal Yardım Rejiminin Oluşumu: Birikim, Denetim, Disiplin*, Ankara: Notabene.

Leisering, L. and Barrientos, A. (2013) 'Social Citizenship for the Global Poor? The Worldwide Spread of Social Assistance', *International Journal of Social Welfare*, 22, 50–67.

Özuğurlu, M. (2005) 'Türkiye'de Sosyal Politikanın Dönüşümü', *Toplum ve Hekim*, 20 (2), 87–93.

Peck, J. (1996) *Work-Place: The Social Regulation of Labor Markets*, New York: Guildford.

Sallan-Gül, S. and Gül, H. (2006) *Poverty Assistance and Employment Study: Relations between Social Assistance and Labour Force Participation*, Report Prepared for the General Directorate of Social Assistance and UNDP.

Standing, G. (1999) *Global Labour Flexibility Seeking Distributive Justice*, London: Macmillan Press.

Topak, O. (2012) *Refah Devleti ve Kapitalizm 2000'li Yıllarda Türkiye'de Refah Devleti*, İstanbul: İletişim Yayınları.

T.R. Ministry of Family, Labour and Social Services (2019) *2018 Year Activity Report (2018 Yılı Faaliyet Raporu)*, Ankara.

T.R. Ministry of Family and Social Policies (2016) *2015 Year Administration Activity Report (2015 Yılı İdare Faaliyet Raporu)*, Ankara.

——(2017) *2016 Year Administration Activity Report (2016 Yılı İdare Faaliyet Raporu)*, Ankara.

Ünlütürk Ulutaş, Ç. (2017) 'Türkiye Refah Rejiminin Dönüşüm Sürecinde Sosyal Yardım Sistemi', *Emek Araştırma Dergisi (GEAD)*, 8 (12), 27–48.

Yentürk, N. (2018) *Sosyal Yardımlardan Güvenliğe Türkiye'nin Kamu Harcamaları (2006–2017)*, İstanbul: Bilgi Üniversitesi Yayınları.

Yücesan-Özdemir, G. and Özdemir, A.M. (2008). *Sermayenin Adaleti Türkiye'de Emek ve Sosyal Politika*, Ankara: Dipnot Yayınları.

Interviews

Interview No. 1. Working poor household. Age: 29. Shanty House. Dostlar Neighbourhood, Mamak, Ankara. Married. With two children. Tenanted. Receiving coal and food assistance from the metropolitan municipality for 1–1.5 years. Date: 21 January 2014.

Interview No. 2. Working poor household. Age 46. Çandarlı Neighbourhood, Hıdırlıktepe, Altındağ, Ankara. Married. With three children. Tenanted. Receiving coal and food assistance from the metropolitan municipality for many years. Date: 2 January 2014.

Interview No. 3. Shanty House. Age 32. Çandarlı Neighbourhood, Hıdırlıktepe, Altındağ, Ankara. Divorced. With three children. Receiving 'Social and Economic Support' assistance for her children, coal and food assistance from the metropolitan municipality for ten years. Date: 8 January 2014.

Interview No. 4. Working poor household. Age 46. Shanty House. Şehit Cengiz Topel Neighbourhood, Mamak, Ankara. Married. With two children. Receiving coal and food assistance from the metropolitan municipality for 15 years. Date: 22 November 2013.

Interview No. 5. Working poor household. Age 31. Shanty House. Çandarlı Neighbourhood, Hıdırlıktepe, Altındağ, Ankara. Married. With two children. Receiving coal and food assistance from the metropolitan municipality for nine years, coal assistance from Social Mutualisation and Solidarity Foundation for eight years. Date: 3 January 2014.

Interview No. 6. Working poor household. Shanty House. Dikmen, Çankaya, Ankara. Married. With two children. Receiving coal and food assistance from the metropolitan municipality for eleven years and also from Social Mutualisation and Solidarity Foundation. Receiving condition cash transfer from the Foundation. Date: 24 January 2014.

Interview No. 7. Working poor household. Shanty House. Plevne Neighbourhood, Yenidoğan, Altındağ, Ankara. Married. With two children. Receiving coal and food assistance from metropolitan municipality, coal assistance from the Foundation. Date: 19 December 2013.

Interview No. 8. Working poor household. Age 29. Shanty House. Çandarlı Neighbourhood, Hıdırlıktepe, Altındağ, Ankara. Married. With two children. Receiving coal and food assistance from the metropolitan municipality for 11–12 years, coal assistance from the Foundation. Receiving 'Social and Economic Support' assistance for her children. Date: 3 January 2014.

9

A View of Precarisation from Turkey: Urban-Rural Dynamics and Intergenerational Precarity

Elif Hacısalihoğlu[1]

9.1 INTRODUCTION

While precarisation is not a recent phenomenon, the term has become more and more prevalent because of the need to conceptualise the current transformations in working life and their impact on masses. While the concept has received attention in academic literature, it seems somehow inadequate to grasp the reality in Turkey. Three important aspects need to be taken into account to overcome this inadequacy: the Eurocentrism of the concept, the urban-rural origins and intergenerationality.

Indeed, the concept of precarisation was developed primarily in a Western-oriented setting, in the light of the developments in Europe. However, the ongoing debates in the mainstream literature are not sufficient to explain the phenomenon of precarity in Turkey as they disregard the unique and immanent features of late capitalist countries in their analysis. The transformation in the capitalist labour process and the accompanying readjustment of the social welfare state are projected differently in advanced capitalist and late capitalist countries, leading to the emergence of processes such as proletarianisation and commodification in diverse forms. The transformation of masses is an integral component of this process. In this context, different answers are given to the questions of 'the rise of proletarianisation', 'the impact of this process on different segments of the working class' and 'the response of the working class to this process'. Hence, it is crucial to focus on the specific dynamics in a late capitalist country being integrated into this process. The fundamental purpose of this chapter is, therefore, to analyse the experience of precarisation in Turkey.

9.2 CONCEPTUALISING PRECARITY

While the concept of precarity is quite prevalent, certain features come to the fore in the common usage of the term in the relevant literature. Firstly, as noted in the works of Mitropoulos (2005), Neilson and Rossiter (2008), Munck (2013), Betti (2016) and Scully (2016), the concept is Eurocentric.[2] In parallel with the critique directed at the Eurocentric approach, the studies focusing on a variety of geographies are on the rise, as demonstrated by the debates on 'developing countries', 'Global South', 'postcolonial countries', 'late capitalist countries' etc. (Barchiesi, 2011; Harris and Scully, 2015, Rogan et al., 2017; Hacısalihoğlu, 2018). Secondly, the Eurocentric view is based on the employment standard of the 'golden age years' of the West – the period of 1945–75. In this framework, another criticism directed towards the term is that it 'excludes' and ignores the state of women and immigrants in the West (Betti, 2016). From a methodological perspective, the Eurocentric understanding of the concept of precarisation suppresses the diverse manifestations of the phenomenon and homogenises the concept. This attempt to universalise the process during analysis ends up in the subordination of the precarisation experience in other geographies. This universalisation obfuscates the specificities in the socio-economic structures in other geographies and the impact of combined and uneven development on precarisation. The geographies mentioned here are connected among themselves as they go through a similar process; however, they reflect their specific features onto the precarisation process and shape this process through relations and dynamics unique to them. The varieties in the formation of a capitalist system may bring forth different issues – and may render them more critical – in different geographical-political contexts during the precarisation process. 'The idea that the Eurocentric evolutionary approach is valid for all societies' (Işık and Pınarcıoğlu , 2011: 31) may cover up these different issues and render them invisible.

Another use of the concept in the literature disregards the histori-cal nature of precarisation and ignores the proletarianisation process. These approaches are individualistic analyses which solely focus on the current state of affairs. The tendency to explain precarisation solely through the current life and working conditions of the workers is based on the methodological inclination to focus solely on the current phenomenon – that is, the appearance by itself. Yet, in order to understand precarisation, the process itself must be the centre of focus. In this sense, precarisation is realised through the proletari-anisation process. Hence, it is also intertwined with the processes of dispossession and commodification. However, some studies which consider the dynamics that characterise precarisation in Turkey and evaluate the precarisation process within the global economic context are worth mentioning: studies by Oğuz (2011), Özuğurlu (2012) and Hacısalihoğlu (2018) belong to this group. Finally, a common approach in the literature discusses precarisation through the insti-tutional/legal regulations and quantitative transformations in the labour market; and focuses solely on the employment dimension of precarisation.

Precarisation is defined through the relations between classes in the capitalist production relations. It is a reality intrinsic to the relation between the capitalist class and the working class. Hence, precarisation needs to be addressed without neglecting the prole-tarianisation process and through its social continuity – otherwise the continuity is neglected and the transformation brought about by precarisation is assumed to be a break from the previous social pro-cesses. At this point, two categories that fill a significant void in the literature acquire further importance: urban-rural origins and inter-generational transmission. The experience of precarisation needs to be discussed through its historical context and continuity – only then can the impact of the precarisation experiences of previous genera-tions on the current lived experience and the struggle given within this experience be debated. This presents us with the last – but not the least – methodological dimension of the analysis: relationality.

The experience of precarity by the working class is shaped through the mutual interaction of socio-economic relations and class rela-tions. Hence, in the current context we need to focus on relations between classes and relations within the working class. The first dimension here is the current precarisation experience in the relationship between the working class and the capitalist class, while the second dimension involves the relations within the class itself. Since precarity is a class experience, precarisation is a process; and while this process takes place between the classes, the relationship networks within the class (which include both working life and non-working life) constitute important dynamics of this process. The conditions experienced by previous generations are also an important determinant of the precarisation of the working class. This leads us to the intergenerational dimension of precarity. What is required in order to discuss this blind spot of current debates on precarity is an approach that focuses on relationality and intra-class relations rather than an approach that focuses on the worker as an individual.

In sum, we need to look at the formation of current precarisation experiences in their historicity and assess them in the context of class relations. To do that, we should start from the area of production, yet include the situation and the relations in non-working life as areas that the precarisation process is diffused in. As shown by Kalleberg (2009), Candeias (2004) and Scully (2015), it is important to look at non-working life and the experiences in this sphere as well as working life when analysing precarity. Looking at both spheres together can be conceptualised as *double precarisation* as Candeias (2004) emphasised. When precarity is understood as such, the responses to precarity from different segments of the working class, their forms of survival or of struggle, or the reproduction of precarity become clear through the story that lies behind. The variety of the precarisation experience in late capitalist and advanced capitalist countries acquire meaning through this approach.

9.3 INQUIRING INTO CURRENT PRECARISATION EXPERIENCES IN TURKEY: FOCUSING ON PROCESS AND INTRA-CLASS RELATIONS

How to locate the past embedded in the present day and how to gauge its impact? Ancelin-Schützenberger (2017) talks about the chain of genealogy, which includes shared ancestors, legacy and transfer. This chain enables the transfer of not only eye colour or various artistic abilities but also experiences, hopes and anxieties between generations; thus, certain traumas may result from individuals' legacies inherited from previous generations. If we can consider precarisation as a socio-economic trauma with an impact on large masses today, looking at precarisation as a process that goes beyond the present day includes looking into the family history as well. To what extent is the current trauma of precarisation in large proletarised masses connected to the experience of the previous generations? What kinds of relations are there among different generations and which type of continuities can be observed in terms of precarisation? These issues are usually neglected in the relevant literature; and this neglect leads to disregarding certain intra-class dimensions of the relations between classes.

Precarisation can occur in different degrees for different parts of the working class. The severity of the precarisation process and the responses it gets may take on different forms. One of the most explicit and universal reasons for this differentiation is the different employment conditions the members of the working class are subject to. As opposed to other geographies, among the most significant reasons of differentiation in Turkey are the migration from rural to urban areas (rural origins) and intergenerational transmission. These two categories constitute the significant determinants of the degree in which the working class in Turkey is subject to precarisation and their methods of dealing with precarity.

The blind spot of the debates on precarisation is the intrinsic connection between current forms of precarisation – which is created by capitalist production relations and constitutes some kind of 'trauma' for different segments of the working class – and the process of proletarianisation. This process makes it necessary to grasp precarity in the context of relations between classes, on the one hand; and, on the other hand, it makes it necessary to look at the dimension of intra-class relations. Intra-class relations include the class relations in the current moment along with relations with previous generations. Ignoring the intergenerational precarity renders invisible the urbanisation process and rural-to-urban migration processes in late capitalist countries and hence overlooks the proletarianisation process as well. Inasmuch as the debates on precarisation take place in the context of urban experiences of precarity, the case of Turkey demonstrates the significance of intergenerationality and rural-to-urban migration in understanding and explaining the current conditions in urban precarity.

The concept was first introduced and discussed in the same sense during the privatisation of TEKEL (Turkish tobacco and alcoholic beverages company) factories in 2009–10.[3] The 78 days of resistance of around 10,000 TEKEL workers from different cities gathered in the streets of the capital city, Ankara, have both factually and symbolically taken a stand against the propagation of precarious employment in the public sector in various forms. The privatisation of TEKEL and the factory shutdowns meant that the workers would occupy more precarious positions and the state of precarity would become more established in the public sector as well. The workers would either be unemployed or they would accept working under 4/C status, defined in the State Personnel Law as 'temporary status'. This temporary status considerably worsened their working conditions. This process eventually led to one of the most significant resistance movements in Turkish labour history. These protests and resistance created an immense break in the course of employment patterns in the public sector; and the concept of precarity became part and parcel of the lexicon describing the conditions of the Turkish working class. The 4/C status became the indicator of precarious employment in the public sector; and the resistance movement of TEKEL workers became the driving force behind the precarity debates that made room for themselves in the relevant literature.

Against this conceptual-theoretical background, the rest of the chapter is based on observations and 28 face-to-face, in-depth interviews with participants from different cities and different positions in the Turkish labour market such as workers from the public sector, private sector, temporary contracted workers, permanent workers, subcontracted workers, outsourced workers, unionised and non-unionised workers, informal sector workers and the unemployed. The interviews were conducted in several sessions with some of the participants; the researcher participated in their protests, performed social activities with them and even attended their weddings. Some of the participants kept in touch with the researcher even after the study was concluded. These different forms of interaction with the participants indicate that the study went beyond a field research conducted through in-depth interviews and acquired an ethnographic quality in some ways. The initiation of this kind of communication with the participants during the research made it possible to follow their account of precarisation even after the research period. Moreover, some interviews were conducted at the homes of the participants and have involved their families as well. Hence, it has become possible to go beyond the individual experience of precarity and to include the closest network of relations (the household) around the individual to broaden the understanding of the basic elements of the study.

9.4 WHAT CAN WE LEARN FROM THE EXPERIENCE OF PRECARITY OF THE WORKING CLASS IN TURKEY?

9.4.1 Rural-to-Urban Migration and Precarity

Recently, the current literature has been increasingly focusing on the relationship between precarity and migration (Schierup et al., 2014; Paret and Gleeson, 2016). However, the migration-precarity relation and manifestations that are the subject of current literature are mostly centred on precarisation through external migration. External migration is indeed a serious issue for Turkey considering the current conditions; but it has been sustained on the basis of the consequences brought upon by the internal migration/rural-to-urban migration process in Turkey. The different reasons for migration have created variety in the characteristics of those who migrate and the processes of participation in the labour market and precarisation. Also, the propagation of precarious forms of employment, patterns of migration and the mobility between urban and rural regions may have an impact on the relationship between proletarianisation and migration (Zhan and Scully, 2018). Hence, the relationship between urban and rural regions and internal migration has to be included in the analysis as a foundational dynamic of the precarisation process.

The dominant tendency for the process of migration from rural to urban areas is the search for jobs due to the restrictive conditions in rural areas. The precarisation of immigrants due to financial hardships is intertwined with the processes of dispossession and proletarianisation. Marriage and concerns about livelihood at times show up as combined reasons for migration. Thus, the experiences relayed in the interviews carry the collective concern with finding a job/earning a living.

Among the interviewees who live in cities, there are those who want to return to their villages or to the countryside and those who do not. While the interviewees do not agree on this point, a common point they make is that they would need a separate regular income to live off their lands in the village. Hence, the answers centre around 'maybe after retirement' or 'if I receive a pension'. The interviewees state that farming is costly, even for the landowners. A participant who has migrated to the city to find work, and who was dismissed from being a subcontracted worker in the municipality, has expressed the cost of this process in his life and what kind of impression it left on him:

> The rise in the prices of oil fuel, the quotas on sugar beet, such state policies, hinders the production of the farmer. These act as an operation or an intervention to stop the farmer from producing an intervention of the state. It had become very difficult to earn a living in the village. People like us, who do not have much land or capital inherited from families, need capital to buy the fertiliser, to buy the seed, the oil, hire the workers, etc. Hence, we were unable to live there, in the village, and we were not the first ones to migrate. The population of the village went down dramatically. In 2004–2005, when I came back from military service, I knew that I wouldn't be able to live in the village. (Interview 1, T., male, aged 30)

Two important features that determine the experience and severity of precarity in terms of class experience and precarisation need to be emphasised: the form and the duration of urbanisation. The form of urbanisation involves the direction of the migration movement. For the working class, whether the form of urbanisation is rural-to-urban or urban-to-urban impacts the precarisation process and the mechanisms employed to deal with this process. More concretely, these two forms impact the process of inclusion in the labour market, accessing the job networks, forming the required connections, becoming part of the social welfare mechanisms and accessing formal networks. Simultaneously, they affect the security networks and how people appeal to informal mechanisms when confronted with precarity, which in turn has an impact on the living conditions and precarisation processes of the next generation.

When rural-to-urban migration occurs through dispossession, it takes place simultaneously with proletarianisation – that is, the loss of all kinds of rural security. In the migration experience of previous generations within Turkey, rural connections had always been maintained and these connections acted as a buffer against the precarity of the migrant segments of the working class. Even for those who did not want to go back, there used to be a continuous financial aid (cash and in-kind) due to income from the land they own in rural areas. However, the experience of the interviewees show that such security mechanisms are dissolving in the face of urban precarisation. Rural connections are gradually severed.

The distinct forms of capital the families bring along with them to the cities are significant in this context. The low level of education, the lack of know-how on the conditions of surviving in the city, and the lack of knowledge about the labour market in particular render it acceptable to be employed in absolutely precarious conditions. These conditions can also make it difficult to be chosen as a party to the employment contract which would form the precarious relation between the working class and the capitalist class. Hence, absolute precarity may become acceptable in the face of continuous unemployment.

The low levels of education of migrant labour and the skill mismatch between rural and urban jobs mean that they are included in the urban labour markets as unskilled workers. Hence, the forms of know-how brought along to the city with proletarianised rural labour – or the lack thereof – may lead to more negative experiences of precarity compared to other members of the working class. For those who have migrated from rural areas to cities, inclusion to city life through precarious work and life conditions is a common characteristic. We can find a similar characteristic among those who come from small towns. The lack of education and skill leads to low wages, informal work etc. – more precarious work in general. The lack of such features also legitimise work under precarious conditions. Those who cannot access formal mechanisms that could be a barrier against precarity (such as work with insurance, unionisation, social benefits) have no choice but to develop informal security mechanisms when confronted with precarity. Such mechanisms are developed both within working life and outside it, as precarity extends to life outside work hours as well.

Coming from the same town or village or being a member of the same extended family is one of the most significant informal security mechanisms in the face of precarity for the migrants in previous generations. These connections are crucial mechanisms in finding a job or finding a place to live in the initial phases of inclusion in city life (Erder, 2001). As Erder (2015) demonstrates, the existence of 'networks based on origins' provides advantages to access skilled and educated jobs in the city and investing in small and medium-sized capital. However, some recent studies argue that such connections are not as efficient as they used to be.[4] This transformation corroborates the information emphasised by Erder (2015: 9) that 'altruistic' relationships of solidarity turn into 'selective and strict power relations' for those who live at the edge of poverty.

The analysis of the fieldwork shows that relations based on personal trust have been replacing relations among countrymen as a new security mechanism. This replacement is crucial in terms of survival practices in the face of precarity and maintaining a certain feeling of security. As the formal employment relation cannot provide grounds for job security, relations of personal trust established with the employer become a way of dealing with insecurity: becoming a reliable employee in the eyes of the employer turns into a method of securing jobs.[5] The expectation that the relationship of trust established with the employer will provide an informal job security, wage security etc. is expressed as follows:

> At first there should be trust ... If I put in my time and effort for this man [the employer], he will give me my due. (Interview 2, S., female, aged 25)

> It's difficult for him to let me go unless I leave of my own accord... There is trust between us. If he hires someone else, that person might steal from the shop. I don't. They actually tried me out for three years. (Interview 2, S., female, aged 25)

In addition to this, employers or the people who are already adjusted to city life are used as mediators for finding higher-paid jobs with insurance and regular hours. Such connections extend beyond working life to non-working life. When confronted with precarity in non-working life, for instance, when there are problems with access to health services, the employers' social connections may make it possible to access qualified health services or accelerate the service. The relationship of affinity and trust established with the employer is used as a coping strategy in the case of precarity that is diffused in all areas of life, including social insecurity. These can be expressed as the informal acquisition of security in some aspects in the lack of formal security through employment.

For those who have migrated to the cities, another issue that affects the precarisation experience is the lack of knowledge about the labour market. The migrants usually lack information about how to find certain types of jobs, how to access the job pools and how to apply for a job; this lack of information limits their access to the labour market. An interviewee has expressed this situation as 'a lack of guidance'. This lack of information about the labour market also includes lack of knowledge about legal conditions and rights in working life and reinforces precarity. One of the participants who has worked without social security for some time says that 'at that time, I had no idea what social security was'.

The lack of knowledge on the labour market following migration and the need for the workplace to be close to home are factors that reinforce precarity in working life, particularly for women. Another female interviewee, who migrated to the city when she got married, has said that she had to choose her first jobs from among those opportunities near her house. Not being familiar with the city and not knowing where to find jobs has directed her towards applying for the jobs that have put up flyers around her house. These are usually low-waged, unskilled jobs in small-scale businesses. The support of kinship or dependence on fellow countrymen seems to have dissolved in this context. Hence, the newcomers to the city tend to apply for the jobs close to their place of residence and tend to imitate others around them to find a place in the labour market and come up with new ways of earning their living. Such conditions steer them towards consenting to be employed in precarious conditions determined by the employer, rather than being unemployed. The longer the migrants stay in the city, the more they get access to better jobs, through their employers, through the internet or through their social circles in workplaces. Examples include becoming apartment complex attendants, caregivers or cleaners for their neighbours or finding jobs through the teachers in their children's schools. Another example is receiving aid-in-kind from the employers, other employees in the workplace or from their children's school networks.

9.4.2 Intergenerational Precarity

Addressing precarity as a process establishes the ground for discussing the links of precarity among different generations and the relation between intergenerational transmission. The current literature argues that there is a crucial divergence between the experience of the working class in the previous generations and the experience of the social segments described as the precariat today. According to this claim, the precariat of the present is employed in precarious conditions as opposed to the secure employment standard of the workers in previous generations. Because of the differences among them, this mass of workers embedded in precarious conditions cannot be described as the working class anymore; it is a new and different class in the process of formation (Standing, 2011). Standing's definition – 'a class in the process of formation' – has been widely discussed in the relevant literature; while there has not been much interest in the intergenerational continuity or transmission of precarity or in monitoring the course of precarisation among different generations.

The interviews I conducted with the members of the working class who are employed under different conditions in the labour market in Turkey show that the experiences that are transmitted from previous generations have an impact on the current experience of precarity. There are instances in which this transmission, like a generational legacy, demonstrates a continuous character in the context of precarity, challenging the current tendency in the relevant literature. These instances are compatible with the findings of other recent studies. The intergenerational continuity of the receivers of social aids in Turkey (Kutlu, 2015) reflects the intergenerational character of precarity (Hacısalihoğlu, 2018).

In parallel with the emphasis that precarity is not a state but a process, an interviewee has relayed that precarity is not about guarantees but about generational processes: 'Security is not about guarantee. Feeling secure in a job is not something about the productivity in one's life circle or the principles one upholds for oneself. It is a process that goes on among generations …' This emphasis made by a member of the working class points to the fact that precarity cannot be negated through formal security at one point of life. The same interviewee continues as follows:

… when I try to see myself from another's eyes, I see that as the child of a family that did not know how to read and write, the best I could do was to be a shopkeeper. However, I took the path to become a journalist, which was quite an ambitious job for me. There are probably many people like me. There should be something that is coded and transferred to you through your family relationships and social relationships, a relationship of belonging … For myself, I see a process that has jumped from the fifth level to the fiftieth. Hence, the feeling of confidence is not strong in me. I am a migrant here from where I was, that takes belonging. As a culture of life, I took a lot from my family to be here. Personally, I think that confidence [security] is something that is transferred from previous generations. (Interview 3, G., male, aged 36)

Raised in an illiterate family with rural origins, this interviewee who is a journalist states that he went beyond the security lines his family could have procured. He has not restricted himself with the areas of employment in which his family could have provided some sort of confidence through their past experience and knowledge. The current network of social relations he is in, one in which he does not know the dominant codes and therefore feels alien to – he is deprived of the feeling of belonging and trust. The interviewee emphasises that this situation can only be understood through a component of precarity that goes beyond formal security and is not restricted to 'guarantees' such as job security and social security. Precarity involves the lack of various forms of security transmitted and provided by previous generations besides the formal and informal security mechanisms of the moment, and these shape the current experience of precarity. Hence, the experience of precarity can only be understood as a whole through the unpacking of the baggage[6] transmitted from the past – that is, through considering the generational legacy and transmission. How this baggage is perceived, what it contains and how the contents are put to use shapes the lived experience in different ways.

As the participant quoted above says, the child of an illiterate family can jump from 'fifth level to the fiftieth' or on the contrary, 'the best he could be' may be a shopkeeper. Or as it is with other examples, the conditions of precarity can be transmitted between generations. The son of another interviewee who has worked in car washing without insurance for years, for example, has also been working in carwash stations, without insurance and with short-term contracts. While the family is not happy with this continuity, they have not yet been able to break it off. There is a similar situation with the daughter of an interviewee who works as a subcontract worker in the municipality – the daughter is also employed as a short-term contract worker in a public institution. There are many other examples to be given for this continuity. This continuity is expressed as follows by an unemployed participant with an elementary level of education, whose father has migrated to Germany for work:

All I try to do is to live a human life. I don't want to work 10–15 hours a day … I want to read a book, I want to spend some time in nature … They ate up my father, my grandfather before him. At least let me live like a human being. What's there to see for my father's work, my grandfather's work? Nothing ... Think about it, not being able to be a person, given the thought ... If he was able to think that would reflect on his son, his son would protect the fruits of his father's labour, and hand it down to his own son. He would be an informed person, he would transfer it to his own son and then on to me. There is a break there, right? It means that the system has left the individual to fend for himself at this point, used the individual for something else. This wave goes on, from him to his child, from him to me. (Interview 4, H., male, aged 40)

What matters here is that being a shopkeeper, or doing similar jobs with their parents are the expected outcomes of the intergenerational continuity, but becoming a journalist is considered an anomalous leap. This diversion from the expected path means that the lines of security the family could provide have been breached. When the socio-economic conditions, social position, knowledge, experiences, relationships etc. of the family is considered, under current conditions the most secure position that can be attained is becoming a teacher under the relatively secure setting of public employment:

> ... If a father is telling his child to 'be a journalist' when the child is taking the university entrance exam, it means that he has some knowledge about journalism. But if your father tells you to 'be a teacher', 'that's what we can do', that's because he knows nothing about journalism. Not because teaching is inherently meaningful for him. That's where he is secure. That's the only role cast for him. The most we can do is to become a teacher. (Interview 3, G., male, aged 36)

The intergenerational legacy and its determinacy have an effect even before participation in the labour market. Evidently, children from households with regular incomes that can pay for the children's education and do not need the income from children's work can be kept within the educational system for a longer period. The experience of participation in the urban labour market of those who work in the educational sector is usually more positive, just like the experience of those who bring their own capital to the city (Erder, 2015: 10–12).

The level of education in the family and their social position, their socio-economic level also determines the education the individual receives, and this education prepares the person for entry to the labour market and the conditions of precarity:

My mother was illiterate and my father has left school after middle school. There are few people around me who have gone to university, so nobody guided me in this process. There was a counselling teacher in the after school courses, she was the one that guided me. (Interview 5, G., female, aged 32)

... My father is a farmer. So it is pure chance that my sister received an education. The ones before her were not so lucky. (Interview 6, O., male, aged 34)

Each generation experiences the precarisation process in the context of the historical conditions of their own period, in interaction with relevant dynamics. Under different socio-economic conditions, the precarisation experience of the members of the working class diverge as well. In historical continuity, the experiences of previous generations and the changes in the conditions of precarity have an impact on shaping the experience of future generations. The change in the conditions of precarity of one generation becomes the determining factor for the employment conditions of the next generation. An interviewee who had an altogether unique vision concerning her children's education before the state-owned factory (TEKEL) he was working in was privatised has said that they have persuaded their children to receive an education in areas with a 'guarantee of employment':

She is the same, she will do the same things. That is all we can do ... nothing else. Our children think like this and live like this as well ... If there had been no privatisation, I had promised my daughter that she could be anything she wanted, an actress, artist, dancer, whatever she wishes. I told her, graduate from high school, then go to any department in the university, any department you wish to go ... But all that has gone up in the air. I had to force her to get into a vocational school of health ... Because she has no other option, otherwise she won't be able to get an education. (Interview 7, H., male, aged 46)

Receiving help from the acquaintances of previous generations in finding a job, that is, providing employment security for the new generations, is another dimension of intergenerational precarity. These networks intervene in the case of getting laid-off and thus are maintained as some passive form of security both during employment and in the case of unemployment. For instance, a participant who works as a research assistant in a public university, and whose father was a local public servant, admitted that his father's position and network at work were influential in his own position at work. While legally he has a secure job, he perceives himself in a precarious position due to the mobbing and academic hierarchy he is subjected to. The impact of his father's work experience and network is revealed in the following quote:

The process at my work, it has helped that my father is an inspector, his past work experience, legal experience, his prestigious network, all those helped me at those points that I would not be able to access, that I would not be able to express myself, at those points he supports me. He has the opportunity to get in touch with some administrative people, he is acquainted with them. He can make the contacts I would not be able to make ... From time to time, he makes it possible for me to voice my problems, softens the impact of the issues directed towards me or postpones certain actions I would be confronted with. (Interview 8, G., male, aged 27)

As all of these examples show, the experiences, ways of struggle and ways of survival shaped by the conditions the previous generations have lived under do not dissolve all of a sudden. The legacy is transmitted and transferred; and it is reshaped in the context of new conditions. This situation embodied by the experience of precarity used to be baggage of the rural-to-urban migration process; but in the next generation it is 'a monkey on their backs. It can be described as temporary baggage that has now become a permanent hump, continuously integrated with the body through an evolutionary process, contorting the posture' (Hacısalihoğlu, 2018: 87).

As can be seen, there are many points of intersection between the issue of rural-to-urban migration and the intergenerational dimension of precarity. As the interviews show, some participants are either rural-to-urban immigrants themselves or come from migrant families. This means that experiences and customs that were formed prior to migration are still maintained in the household; because either they are the first generation of migrants or they are in active communication and interaction with the first generation of migrants. The social norms are shaped in accordance with the rural relationships. However, there is an incompatibility between rural and urban values; there are different behavioural patterns, different forms and levels of communication in the city. The support mechanisms derived from previous generations in the city can contribute to overcoming this incompatibility. If not, the inadequacy of the experience of the previous generations comes to mean a lack of guidance in the labour market. The experiences in a brand-new world may bring along mistakes and deepening conditions of precarity. One of the interviewees who was unable to receive such a support from his family has stated that he consults his more experienced spouse about how to communicate with the employer and other employees in the workplace. Another interviewee has said that he has been counselling his sister about similar problems. Hence, the intergenerational transmission of precarity, on the one hand, has an impact on the life cycles of the new generations, and on the other, it functions as an adaptation strategy in the context of the transmitted experience.

9.5 CONCLUSION

The theoretical and methodological contribution of this chapter is that it addresses precarity as a process. Thus, the context is extended beyond an individual and her/his precarious state and theoretically broadened. Precarity is conceptualised as a process and the role of intra-class relations in the production and continuation of precarity highlighted. According to the analysis of the qualitative data obtained, two main dynamics of precarity are identified in the Turkish case:

urban/rural origins and intergenerationality. These two dynamics are intertwined in some cases.

Having urban or rural origins still has an effect on the precarisation process in Turkey. The form and process of urbanisation is a determining factor. Distance from the urban labour market and the lack of information on security leads to settling for the current conditions of absolute precarity. These factors also have an impact on relations with the institutionalised labour market and integration under formal conditions. As a result, precarious workers fall back onto informal mechanisms, which in turn they reproduce and even create new mechanisms. Without access to formal protection mechanisms such as job security, employment security and health services, workers appeal to their relationship with the employer as a mechanism for feeling secure in their employment relations. Precarity is dealt with through building relationships based on trust with the employer. It is interesting to observe that the sphere that creates precarity is transformed into the sphere through which the worker seeks the feeling of security.

Another factor in the precarisation process is the precarity experiences of the previous generations. The current experiences of precarity are shaped through both current social, economic and political conditions and those that are transferred from the past. This process begins even prior to the participation in the labour market and shapes the conditions of entrance to the labour market and the attempts to deal with different dimensions of the precarisation process. The interviews reveal that a sudden break in the process of precarisation of the previous generation has a direct impact on the future of the next generation.

The conceptualisation of precarity presents us with an extensive understanding regarding modern capitalism. To broaden the term to include the experience of large masses, a plurality of cases should be analysed and the accumulation of knowledge should encompass the unique forms of integration and specificities. The dynamics of intergenerationality and urban/rural origins point to the importance of analysing precarity in a context rather than individual experience and the significance of a historical and process-based outlook.

BIBLIOGRAPHY

Ancelin-Schützenberger, A. (2017) *Psikosoybilim*, trans. K. Kahveci, 3, Basım, İstanbul: Türkiye İş Bankası Kültür Yayınları.

Barchiesi, F. (2011) *Precarious Liberation: Workers, the State, and Contested Social Citizenship in Postapartheid South Africa*, Albany, NY: State University of New York Press.

Betti, E. (2016) 'Precarious Work: Norm or Exception of Capitalism? Historicizing a Contemporary Debate: A Global Gendered Perspective', in Betti, E. and Miller, K. (eds), *The Power of the Norm. Fragile Rules and Significant Exceptions*, Vienna: IWM Junior Visiting Fellows' Conferences, Vol. 35.

Candeias, M. (2004) 'Double Precarisation of Labour and Reproduction – Perspectives of Expanded (Re)appropriation', https://tinyurl.com/y6sk7kr4 (accessed 1 December 2018).

Çerkezoğlu, A. and Göztepe, Ö. (2010) 'Sınıfını Arayan Siyasetten Siyasetini Arayan Sınıfa: Güvencesizler', in Bulut, G. (ed.), *TEKEL Direnişinin Işığında Gelenekselden Yeniye İşçi Sınıfı Hareketi*, 2, Baskı, Ankara: Nota Bene Yayınları, 67–95.

Erder, S. (2001) *İstanbul'a Bir Kent Kondu* Ümraniye, 2, Baskı, İstanbul: İletişim Yayınları.

—— (2015) İstanbul *Bir Kervansaray (Mı?) Göç Yazıları*, İstanbul: İstanbul Bilgi.Üniversitesi Yayınları.

Hacısalihoğlu (2014) *Türkiye'de İşçi Sınıfı Haritasında Güvencesizlik Deneyimleri*, Yayınlanmamış Doktora Tezi, Ankara Üniversitesi SBE.

—— (2018) 'Güvencesizlik Döngüsünde Vazgeçil(e)meyen Güvence Arayışı: Çalışma, Geçim ve Sosyal Yardım Bağı', in Kutlu, D. (edt), *Sosyal Yardım Alanlar- Emek, Geçim, Siyaset ve Toplumsal Cinsiyet*, İstanbul: İletişim Yayınları, 77–101.

Harris, K. and Scully, B. (2015) 'A Hidden Counter-movement? Precarity, Politics, and Social Protection Before and Beyond the Neoliberal Era', *Theory and Society*, 44 (5), 415–44.

Işık, O. and Pınarcıoğlu, M.M. (2011) *Nöbetleşe Yoksulluk - Gecekondulaşma ve Kent Yoksulları: Sultanbeyli* Örneği, 8, Baskı, İstanbul: İletişim Yayınları

Kalleberg, A.L. (2009) 'Precarious Work, Insecure Workers: Employment Relations in Transition', *American Sociological Review*, 74 (1), 1–22.

Kutlu, D. (2015) *Türkiye'de Sosyal Yardım Rejiminin Oluşumu*, Ankara: Nota Bene Yayınları.

Mitropoulos, A. (2005) 'Precari-Us?', http://eipcp.net/transversal/0704/mitropoulos/en (accessed 10 May 2020).

Munck, R. (2013) 'The Precariat: A View from the South', *Third World Quarterly*, 34 (5), 747–62.

Neilson, B. and Rossiter, N. (2008) 'Precarity as a Political Concept, or, Fordism as Exception', *Theory, Culture & Society*, 25 (7–8), 51–72.

Oğuz, Ş. (2011) 'Tekel Direnişinin Işığında Güvencesiz Çalışma/Yaşama: Proleteryadan 'Prekarya'ya mı?', *Mülkiye Dergisi*, Cilt 35, Sayı 271, 7–24.

Özatalay, K.C. (2016) 'Neoliberalleşen Türkiye'de İşçi Sınıfının Parçalanması', in Sunar, L. (ed.), *Türkiye'de Toplumsal Tabakalaşma ve Eşitsizlik*, İstanbul: Matbu Kitap, 139–61.

Özuğurlu, M. (2011) 'The TEKEL Resistance Movement: Reminiscences on Class Struggle', *Capital & Class* 35 (2), 179–87.

—— (2012) 'Emeğin Güvencesizleşmesi Penceresinden Türkiye Tarımı', in Göktepe, Ö. (ed.), *Güvencesizleştirme Süreç, Yanılgı, Olanak*, Ankara: Nota Bene Yayınları, 159–65.

Paret, M. and Gleeson, S. (2016) 'Precarity and Agency Through a Migration Lens', *Citizenship Studies*, 20 (3–4), 277–94.

Rogan, M., Roever, S., Chen, M.A. and Carré, F. (2017), 'Informal Employment in the Global South: Globalization, Production Relations, and "Precarity"', in Kalleberg, A.L. and Vallas, S.P. (eds), *Precarious Work (Research in the Sociology of Work, Vol. 31)*, Bingley, UK: Emerald Publishing, 307–33.

Savran, S. (2010) 'The TEKEL Strike in Turkey', *Socialist Project*, http://www.socialistproject.ca/bullet/326.php (accessed 21 July 2020).

Schierup, C.U., Alund, A. and Likić-Brborić, B. (2014) 'Migration, Precarization and the Democratic Deficit in Global Governance', *International Migration*, 53 (3), 50–63.

Scully, B. (2015) 'From the Shop Floor to the Kitchen Table: The Shifting Centre of Precarious Workers' Politics in South Africa', *Review of African Political Economy*, 43 (148), 1–17.

—— (2016) 'Precarity North and South: A Southern Critique of Guy Standing', *Global Labour Journal*, 7 (2), 160–73.

Standing, G. (2011) *The Precariat: The New Dangerous Class*, London: Bloomsbury Academic.

Suğur, N., Suğur, S., Gönç, T. and Beklan-Çetin, O. (2010) 'Hizmet Sektöründe Çalışan Yoksulların Geçim Stratejileri ve Sosyal İlişki Ağları: Eskişehir Örneği', *İş, Güç Endüstri İlişkileri ve İnsan Kaynakları Dergisi*, 12 (1), 59–84.

Yalman, G.L. and Topal, A. (2017) 'Labour Containment Strategies and Working Class Struggles in the Neoliberal Era: The Case of TEKEL Workers in Turkey', *Critical Sociology*, 45 (3), 447–61.

Zhan, S. and Scully, B. (2018) 'From South Africa to China: Land, Migrant Labor and the –Semi-proletarian Thesis Revisited', *The Journal of Peasant Studies*, 45 (5–6), 1018–38.

Interviews

Interview 1. T., male, aged 30, Ankara. November 2013.
Interview 2. S., female, aged 25, Ankara. November 2013.
Interview 3. G., male, aged 36, Ankara. November 2013.
Interview 4. H., male, aged 40, Ankara. December 2013.
Interview 5. G., female, aged 32, Ankara. January 2014.
Interview 6. O., male, aged 34, Ankara. January 2014.
Interview 7. H., male, aged 46, Samsun. February 2014.
Interview 8. G., male, aged 27, Ankara. March 2014.

10

When the Law is Not Enough: 'Work Accidents', Profit Maximisation and the Unwritten Rules of Workers' Health and Safety in 'New' Turkey

Murat Özveri

10.1 INTRODUCTION

Health and safety at work is a system. Like every system, it includes a series of purposes, as well as policies that are related to these purposes, and a distinctive legal framework to put these policies into practice. The purpose of the legal rules regarding the health and safety at work is the regulation of the workplace environment. These rules aim to facilitate such a work environment where even the least experienced, the least educated and the least cautious workers would not have or cause an accident. Yet, the legal framework to provide health and safety at work in Turkey proved to be not effective in terms of its purpose; i.e. preventing work accidents.

The main specific legal regulation on health and safety at work in Turkey is the Occupational Health and Safety Law No. 6331, dated 20 June 2012. However, the regulation has remained insufficient so far to change the reality of ineffective laws in this area in Turkey. There are political, economic and social reasons for this ineffectiveness in 'new Turkey' under the AKP governments. The typical manifestation of this inter-connectedness of all these reasons is the Soma mining disaster of 2014 (Manisa city) where 301 workers died.

This chapter first conceptualises 'work accidents' from a critical perspective. Then it discusses the contradictions in official numbers regarding the work accidents in Turkey. Following this, the reasons for the ineffectiveness of laws regarding work accidents, and then the legal system and its consequences are addressed by analysing a number of labour court cases from various industries. The chapter then debates the political economy of 'work accidents' under neoliberalism in Turkey with a specific focus on the Soma case. A critical conclusion summarises the argument.

10.2 WHY IS IT 'WORK MURDER', BUT NOT WORK ACCIDENT?

Turkey is ranked third in the list of reported work accidents in the world. Unreported work accidents are, however, at least as many as the reported ones (Akkurt, 2015). According to the preamble of a law proposal related to work accidents, between 1983 and May 2014[1] – when the Soma disaster happened, the recorded number of deadly work accidents with at least three deaths were 20 in the mining sector alone. The total number of deaths in the same period in the mining sector is 948. Four work accidents happened in a single workplace in 30 years and the same reason caused three of these four accidents. The preamble of the law also states that these figures prove that the measures of health and safety at work were ignored (Hamzaçebi, 2014). Therefore, it is not possible to call these incidents 'accidents'. They are already predicted by almost everyone including policymakers, the ones who are supposed to take relevant measures, but still no measures are taken despite recurring work accidents. Since the required measures were not taken, we cannot explain these deaths with the notion of the accident. It could be understood in the context of what Friedrich Engels calls 'social murder' (1845 [2008]: 95–6):

> But when society places hundreds of proletarians in such a position that they inevitably meet a too early and an unnatural death, one is quite as much a death by violence as that by the sword or bullet; when it deprives thousands of the necessaries of life, places them under conditions in which they cannot live – forces them, through the strong arm of the law, to remain in such conditions until that death ensues which is the inevitable consequence – knows that

these thousands of victims must perish, and yet permits these conditions to remain, its deed is murder just as surely as the deed of the single individual; disguised, malicious murder, murder against which none can defend himself, which does not seem what it is, because no man sees the murderer, because the death of the victim seems a natural one, since the offence is more one of omission than of commission. But murder it remains.

Therefore, it is more appropriate to call them *murders*. Initiatives such as Health and Safety Labour Watch (*ISIG Meclisi*),[2] a workers-led network organisation fighting for a healthy and safe life and working conditions, also call them 'work murders' (see ISIG, 2015a; Hazards, 2019). Although this could sound disturbing, 'accident' in this context trivialises the severity of the social reality and omits the dynamics of Turkey's political economy which paves the way for these widespread 'accidents'.

10.3 UNREPORTED WORK ACCIDENTS AND OCCUPATIONAL DISEASES

The most important database for deadly work accidents in Turkey is the Social Insurance Institution (SGK) records, which are based on the employer notices according to Law No. 5510. Since the SGK records are based only on employer notices, unions and worker representatives do not have a right to declare, inform or report work accidents. Thus, the legal framework prevents documenting all accidents and the official number of work accidents and occupational diseases remain underreported.

The misleading figures in SGK database can be observed through a comparison with other data of SGK; that is, the number of right-holders (wife or children) who are entitled to payments after a worker dies because of a 'work accident'. When the number of deaths due to work accidents and the number of right-holder files are compared, it could be seen that the number of deadly work accidents is way above the formal numbers in SGK records, according to SGK statistics covering the period of 2005–18.[3] According to SGK statistics, while

1227 workers die on average annually because of work murders, the number of deaths is 2311 according to SGK right-holders' files.

As for the occupational diseases, the situation seems even more desperate. International Labour Organization (ILO) data state that every year 160 million people are exposed to work-related diseases worldwide and 1 million 950,000 people die because of occupational diseases. According to these calculations, 'from 4 to 12 new occupational diseases are expected for each thousand workers every year'. In other words, according to these estimations, between 120,000 to 360,000 workers would normally catch an occupational disease every year in Turkey. Considering the long working hours and the prevalence of insecure and flexible working conditions in Turkey, it is safe to argue that the expected number of occupational diseases in a year is expected to be over 300,000. According to SGK data, however, annual diagnosis in occupational diseases in Turkey has been decreasing since 2003. Less than 600 cases have been recorded in every year, except 2007, 2011, 2017 and 2018, with 1208, 697, 691 and 1044 diagnosed cases, respectively (ISIG, 2015b; SGK, 2018; Çeri, 2019).

A clear controversy appears when one considers that 'the world level average proportions of work accidents and occupational diseases are 44 percent and 56 percent, but the same proportion in Turkey are 99,998 percent and 0,002 percent' (TMMOB, 2015: 73). While the ILO reports that 1 million 950,000 people die because of occupational diseases every year, the same official incidence rate is quite insignificant in Turkey. For instance, quite interestingly, SGK reported no occupational disease-related deaths between 2013 and 2018 (see SGK, 2018). In the light of this comparison, the official SGK data prove to be unreliable.

In countries such as Turkey, where the official data could be considered unreliable especially for some sensitive topics such as fatal work accidents, the data collected by independent initiatives such as ISIG are more helpful to make sense of the severity of the situation:

> According to ILO data, deadly occupational diseases are approximately 5–6 times more than deadly work murders. Since at least 1500 people die because of work murders every year in Turkey, there would be at least 10 thousand deaths related to occupa-

tional diseases. However, according to SGK data, the annual average of deaths related to occupational diseases in Turkey are less than a dozen. When we compare ILO data with SGK data, we can conclude that there is no diagnosis system for occupational diseases in Turkey. Apart from the poor structure of Turkey's health system, which makes it impossible to diagnose occupational diseases, the features of working life prevent diagnosing the occupational diseases. (ISIG, 2015b)

The ISIG publishes the data it collects on a monthly basis. Even though the ISIG data are collected by a wide network of experts as well as workers and their families on a voluntary basis, it should be noted that the numbers of fatalities provide only an approximate calcuation (see ISIG, 2020a).

10.4 MEASURES OF HEALTH AND SAFETY AT WORK IS CONSIDERED TO BE A COST INCREASING COMPONENT

Measures of health and safety at work include a certain amount of cost for employers. As Özgümüş (2013: 35) argues, 'according to the common belief, the cost of taking the required measures to prevent work accidents is more costly than the cost of damage or legal obligations etc. that would occur after the accidents', and this belief leads to lack of required measures, when the cost of these measures is considered to be higher than the monetary costs of deadly accidents. Here, a clear contradiction between profit maximisation and workers' health and safety could be observed.

Since Turkey pursued neoliberal policies for integration into the global economy since 1980 and intensified them especially after 2002 under the AKP governments, competitiveness provided by cheap labour to survive in global markets became of vital importance; and keeping the labour force under control with minimum cost is the unavoidable outcome of this preference. Having the legal regulations regarding health and safety at work on paper but no practical use of them is a clear sign that it is not a coincidence to sacrifice the policies of health and safety at work over cost. For instance, according to the justification of the Supreme Court's decision about a firedamp explosion in Bursa:

> the employer and employers' procurators, who are judged as defendants, are well-experienced in the sector and although they are aware of the presence of methane gas in the operation, they disregarded it. They did not build an early warning system, which they were supposed to in the first place, and they did not provide the sufficient number of gas-measuring devices. (Case No. 1)

According to the Supreme Court's decision, defendants acted negligently, took no measures intentionally and did not even feel the need to take them.

Employers not only decrease their costs through these ways but they also take less responsibility than they normally would have, thanks to the measures taken only on paper. Employers who force workers to work faster without safety measures for the sake of profit may easily turn this into a 'just cause' for dismissal by making it look like it is the own initiative of the worker:

> Relying on the expert reports derived from criminal and compensation cases, it is understood that the complainant deactivated the safety mechanisms to enable working faster. The complainant had the related fault in the occurrence of the work accident. On the ground of the Article 25/II-i of the Labour Law No. 4857, the act of the complainant has the characteristics of endangering work safety by his own will or by laying it down and the termination by the employer by relying on this was fair ... (Case No. 2)

The question whether deactivation of a safety mechanism by the worker who does not work on a piecework basis, at the risk of her/his own health to work faster is logical without any explicit or hidden order of the employer was not mentioned in this incident.

The ineffective implementation or subordination of Law No. 6331 to profit maximisation manifested itself once again with the Soma mine disaster in 2014. In fact, work accidents and work murders taking place almost everyday are the most reliable indication of whether the law provides an effective protection of health and safety at work. Even disasters like Soma cannot bring about change on this issue. Indeed, according to ISIG reports, at least 11,219 workers died in work murders after the Soma disaster until May 2020 (ISIG, 2020b).

The Turkish experts who analyse the problem from the point of labour law explain this phenomenon with both workers' and employers' lack of compliance to the legal rules, and see the problem about workers' health and safety as a *behavioural disorder*; and they simply ignore the connection between workers' health and safety and economic and political preferences of political power.[4] Some other scholars (i.e. Taner et al., 2015), argue that 'all occupational illnesses and injuries are preventable' and relate this phenomenon with Turkey's low Human Development Index level vis-à-vis EU countries. According to this explanation: (1) work accidents can be reduced by taking effective and preventive measures including training of workers on safety and health by employers; (2) Turkey needs to have a large trained force of Occupational Health and Safety (OHS) professionals and this can be achieved through governmental and corporate initiatives; and (3) firms should give more importance to work safety rather than the maximisation of their profits.

Even though these suggestions are important, they largely neglect the essentials of the capital accumulation regime in contemporary Turkey. The neoliberal growth strategy implemented in the last 40 years is based on a cheap reserve army of labour in Turkey. So the problem here is much deeper and entails putting an end to neoliberal and extractivist growth orientation.

10.5 PRINCIPLES AND LEGAL FRAMEWORK EXISTING ONLY ON PAPER

As mentioned in the introduction of this chapter, workers' health and safety is a system, with its own purposes. It also includes the policies regarding these purposes and distinctive legal framework to put these policies into practice. In this context, Law No. 6331 puts employers under several obligations. As such, employers have to perform risk assessment, take and implement measures regarding workers' health and safety on a workplace-specific basis, provide training for workers and enable them to follow these measures. While taking these measures, employers have to use the most advanced technology, which reduces the 'risk of work accidents and occupational diseases' to a minimum. The legal framework does not envisage any 'excuses' as far as the obligation of the employer is concerned in terms of following the innovations and using the most advanced technology available. According to various Turkish laws, reasons such as inadequacy of business capital and increased production costs are not considered valid in terms of employers' given responsibility.

Even though the language of the law seems to cover fundamental principles, it mainly exists on paper only since it does not guarantee the internal inspection mechanisms of workplaces which are supposed to put into practice their own regulations of workers' health and safety. Indeed, two shortcomings draw attention. Firstly, there is no assurance for workplace doctors and occupational safety specialists, who are given the key role in the determination and implementation of measures of workers' health and safety, and to limit the employer's authority. Secondly, according to Law No. 6331, employers can receive workers' health and safety services from Common Health and Safety Units (CHSUs).

This opportunity given to the employer by law is nothing but the subcontracting of workers' health and safety system. The general problems of the subcontracting system can also be observed here. Each CHSU is in stiff competition to have a contract with as many workplaces as possible and pretend as if they are taking required measures; tailoring to the needs of the employers with minimum costs. Commodification and marketisation of internal inspection of workers' health and safety conditions lead inevitably to lack of inspection.

A proper inspection of workers' health and safety by labour inspectors, who are assigned by Law No. 6331, does not seem possible because of several obstacles. Firstly, the number of inspectors is not sufficient. Secondly, the inspectors are not trained properly. Many of them self-trained through their own efforts in the field. Thirdly, the inspectors' personal rights are not protected sufficiently by the law. Fourthly, the reports they prepare after the inspection are open to external interventions. Finally, because Law No. 6331 paves the way for marketisation, many of the class-A senior inspectors are retired and transferred to the CHSUs.

Since the export-oriented growth period started in the 1980s, wages were considered primarily as a cost factor for the employers. Organised labour was weakened coercively to cheapen labour to increase the competitiveness. The authoritarian union legislation, which hinders effective organisation of workers to challenge the cheap labour orientation, also serves as a legislation which implicitly obstructs legal regulations regarding workers' health and safety. Unionisation has a crucial role in the internal inspection of workplaces in terms of workers' health and safety. While unionisation is in decline, conciliatory unions which do not organise without the permission of the employers are strengthened.[5] Once these unions are organised, their role is only limited to providing a simple majority for collective labour agreements, which mostly focus on wage increases. Thus, other necessary elements such as workers' health and safety become less important for the unions during the bargaining process. When the work accidents happen, this negligent position of the unions also leads to various disadvantages during the legal processes for workers and their families.

10.6 THE PROTRACTED JUDICIAL PROCESS FOR DETERMINATION AND COMPENSATION FOR OCCUPATIONAL DISEASES AND WORK ACCIDENTS

The legal system, which is ineffective in terms of protecting workers' health in terms of enforcing workers' health and safety measures, cannot also provide adequate protection during the determination of work accidents and occupational diseases as well as compensation for the damage to victims.

10.6.1 Occupational Diseases

The legal process regarding the determination of occupational diseases suffers from the lack of technical and legal tools; and it functions ineffectively, arbitrarily and with delays. SGK's health providers avoid taking responsibilities in the process of detecting occupational diseases and they send the workers to hospitals of occupational diseases. The hospitals of occupational diseases are seriously ill-equipped in terms of their insufficient staff and knowledge.

The SGK Health Council acts with the motivation of protecting the SGK and in the context of detecting occupational diseases, it decides on the basis of previously prepared list of occupational diseases. Hence, it does not acknowledge any disease as occupational unless it is on that list.

Legal objections to the SGK Health Council reports have to pass through the stages of Regional Forensic Medicine Directorship, Forensic Medicine Expert Department and Forensic Medicine General Board separately. At the end of this costly and time-consuming process, reversal of the initial decisions of 'not qualified as an occupational disease' or 'occupational disease has caused no disability' is very rare. SGK's data for 2013–18 report only 3707 occupational diseases (SGK, 2018). This dubious figure describes a work environment in which only 3707 workers were affected by poor working conditions between 2013 and 2018. Even if only two publicly known mass diseases of the last two decades, chronic obstructive pulmonary disease (COPD) incidences caught by coal miners (see Tor et al., 2010) and silicosis incidences caused by sandblasting operation in textile industry (see Akgün and Ergan, 2018; Akgün et al., 2008), had been taken into account for the same period, these data would have been way above the declared figures. These figures show us that occupational diseases cannot be detected properly unless some other research is conducted, thus the legislation definitely stays only on paper.

10.6.1.1 The Unwritten Rules of the Occupational Disease Cases   Occupational diseases are described in Laws No. 5510 and No. 6331. According to these definitions, occupational diseases could occur in two different ways. Firstly, they can be a result of being exposed to noise, dust, gas etc., that are produced at the workplace. Secondly, occupational diseases can emerge as a result of repeated movements of the worker because of work conditions.

Thus, to detect an occupational disease, the following conditions should be looked for: disease, hazardous materials in the work environment, and repeated movements due to the execution of the work. The incident ought to be accepted as an occupational disease if it is possible to link the disease with at least one of these conditions. However, determination of an occupational disease in practice is unfortunately not as simple as described above. This is due to some 'unwritten rules', discussed below.

Unwritten Rule No. 1: Determination of Occupational Disease Is Against the 'Customary Law'

Various reasons can cause diseases and it is generally possible to conceive which one of these reasons is present and effective in the occurrence of a disease. However, this process is not easy in practice in Turkey. As observed in the case study below, although the only reason causing the deterioration of workers' health is the repeated movements of her/him while doing the job, still the disease is not acknowledged as an occupational disease. As for the justification, an excuse which is not present in legal legislation is applied and it is argued that acknowledgement of the disease as occupational is 'against customs'.

Case No. 3: The worker worked for the same employer for 24 years between 1987 and 2011. After removing the tyres from the machine manually, he piles them in the carrier vehicle, putting four tyres on top and another four tyres at the bottom. If the piling is not good enough, he places the tyres again in the gap on the vehicle by lifting them manually.

It is revealed by the experts that in the given workplace, 76 tyres are produced in one shift and three or four workers in the tyre machine work in every step of the production; they lift treads which weigh between 15.43 and 25.95 kg and push tyres weighing between 42.12 and 82.34 kg with the help of a slope. The workers repeat these movements throughout their shifts. All these overlap with the conditions of repeated movements envisaged by the law to identify the disease as occupational.

However, the experts did the opposite and despite all the facts in the worker's file (i.e. that there is no medical evidence that the worker has a 'genetic predisposition'), they reached the conclusion below:

After the investigation of the workplace, even if the complainant did the movements of pushing, pulling, lifting, landing, as described in the Regulations of Manual Handling Jobs, because of several reasons such as the complainant's continuation of work after the surgery, the disease of cervical disc herniation has multiple genetic, congenital, degenerative and traumatic reasons, and also is not more common in the workplace than the general society, and sarcoidosis as an immune-derived rheumatic disease with some unknown reasons which can regress by itself; considering the custom, legislation, and medical information, it is decided with majority voting that it is not possible to prove the diseases occurred only due to the working conditions in the workplace and these diseases cannot be included in occupational diseases.

We should highlight once again that among the factors that experts referred to as the reasons of the disease in this case, the one which is detected concretely by the experts themselves stemmed directly from workplace conditions. There are testimonies in the file indicating that the workers who do the same job also suffer from the same disorders. Furthermore, the Turkish legislation does not include customary practices as part of official criteria for the determination of occupational disease under any circumstances.

Customary practices, as a phenomenon used by the experts, explain the situation well even if not regulated by the legislation. Turkish employers and SGK created various customary practices of preventing the determination of occupational diseases because of the burden it would cause, even if it is based on unreasonable motives.

Unwritten Rule No. 2: Even If the Reason Is Proven to be Work Originated, the Disease Is Not Occupational Because of the Specific Anatomy of the Worker

Case No. 4: The worker started to work in a company on 1 April 2005 and quit on 4 September 2012. He worked there for more than seven years. Experts' view was as follows:

> As a conclusion, it is understood that the complainant conducted manual handling work and continuously repeated his movements as a matter of his work, the employer made some improvements such as 'using mechanical systems' and 'decreasing the number of repeated movements' over time, but the movements could not be ceased completely.

Worker's impingement syndrome is the result of the rotator cuff rupture. There are genetic and anatomic factors, such as narrow spaced by birth, the specific shape of the acromion, working long hours by raising both arms up constantly, doing intensive, but wrong exercises, wrong sleeping habits, daily life activities causing long-lasting shoulder rotation, and repeating throwing actions may lead to this syndrome by causing oedema in the shoulder muscles. Although it is possible to add new factors to this list, being exposed to one or more of these factors is sufficient for the development of the impingement syndrome.

Since the complainant Ş.T. conducted manual handling works and repeated movements with the risk of muscular and skeletal diseases as an inevitable matter of his job, the employer made some improvements in the form of 'using mechanical systems' and 'decreasing the number of repeated movements' over time, but these were not sufficient to eliminate these movements completely. Working at the *tyre production machine*, where the complainant works by raising both his hands up repeatedly could lead to the impingement syndrome. However, many other factors, such as the specific anatomy and genetic structure of the individual as well as daily habits, may cause the syndrome as well. Therefore, according to the experts, it does not seem possible to link the syndrome only to the working conditions and the current work of the complainant, so the impingement syndrome of the complainant cannot be considered as an occupational disease.

However, there is no physical evidence for anatomy and genetic structure of the worker in this case. Despite the clear cause-and-effect relationship between the working conditions and the disease, the occupational disease could not be determined by the experts. As is seen in this case, the unwritten but valid rule in the determination of occupational diseases is to avoid identifying the occupational diseases.

Unwritten Rule No. 3: The Disease Is Not Occupational since the 'The Earning Capacity of the Worker' Is Not Affected

Case No. 5: The worker works at a tube filling facility. During his work, he has to lift 300 tubes weighing 25 kg each, every day. Istanbul Occupational Diseases Hospital confirms his low back pain started in 2007 and diagnosed him with disk degeneration. SGK acknowledged the disease as occupational, but after an investigation it also reached the conclusion that the disease does not affect the earning capacity of the worker because of the limited rate of permanent disability.

The worker stated that the medical reports and examinations revealed the causal connection between his work conditions and the disease. He objected to the institutions' conclusion by adding to his claim that he had no prior disease. After his objection, his case was sent to the Forensic Medicine Experts Board, and the Board rejected the worker's request on 20 November 2013 with the reason that 'the disability rate could not be detected; as deciding whether it is work related or an already existing disease of the worker with the available medical data was not possible'.

The case came before the General Board of Institution of Forensic Medicine where it ought to be considered with the participation of experts. However, the General Board does not have enough time to discuss the rate of disability of a worker as it is inferred from the decision. In the verdict of the General Board, the judgement of the expertise department is repeated with no further justification.

10.6.2 WORK ACCIDENTS

By definition, it is more difficult to conceal work accidents compared to occupational diseases. However, prevention of work accidents as well as the treatment and compensation process following the accident include a series of problems and legal impasse. The exact moment of the accident, lack of measures against it and the condition of the machine that led to the accident are mostly determined after the accident. Therefore, employers have the chance to make necessary amendments to reduce their responsibility.

The experts, who are responsible for revealing the causal factors of the accident, are also expected to detect the proportion of responsibility between parties as a legal matter. The investigation of responsibility is left to the experts and their reports of the accident could be against the fundamental logic of workers' health and safety rules. For instance, even if the responsibility to take measures belongs to employers legally, attribution of the fault to the worker for the professional experience of him/her is common practice.

The employers have a legal responsibility to use the latest technology to establish a workplace environment to prevent even the most inexperienced and the most careless worker having a work accident. This obligation is ignored and workers are considered responsible by principle; even because of not using the safety equipment, which is in fact ineffective in the prevention of accidents in the first place.

10.6.2.1 What Happened in Soma Was a Mass Work Murder Manifesting the Non-existence of Workers' Health and Safety System The Soma disaster was Turkey's worst industrial disaster and the world's biggest mining disaster in this century. However, local people, unions and opposition parties rightly described it as a massacre. The reason for this could be seen in the process prior to the disaster. Before the disaster, the company's CEO boasted that he had lowered the coal extraction cost per ton from $US 140 to $US 24, while the output doubled. While the CEO explains this with 'the business style of the private sector', there are three obvious reasons for this increased profit. Firstly, the main source of profits is extreme pressures on the workers to maximise production per person. The workers are mostly unskilled, recruited from the countryside through subcontractors also known as 'head uncles', and worked under pre-capitalist mechanisms of labour control within a capitalist setting (Ercan & Oğuz, 2014: 117–18). The second reason is related to insufficient safety regulations such as poor ventilation, unfunctional gas masks, absence of gas sensors and rescue chambers and flammable equipment, which are reminiscent of common work and labour practices in the nineteenth century. Finally, a new form of neoliberal developmentalism pursued by the AKP government based on rapid economic growth as a solution to all social woes, which also proceeded side by side with an intensified transformation of the countryside towards dispossession and deagrarianisation (Adaman et al., 2019).

With the mass work murders in Soma in May 2014 and later in Ermenek in October 2014, it proved once again that implementing legal regulations regarding workers' health and safety is left to employers' mercy. Therefore, the measures taken at workplaces and their inspection exist on paper only.

After the mass work murder in Soma, Ministry of Labour and mining officials stated in their first statements that there was nothing wrong with the legal legislation and audit reports of the mine (see DW, 2014). These statements led to the ironical conclusion that the death of workers is in compliance with the legislation. The documents and workers' testimonies revealed shortly after the disaster in Soma, however, showed that nothing was in compliance with the legislation.

What happened in Soma is a mass work murder whose facilitator is the neoliberal state; because it did not perform executive power to put social rights into practice, and commodified the authority of the inspection of workers' health and safety measures. It also did not employ enough inspectors to conduct the external inspection, paved the way for its own laws to exist on paper only, broke down all kinds of intervention and limited experts' authority by abolishing the legal protection of the staff who are in charge of making these interventions.

What happened in Soma is a mass work murder which is committed by the hitman, the so-called employer who takes his courage from his instigator state, who praises himself about making the most production with minimum cost, and who sees labour as a production input and as a cost element only.

What happened in Soma is a mass work murder where the Joint Health and Safety Units (JHSU) took over the 'stand guard' position, provided the logistics support and redefined the duty of 'taking and inspection of workers' health and safety measures' as 'the more you pay, the less I inspect'.

What happened in Soma is a mass work murder where the shift supervisors, workers' health and safety experts, and workplace doctors who do not have the luxury of saying no to the employer were held up as scapegoats to conceal actual murderers, instigators and stand guards.

What happened in Soma is a mass work murder where the murderers attempted to be cleared of the murder by shamelessly alleging and implying that the victims are responsible for the existence of the conditions of murder and, therefore, defendants should benefit from 'grievous provocation abatement'.

What happened in Soma is a mass work murder where a choir – composed of scientists, labour lawyers, trade unionists, journalists and politicians – takes over the duty of defending the murderers by keeping quiet about deunionisation, being silent about the insecurity through the fragmentation of the labour market, by defending deregulation with the slogans of 'security only as much as to protect worker' and 'flexibility only as much as to protect employment' and by calling the process of the elimination of security through flexibility as modernity.

What happened in Soma is a mass work murder where the 'conciliatory unions' just watched it by locking themselves within legal boundaries, extending their fears as they get downsized, displaying only empty threats to stop the processes, and closing their eyes not to see the murders.

10.7 COMMON GROUND OF WORK MURDERS
IN NEOLIBERAL TURKEY

Turkey debated work murders that happened in Istanbul/Tuzla shipyards intensely for a long time before the disasters in Soma and Ermenek happened. Subcontracting, cheap labour, cost reduction concerns and lack of inspection were the major topics in these debates. What makes the Tuzla shipyards special, however, is its density as an industrial zone where about 40 shipyards are located side by side in a relatively small area. While the Turkish shipbuilding sector rapidly grew by 2006, work accidents in Tuzla shipyards took place frequently and regularly, and this allowed the work accidents to be considered and problematised not as singular cases anymore but as a structural and chronic issue (see Güney, 2016, 2019).

In light of the distribution of work murders among economic sectors so far, it is possible to assert that whenever a sector grows and becomes more profitable for employers, work accidents specifically increase in that sector. The common feature of these sectors is the rapid increase both in profit rates and in the entrance of capital. This capital avoids using high technology, and the required labour force is met by a subcontracting system. The common point of all these policies is the goal of reducing the cost of labour. To achieve this goal, capital avoids inspections, especially where it grows and increases its profit mostly (BOUN, 2014: 78–85). A distinctive work environment occurs in these sectors where the laws are not fully implemented because of the subcontracting system and workers cannot claim their legal rights. The capitalist state is the facilitator of all of these mechanisms.

The common ground of all accidents is the failing labour relations system, where workers are controlled and disciplined through insecurity, capital aiming to grow through cheap labour, political will adopting the model of enabling national capital accumulation through cheap labour strategy, and the industrial relations system which is formed exactly upon applying all these preferences and confines workers to insecurity.

10.8 CONCLUSION

It is not possible to explain the problems of workers' health and safety in Turkey without questioning the long-lasting policy of 'gaining competitive advantages' in global markets through a cheap labour force since 24 January 1980. Since the export-oriented economy model started in 1980, wages were mainly considered only as a cost. In order to cheapen the cost of labour, the aim is for the formation of a special kind of labour force: disciplined by the insecurity produced by the free labour market conditions. Hence, the working class was disorganised for this purpose. The working class is divided into various groups, such as white-collar and blue-collar, subcontracted worker, day labourer, apprentice, intern, workers working under a contract of a specific work, and these groups pushed to compete.

Without doubt, the workers' health and safety system has been affected by these labour market restructuring policies. This restructuring increased especially in the 2000s under the AKP rule. As a result, the consequences of this policy become more visible during the 2000s via accelerating fatal work accidents. Indeed, over 21,800 workers died in 'workplace homicides' between 2002 and 2018, the first 16 years of the AKP rule (BirGün Daily, 2018).

Although the concepts and processes are described properly in the legal legislation of workers' health and safety, the inspection and enforcement institutions aiming to create the proper work environments for these notions and processes have not been constituted successfully in the legislation. Moreover, the obligation of starting a business by taking the required measures of workers' health and safety was abolished on the discourse of 'decreasing the bureaucracy' and the statement of employers claiming that the required measures are taken fully was considered enough to give the employer a business operating licence. The workers' health and safety experts and workplace doctors, who are capable of internal inspections, became precarious. The duty of internal inspection is left to JHSUs, which have to work according to the market conditions. Labour inspectors and SGK inspectors are deprived of the technical conditions and guarantees for making an effective inspection.

In sum, considering the problematic legal process of the compensation of occupational diseases, existing problems became even more complicated: (1) the legal process of the determination of occupational diseases functions inadequately and arbitrarily because of the lack of the technical and legal tools; (2) the SGK health providers avoid taking responsibilities and pass the cases to the occupational disease hospitals; (3) occupational disease hospitals suffer from a lack of qualified staff and knowledge; (4) the SGK Health Council decides with the intention of protection of the entire institution and does not reach the conclusion of occupational disease in most of the cases, except for certain traditional cases; and (5) the legal objections to the reports of the SGK Health Council need to pass through all the stages of the forensic medicine institution, forensic medicine expert department and forensic medicine general board successively. Only a small number of these objections results in a change in the initial decision at the end of this costly and time-consuming process.

Although the primary responsibility is given to the employer by the law, quite often the fault is linked to workers' own acts just because they are considered to have enough experience. Using the latest technology is widely ignored and workers are considered responsible just because she/he does not use the safety equipment, while it is not even certain if using them would be effective or not.

Most of the time, where subcontracted employment takes place, the determination of the actual employer is an issue. Even though there is a legal relationship between the employer and the workplace which is based on responsibility, the connection between the employer and the responsibility of work accident may be lost time and again and it may take a very long time to prove the contrary.

As the actual wage of the worker is unclear, the determination of the level of wage becomes difficult. This is important because it is the basis for the compensation of an accident. It may take years to determine the work accidents which occurred in unregistered works. Because of the methods of abusing the legal entity, workers may not receive their compensations even if they win the court case for compensation. These methods include changing the ownership of the workplace, evasion of the assets through a different legal entity, and transferring assets of the limited company to personal assets of company partners. Thus, there is no guarantee for workers' specified receivables. After a long marathon of legal process, workers may receive nothing but a disability, such as a disconnected arm, a blind eye or a burned face, if they are fortunate enough to survive.

BIBLIOGRAPHY

Act No. 4857 *Labour Act of Turkey*, 22 May 2003, https://tinyurl.com/yyo65xby (accessed 22 October 2020).
Act No. 5510 *Social Insurance and General Health Insurance*, 31 May 2006, https://tinyurl.com/ycj6eq4f (accessed 22 October 2020).

Act No. 6331 *Occupational Health and Safety*, 20 June 2012, https://tinyurl. com/yawp33z5 (accessed 1 January 2020).

Adaman, F., Arsel, M. and Akbulut, B. (2019) 'Neoliberal Developmentalism, Authoritarian Populism, and Extractivism in the Countryside: The Soma Mining Disaster in Turkey', *The Journal of Peasant Studies*, 46 (3), 514–36.

Akgün, M. and Ergan, B. (2018) 'Silicosis in Turkey: Is it an Endless Nightmare or Is There Still Hope?', *Turk Thorac Journal*, 19 (2), 89–93.

Akgun, M., Araz, O., Akkurt, I.et al. (2008) 'An Epidemic of Silicosis among Former Denim Sandblasters', *European Respiratory Journal*, 32, 1295–303.

Akkurt, İ. (2015) 'Yılda En Az 20 Bin Ölümün Asıl Nedeni Meslek Hastalığı', *Evrensel Gazetesi*, 28 September 2015.

BirGün Daily (2018) 'AKP İktidarında 21 bin 800 İşçi Hayatını Kaybetti', https://tinyurl.com/y48c63lq (accessed 10 June 2020).

BOUN (2014) 'Boğaziçi Soma Dayanışması, İş Cinayeti/Kazası Gözlem, Aktarım ve Teknik İnceleme Raporu', November 2014, www.bogazicisomadayanismasi.boun.edu.tr (accessed 18 September 2017).

Çeri, U. (2019) 'Occupational Diseases: Turkey's Hidden Epidemic', *Inside Turkey*, https://tinyurl.com/ycrprd2m (accessed 15 May 2020).

Durmuş, H.O. (2012) 'İş Güvenliği Kültürü', https://tinyurl.com/ydy58qet (accessed 16 July 2012).

DW (2014) 'Turkey Coalmine Rescue Called Off as Investigation Gets Underway', *Deutsche Welle*, 17 May 2014, https://tinyurl.com/yazmew8o (accessed 20 May 2020).

Engels, F. (2008) [1845] *The Condition of the Working-class in England in 1844*, trans. F. Kelley-Wischnewetzky, New York: Cosimo Classics.

Ercan, F and Oğuz, Ş. (2014) 'From Gezi Resistance to Soma Massacre: Capital Accumulation and Class Struggle in Turkey', *Socialist Register*, 51, 114–35.

Güney, K.M. (2016) *Fatal Workplace Injuries in the İstanbul Tuzla Shipyards and the Obsession with Economic Development in Turkey*, PhD Thesis, Graduate School of Arts and Sciences, Columbia University.

—— (2019) 'The Paradox of Development: Rapid Economic Growth and Fatal Workplace Accidents in Turkey', *'IS, GUC' Industrial Relations and Human Resources Journal*, 21 (1), 5–22.

Hamzaçebi, M.A. (2014) '657 Sayılı Devlet Memurları Kanunu ile Bazı Kanun ve Kanun Hükmünde Kararnamelerde Değişiklik Yapılmasına Dair Kanun Teklifi'o, 24 July 2014, Genel Gerekçe, tbmm.gov.tr/gelenkagitler/metinler/in.t (accessed 22 October 2017).

Hazards (2019) 'IWMD19 Special Report: Making Work-related Murders Visible in Turkey', http://www.hazards.org/workingworld/turkeyreport. htm (accessed 12 June 2020).
ISIG Council of Turkey (2015a) Work Murders Report 2015 (1. Term), http://www.guvenlicalisma.org/icerik/haber/dosyalar/oisig.pdf (accessed 22 October 2016).
—— (2015b) 'Written Statement on Occupational Diseases', https://tinyurl. com/yajr8bc9 (accessed 23 October 2016).
—— (2020a) 'Principles & Functioning of HESA Labour Watch Turkey', http://isigmeclisi.org/hakkimizda (accessed 5 May 2020).
—— (2020b) 'İş Cinayetleri Raporları', http://isigmeclisi.org/iscinayetleri-raporlari?sayfa=1 (accessed 20 June 2020).
Özgümüş, H. (2013) 'İşçi Sağlığı ve İş Güvenliğine Hatalı Yaklaşımlar', *TMMOB Elektrik Mühendisleri Odası İstanbul Şubesi Bülteni*, Sayı 55, May 2013.
SGK (2018) *SGK Statistics Yearbooks*, https://tinyurl.com/y9xj2tv6 (accessed 3 March 2020).
Taner, M.T., Mıhcı, H., Sezen, B. and Kağan, G. (2015) 'A Comparative Study between Human Development Index and Work Accidents in Turkey and the EU Member Countries', *Journal of Research in Business, Economics and Management (JRBEM)*, 4 (1), https://tinyurl.com/y86jng2m (accessed 6 June 2019).
TMMOB (2015) *TMMOB – Makina Mühendisleri Odası, Oda Raporu İşçi Sağlığı ve İş Güvenliği*, Genişletilmiş 6, Baskı, Yayın No. MMO/617, Ankara.
Tor, M., Öztürk, M., Altin, R. and Çimrin, A.H. (2010) 'Working Conditions and Pneumoconiosis in Turkish Coal Miners between 1985 and 2004: A report from Zonguldak Coal Basin, Turkey', July 2010, *Tuberkuloz ve Toraks*, 58 (3), 252–60.

Court Cases

Case No. 1. Penal Department No. 12 of the Supreme Court, 2012/21104, 2013/25712 Numbered Decision (accessed 14 November 2013).
Case No. 2. Civil Chamber No. 9 of the Supreme Court 2012/9461, 2014/14283 Numbered Decision (accessed 5 May 2014), Decree on File.
Case No. 3. Kocaeli 1. Labour Court, 2013/387 Numbered Decision.
Case No. 4. Kocaeli 1. Labour Court, 2014/409 Numbered Decision.
Case No. 5. Kocaeli 6. Labour Court, 2012/574 Numbered Decision.

11
Are We All in the Same Boat? Covid-19 and the Working Class in Turkey

Yeliz Sarıöz-Gökten

This contrast between wealth that does not labour and poverty that labours in order to live also gives rise to a contrast of knowledge. Knowledge and labour become separated. The former confronts the latter as capital, or as a luxury article for the rich.
(Karl Marx, *Theories of Surplus-Value*)

11.1 INTRODUCTION: COVID-19 AND THE GLOBAL POLITICAL ECONOMY

When Chinese authorities informed the World Health Organization (WHO) about a novel coronavirus on the last day of 2019, global capitalism was still suffering from the economic, political and geopolitical impacts of the 2008 financial crisis. This crisis-ridden condition of the world market has entered a new phase following the Covid-19 pandemic; and it is widely accepted that our world and daily lives will not be the same – at least for the foreseeable future.

Starting in China and spreading throughout the world, Covid-19 was declared as a pandemic by the WHO on 11 March 2020, after 118,000 cases and 4291 deaths in 114 countries. The virus affected over 169 million people worldwide and caused more than 3,500,000 deaths by the end of May 2021 (Worldometers, 2021). The economic crisis caused by Covid-19 is possibly the most unique crisis in the history of capitalism. This crisis contains uncertainties in terms of the impact on people's lives, and results in a collapse of health systems, decline in finance, production and consumption in many countries regardless of their level of development. According to the *Financial*

Times (2020), the coronavirus pandemic has resulted in the most severe global economic contraction since at least the 1930s, triggered by the 1929 crash, and it is safe to argue that it will have much deeper impacts than the 2008 Great Recession.[1]

At the end of 2020, the effects of the pandemic on human life and global capitalism became clearer. Almost all of the world economies have shrunk due to the pandemic. The contraction in 2020 is among the deepest of the global economic crises (World Bank, 2020; IMF, 2021: 8, see Figure 11.1). As such, global economic growth was realised as −3.3 per cent (IMF, 2021: 8). For developed capitalist countries, the decline was 4.7 per cent. In the long term, the stagnation triggered by the pandemic is expected to lead to a decrease in investments, rise in unemployment, a decline in human capital, problems in global trade and broken supply chains.

The already crisis-ridden globalisation process has received a fresh wound with the pandemic; long supply chains that have long been viewed as the only 'rational' way to organise production have collapsed. Also, in this period, international trade has decreased to a great extent and serious restrictions have been imposed on inter-

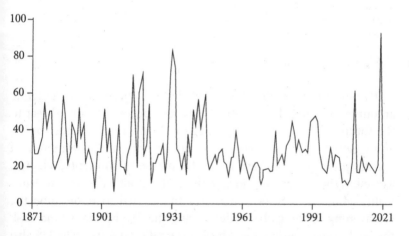

Figure 11.1   Share of Economies in Recession (1870–2021)

Note: Data for 2020 and 2021 are estimates.

Source: World Bank (2020), The Global Economic Outlook During the COVID-19 Pandemic: A Changed World, www.worldbank.org/en/news/feature/2020/06/08/the-global-economic-outlook-during-the-covid-19-pandemic-a-changed-world (accessed 9 June 2020).

national travel. Within a few weeks, tens of millions of people were left unemployed and millions of businesses lost their employees, customers, suppliers and credit lines (Saad-Filho, 2020). Table 11.1 shows the estimated real GDP growth rates in selected countries. The annual real GDP rate for 2020 is negative in leading economies other than China. Though it is optimistically predicted that there will be a global recovery in 2021.

Table 11.1   Real GDP Growth, Annual Per Cent Change and Projections

	2019	*2020*	*2021*
World Output	2.3	4.3	4.0
United States	2.2	–3.6	3.5
Germany	0.6	–7.0	5.2
France	1.3	–7.2	4.5
Italy	0.3	–9.1	4.8
Japan	0.7	–5.2	3.0
United Kingdom	1.4	–6.5	4.0
China	6.1	2.0	7.9
India	4.2	–9.6	5.4
Russia	1.3	–4.0	2.6
Brazil	1.4	–4.5	3.0
Turkey	0.9	0.5	4.5

Source: IMF (2020); World Bank (2021).

It would not be an overstatement that the coronavirus pandemic amounts to a 'global existential crisis' and poses an actual threat to the future of capitalism (Burgin, 2020). With the pandemic threatening global capitalism, relations of production, labour relations and consumption patterns have entered a period of substantial change, as well as the power dynamics in the global political economy. Ironically, while the US took measures that aimed to undermine the functioning of the global order during the Trump era, China took the lead in maintaining the 'liberal international order'. The US also blamed China for the global losses it caused, and argued that this damage should be compensated. On the other hand, China cooperates with other countries in the development of vaccines and in the fight against the virus, and carries out a kind of health diplomacy.

However, despite the examples of solidarity, the pandemic conditions led to an increase of nationalism and the intensification of the imperial power struggle.

Although the pandemic affects every segment of the global community, the biggest impact is on the (global) working class, which has to sell its labour power to survive. Since the outbreak of the pandemic, the phrase 'we are all in this together' was frequently repeated (see, for instance, UN General Secretary Guterres, 2020). This implies that the global pandemic is 'classless', it is blind to social class differences. This chapter sharply contradicts this sentiment, with a specific focus on the case of Turkey. Against this backdrop, the next section examines whether Covid-19 is really 'classless'. Following that, the measures taken by Turkey's AKP government against the economic impact caused by the pandemic are dealt with and their implications for the working class of the country are revealed.

11.2 ARE THE EFFECTS OF COVID-19 CLASS-BLIND?

The fact that coronavirus has infected the rich and powerful, from British establishment figures Prince Charles and Prime Minister Boris Johnson to Hollywood stars like Tom Hanks, is used as an example to prove that the virus does not choose class. However, although the risk is valid for all segments of society regardless of status and class, it does not mean that the effects of the pandemic would be exactly the same. Hence, although the virus does not choose classes, its effects could not be explained without the notion of class. Indeed, the effects of the pandemic so far once again show that today's societies are above all class societies (Fuchs, 2020), based on exploitation, inequality and injustice.

The rich capitalists moved to their yachts or took refuge in their second home; while the lower classes either struggled to work from their not very spacious homes with various responsibilities such as child care, or lost their jobs. The pandemic also proved how some jobs hitherto considered 'low skilled' or 'unskilled' are strategic for the continuity of capitalism. From truck drivers to supermarket cashiers, and from cleaning to agricultural workers, the precarious and low-paid workers took the front line by putting their lives at risk for the continuity of the system, and lost or risk losing their income altogether because of the economic collapse triggered by the pandemic (Harvey, 2020; Saad-Filho, 2020). The preference of the working class whether to work is almost like a knife edge. If she works, she would work in the face of the virus, and if she chooses not to work, she would risk losing her income, as most capitalist states (especially in the Global South) do not provide meaningful support. In both cases, the working class is struggling to survive. In fact, the questions of who can work from home and who cannot, who can self-isolate (paid or unpaid) or be under quarantine against close contact or infection are very significant, and deserve a class-based approach.

As the global spread of coronavirus has increased steadily, quarantine measures have affected 2.7 billion workers, representing 81 per cent of global labour. Firms operating in various sectors face a process threatening their operations and payments, while millions of workers are vulnerable to loss of income and the threat of layoff. Specifically, precarious and unregistered workers are the most affected class components by this process (ILO, 2020a: 1). Therefore, it is evident that the effects of Covid-19 are pertinent to class. The pandemic did not catch different classes in the same manner and under the same conditions; and it affects them differently.

Against this background, the economic measures taken against the pandemic shock in Turkey and the devastating effects of these measures on the working class are examined in the following section.

11.3 MEASURES AND POLICIES RELATED TO THE COVID-19 CRISIS IN TURKEY AND THEIR CLASS CONTENT

The first cases of Covid-19 in Turkey were announced on 11 March. The virus spread rapidly in the following period and the transmission rate remained high until the end of April. During this initial phase of the pandemic, a lockdown covering under the ages of 20 and over 65 was introduced, and the affected neighbourhoods and villages were quarantined. In 30 provinces, prohibitions for going out at weekends were put in place, international flights were suspended and travelling between provinces was not allowed. Until June, schools, universities, cafes, restaurants, entertainment centres, shopping malls were closed, mass worship was not allowed, and it was obligatory to wear masks in public areas. Initially, a voluntary quarantine system was suggested to citizens. Then, a mixed policy against coronavirus was introduced, with weekend and four day-long 'curfews' on official holidays. The government encouraged people to stay home with campaigns such as 'stay home Turkey' and 'everyone should declare their own state of emergency'. It is important to emphasise, however, that in sectors that were considered of vital importance for the economy, such as metal, textile, mining and construction, and logistics, millions of workers were forced to go to work or faced losing their jobs (Gökay, 2020).

To combat the economic effects of the pandemic, a package of measures called the 'Economic Stability Shield' were announced on 18 March. The stimulus package amounted to 100 billion liras (around US $15.5 billion) coverage, which remained rather limited compared to other capitalist countries. Accordingly, a six-month VAT deferral was provided for companies, and social security premium payments by employers were postponed. Loan repayments of firms whose cash flows deteriorated were delayed for three months as well. The interest payments of the craftsmen who declared that their business had deteriorated were suspended, and it was decided that the credit registers of the companies that could not pay their debts would not be affected negatively. Implementations such as stock financing support for exporters have been put into practice. Again, to keep the demand alive in the housing and construction sector, the upper limit of mortgage credits increased from 80 per cent to 90 per cent provided that it is valid for houses below 500,000 liras. Somewhat controversally, VAT discounts were introduced for three months in domestic air transportation. For the workers, it was decided to activate the short-time work allowance,[2] increase the lowest pension payments to 1500 liras per month and continue to support minimum wages. An additional 2 billion Turkish liras were provided for cash assistance to families in need, and to increase the two months 'compensatory working period' to four months in order to ensure continuity in employment. In addition, the AKP government encouraged flexible and teleworking models (Anadolu Ajansı, 2020). In December 2020, President Erdoğan announced that craftsmen would be given 1000 liras of income loss support for three months, 750 liras in metropolitan cities, and 500 liras in other cities. However, sufficient support was not provided for the craftsmen to fight against the pandemic (Evrensel Daily, 2020a).

Again, with the circular of the Ministry of Interior dated 3 April 2020, public sector employees between the ages of 18 and 20, those working in a regular and registered job in the private sector and seasonal agricultural workers were exempted from the lockdown (Ministry of Interior, 2020). Thus, hundreds of thousands of workers between the ages of 18 and 20 were exempted from the lockdown and encouraged to work. Following this, a provisional article was added to Law No. 4447 on 17 April, which introduced a daily 39.24 Turkish liras cash support to the workers who are sent for unpaid leave and who cannot benefit from the short-time work allowance and those who have not been able to benefit from unemployment benefits. Under the law, the employer cannot end any employment contract for three months, except in cases of non-compliance with moral and goodwill principles (Law No. 4447). The law also envisaged that this prohibition of layoff could be extended up to six months if necessary (İŞKUR, 2020). However, the employers took advantage of the exceptions mentioned above through what is known as 'Code-29'. Normally, dismissed workers are given a code for the reason for dismissal (which is mentioned in employers notice to the Social Security Institution after the dismissal). Code-29 demonstrates that the contract is terminated on the grounds that the behaviour of the worker 'did not comply with moral and goodwill principles', regulated by Labour Law No. 4857. The employers laid off 233,400 workers through this code in 2020, while it was 194,524 in 2019. Since unemployment aid is not granted on a dismissal issued through Code-29, the workers who were dismissed this way were deprived of their jobs, income, short-time work allowance and wage support, severance pays and termination benefits as well as unemployment aid (Aysoy, 2021; Bakır, 2021). Furthermore, although the layoffs have been prohibited on paper, no measures have been taken to prevent workers from being released on unpaid leave. Workers on unpaid leave are expected to make a living with an amount nearly equal to half the minimum wage (39 liras daily or 1170 Turkish liras monthly).

Another significant development was the circular published by the Social Security Institution (SGK) on 7 May 2020, which declared that Covid-19 is not considered to be an occupational disease or a work accident. Covid-19 has been recognised as 'discomfort and illness that causes incapacity' instead of occupational disease (SGK, 2020). With this regulation, the possibility of a compensation mechanism that workers could apply in case of death or permanent illness related to Covid-19 has been eliminated, as it is not recognised as an occupational disease.[3]

During this process, Turkish President Erdoğan repeatedly emphasised the need to 'keep wheels of the economy turning'; and as a consequence the AKP government rushed to reopen the economy which was already fragile before the pandemic as a result of the 2018–19 currency crisis and a short recession following this. Hence, from 11 May 2020, shopping malls and hairdressers were allowed to reopen, in line with the return to normal. On 1 June, restaurants, beaches, parks and nurseries were reopened, and transportation within the country was allowed again. Foreign tourism was encouraged to resume.

Despite the continuation of unrealistic slogans such as 'stay at home Turkey' and 'declare your own state of emergency', especially following 'normalisation', the working class is forced to go to work in crowded transportation vehicles, perhaps by changing a few vehicles and working under conditions where the necessary measures are not taken sufficiently. While the risk of transmission of the virus to those who can voluntarily self-quarantine in this process is low, for the significant proportion of workers who cannot work from home and depend on daily earnings, the risk of becoming infected is very high. In this sense, it is clear that the virus has a class dimension and the outbreak will leave deep traces on the physical continuity conditions of the working class.

For example, the Food Industry Workers' Union of Turkey (Gıda-İş) has prepared a report examining the measures concerned with the health and safety of workers during the Covid-19 outbreak. For the report, interviews were conducted at 45 food factories where 150 to 4000 workers worked. Accordingly, 70 per cent of the businesses experienced an increase in production, while the rest did not experience any decrease in production. In order to meet the increase in the demand for food products and to create stocks, workers' overtime work has been increased. In other words, firms preferred to meet the demand with existing workers instead of recruiting new workers. Apart from businesses that operate in two or three shifts, some businesses have also removed their weekend leave. In addition, the report states that the physical distance is not observed during the production process, which takes place under conditions of absolute exploitation, and that workers do not have adequate access to paper towels, soap and cleaning materials (Gıda-İş Sendikası, 2020).

While the workers continue to work under unsanitary and bad conditions, some measures taken by the companies against the virus also aggravate the burden of the worker. For example, with the introduction of 'one day work, one day leave' rule, the food and travel allowances of the workers are not paid on the days when they are not working. Measures to ensure the health of workers who continue to work in many sectors have been insufficient. In some sectors, workers continue to work close to each other, and the use of shared bathrooms, toilets and dining halls increase the risk of infection. Increasing working hours and having to use the machines they are not trained for increase the risk of both infection and injury as well. In addition, despite the increase in working hours, there has not been any pay rises.

This process also increased the attempts of capitalists to strengthen control and discipline over the working class even under pandemic conditions. An example of the control mechanisms implemented by the capitalist class over labour during this process in Turkey is the system introduced by the Metal Employers' Union (MESS) which is called 'MESS Safe'. With this system presented as the 'technology of tomorrow', a device will be attached to the neck of workers. With this device installed, the movements of workers will be monitored constantly and the device will warn the worker and the employer if one worker approaches another worker or a machine more than necessary. In this way, it will be ensured that all the movements of the worker are monitored (Özveri, 2020). Some factory workers now report that the employers started using these devices by the end of 2020 (Evrensel Daily, 2020b).

Another striking example of capital's attempt to turn the crisis into an opportunity and increase control over labour is the project of 'isolated production bases' or 'labour camps'. This project was announced by MÜSİAD (Independent Industrialists and Business-men's Association), which represents the Islamist fraction of the Turkish bourgeoisie, in May 2020, as a response to the 'disruption' caused by the pandemic. This controversial project aims to create 'isolated' living and working bases (camps) for 1000 families and 4500 people with the aim of continuing 'production inside by closing their doors in an outbreak or possible natural disaster' (Atesci, 2020). This dystopian project, which led to a reaction from the unions, reveals capitalists' dreams of uninterrupted and intensified exploitation of labour. Indeed, some other incidences support this expectation. For instance, after more than 40 of its workers tested positive for coro-navirus, the Dardanel canned fish factory in Çanakkale city, which is known for its union busting efforts, decided to carry on with a 'closed-circuit production system', forcing its 1000 workers to work – the majority of which are women – in the factory during the 14-day quarantine period (Evrensel Daily, 2020c). It is apparent that the cap-italist class 'never lets a good crisis go to waste'.

11.4 THE EXPERIENCE OF THE TURKISH ECONOMY WITH THE PANDEMIC

Although the Turkish capitalist state and class want to turn the crisis into an opportunity through capitalising on a possible shake-up of global supply chains (Pitel, 2020), with the decline in domestic and international demand due to the pandemic, production and employ-ment losses would inevitably occur. With a 'sudden stop' and reversal of financial capital inflows, the main expectation was that the crisis would deepen in Turkey (Voyvoda and Yeldan, 2020: 5), and these dynamics have manifested themselves in the course of time. Despite heavy intervention by policy makers and replacement of the central bank governor twice since 7 November 2020, the Turkish lira has depreciated by about 40 percent since the start of the pandemic (TCMB, 2021).

As far as the first impact of the pandemic on production is concerned, key indicators show a significant decline as electricity production decreased by 16 per cent, automotive production decreased by 90.7 per cent and white goods production decreased by 52.3 per cent in April 2020, compared to the same month of the previous year. As of May 2020, real sector confidence index decreased by 22.2 per cent. In terms of changes in demand, electricity demand decreased by 15.4 per cent in April 2020 compared to the same month of the previous year. Automobile sales decreased by 7.6 per cent in May compared to the previous month, and exports decreased 85.9 per cent. Again, for the same month, white goods sales decreased by 11.4 per cent and exports decreased by 48.9 per cent (Strateji ve Bütçe Başkanlığı, 2020: 15–16).

The Covid-19 pandemic also had an impact on the consumption patterns of households in Turkey. As such, demand for gasoline and fuel decreased by 23.21 per cent. As observed elsewhere, food consumption was the major part of the demand, with online shopping reaching its highest level at the beginning of May, with an increase of 42.97 per cent. A decrease of 27.29 per cent was observed in supermarkets and shopping malls, however; and demand for electronic goods decreased by 8.81 per cent as of May. It is observed that household spending has decreased in general terms, as credit card expenditures decreased by 33.32 per cent as of May 29 (TCMB, 2020).

The OECD initially made two different estimates regarding the damage to the Turkish economy from the pandemic. Depending on the number of waves, the OECD estimated that the Turkish economy would shrink by 4.8 per cent (only one wave) to 8.1 per cent (if there would be a second wave). However, according to the official data, the performance was not as bad as the OECD estimates. The country's economy recovered in the last two quarters of 2020 and achieved a small growth (1.8 per cent – though this was achieved at the cost of price and currency stability and burning through almost all foreign reserves). Moreover, the effects of the pandemic are deeply felt particularly in distribution; as the share of labour in the national income decreased from 39 per cent to 35.5 per cent, and the share of capital increased to 45.8 per cent by the end of the first quarter of 2021 (OECD, 2020; DISK-AR, 2021a).

As mentioned, considering the situation of a significant number of workers who are stuck between being unemployed and losing their health, the class character of the consequences of the outbreak emerges. With the pandemic, the unemployment rate has soared globally. Many workers have lost their health insurance, and many have difficulty in accessing unemployment benefits. Households who have difficulty in repaying their housing or consumer loans have faced the risk of losing their assets. The debt society, built on the credit debt of most households, reproduces itself as a result of unemployment or wage default. Reflecting the financialisation trends since the 2000s under the AKP rule in Turkey, so-called 'financial inclusion' was once again offered as a solution to vulnerable segments of society by encouraging the use of credit (through lowering the interest rates consistently) instead of cash assistance programmes. As such, in April 2020 alone, approximately 1 million new people joined the financial system; 920,000 of them were first-time consumer loan users. Almost all the remaining new participants opened their credit cards and overdraft accounts (TBB, 2020).

The already bleak picture for the condition of unemployment and employment worsened with the pandemic in Turkey. According to a report published by BETAM (Bahcesehir University's Economic and Social Research Centre) in June 2020, the decline in employment was 21,000 in agriculture, 85,000 in industry and 202,000 in the construction sector. The sector with the highest decrease in employment is the services sector at 694,000. A significant portion of income and employment in Turkey is based on tourism, and 45 per cent employment loss is expected in this sector due to the pandemic; these losses will hinder the recovery of the economy for a long time. According to seasonally adjusted data, the decrease in female employment is 245,000 and the decrease in male workforce is 368,000 (Gürsel and Mutluay, 2020: 1). Employment hit rock bottom with 25 million 807,000 in the second quarter of 2020 and the total loss increased to about 3 million people. In the remaining period of the Covid pandemic since mid-2020 with a rhythm of closing-opening-closing, Turkey's net employment loss settled at roughly 1 million people (Yeldan, 2021).

Table 11.2 shows the basic labour indicators. As shown in Table 11.2, the employment rate fell significantly to 41.1 per cent, which makes Turkey the worst-performing OECD country in this area. The unemployment rate decreased slightly to 12.8 per cent as a result of more than 3 million people who abandoned the workforce. It is important to note that these figures are estimated to be much higher by the unions, as the official statistics are considered to be highly controversial because they are based on a narrow definition of unemployment.[4] Hence, according to the calculations made by DİSK-AR based on the broad definition of unemployment, the unemployment rate is 28.7 per cent. Broadly defined unemployment rate with the Covid-19 effect was calculated as 52.2 per cent. According to the same report, due to unpaid leave and short-time working, working hours have decreased from 44.6 to 39.5 per week and a loss of approximately five hours has occurred (DİSK-AR, 2020a: 5).

Table 11.2 Unemployment and Employment Data with the Effect of Covid-19

	April 2019	April 2020
Labour force	32.401	29.388
Discouraged (000) (1)	553	1.310
Available to start a job (000) (2)	1.732	3.150
Working seasonally (000) (3)	102	123
Unemployment (000) (4)	4.202	3.775
Persons at work (000) (5)	27.565	20.456
Persons not at work (000) (6)	634	5.158
Employment (000) (5+6)	28.199	25.614
Employment rate (%)	46	41.1
Time depended underemployment (000) (7)	374	1.398
Broad definition of unemployment (000) (1+2+3+4+7)	6.963	9.756
Equivalent Full-Time Jobs Loss (000) (8)	–	9.364
Broadly Defined Unemployment Revised with the Covıd-19 Effect (000) (1+2+3+4+8)	–	17.722
Broadly Defined Unemployment Increase Revised with the Covıd-19 Effect (000) (from April 2019 to April 2020)	–	10.759

Source: DİSK-AR (2020a).

When the effects of Covid-19 on employment are analysed by gender, it can be claimed that women are in a worse situation compared to men. As of April 2020, female labour force participation rate was 29.2 per cent with a decline exceeding 5 points compared to the same month of the previous year, and it only reached 31.2 per cent by the end of the first quarter of 2021. The real negative impact on women can be seen with broadly defined unemployment rates. The broadly defined female unemployment rate, revised with the effect of Covid-19, was 56.4 per cent. This rate was around 25–30 per cent before the pandemic. In summary, it is safe to argue that the majority of women of working age are unemployed (DİSK-AR, 2020a: 7, 2020b: 3, 2021b: 1–7).

Another structural problem in Turkey is youth unemployment. This problem deepened with the pandemic. As of May 2021, Turkey ranks eighth among the OECD countries in youth unemployment with 22.9 per cent (DİSK-AR, 2021b). In general, young people have difficulty in finding jobs compared to workers with work experience during times of crisis. In addition, as the lack of experience makes it difficult to find good jobs, young workers may turn to informal and insecure jobs. Three out of every four young workers can find employment in either the informal or service sectors. In addition, most young workers are in precarious jobs; working in part-time and temporary jobs. They work in jobs with a low wage, irregular working hours and insufficient job security, without any rights such as paid leave, pensions and sick leave. Due to lack of experience, young people are concentrated in particularly vulnerable sectors vis-à-vis the Covid-19 outbreak, such as the wholesale and retail, accommodation and food industries. The ILO (2020b) points out that there should be policies for young people in prevention plans, and if the young people are not supported, the economic effects of Covid-19 will last for decades.

11.5 CONCLUSION

The Covid-19 crisis once again revealed the class inequalities under neoliberal capitalism. The working class, which is vital for the maintenance of capitalism, has been the most affected by this process, either through directly putting their health at risk or bearing the burden of adjustment. The process proves this motto: 'the wealthier you are, the heathier you are'. In this process, protecting the capitalist class and the capitalist system has been the main duty of governments. The measures taken to combat the pandemic in Turkey lend support to employers rather than workers. With the pandemic, even though we have realised the irrelevance of the passion for consumption and the fact that living in a world dominated by capital threatens the existence of the human species, policies have been adopted to restore the system and to reproduce the norms of the consumer society. As observed in Turkey throughout the pandemic, further financialisation and indebtedness are encouraged with various mechanisms including increasing the credit card limit to 2000 liras for consumers who do not even declare an income. This will mean a new debt burden, not a solution for the working class who try to live their lives in a debt-ridden condition, especially under the worse economic atmosphere after the 2018 crisis. More progressive policies are urgently needed. A deferral programme similar to the loan deferral provided to employers is required. In addition to income support, basic services such as water and electricity should be provided free of charge.

Although neoliberalism is widely questioned once again (as in the 2008 crisis) following the pandemic, the measures taken to reduce the effects of the crisis caused by coronavirus do not seem to go beyond some sort of 'hesitant' Keynesian intervention. The revision of neoliberalism does not respond to the needs of the working class, however. To support the working class in Turkey, measures such as a temporary ban on layoffs and income support for the unemployed to 1170 liras are consistent with this framework – 1170 liras of cash support per month is not even half the hunger limit for a family of four. After a cycle of closing and opening, a 17-day full closure was implemented as of 29 April 2021 in Turkey, but no aid or support package has been implemented in this process. The closure process has left the economically affected classes in an even more difficult situation. Almost a month later, a new grant package was implemented on 25 May 2021. In this grant package, craftsmen were divided into two groups and paid either 3000 or 5000 lira support (Resmi Gazete, 2021). However, this support was given only once and was found to be unsatisfactory by the people to compensate for their losses. As Taymaz (2020) and Voyvoda and Yeldan (2020) highlighted in the initial months of the pandemic, for the Turkish economy, the most important step to mitigate the effects of Covid-19 will be adequate income support for those in need. Giving demand support will not only benefit the masses with basic needs, but will also act as a leverage for the economy. Besides generating surplus value, workers, who are an important element of effective demand, can only survive this way. However, the class character of the government is in contradiction with these demands. While the government prevented layoffs, unpaid leave policy is a major threat to the working class. In the months when the economic crisis combined with the pandemic, more than 10 million workers lost their jobs. This means an unemployment rate (informal) at around 30 per cent. Reducing the number of workdays during the Covid-19 process and therefore unpaid food and transportation allowances affect workers deeply.

A small portion of the economic measures taken against Covid-19 in Turkey would be needed to meet the needs and demands of the working class. The announced economic packages are mostly to do with keeping capital afloat. The life of the worker is subordinated to the needs of capital accumulation. It is important to emphasise once again that campaigns such as 'stay at home' or 'declare your own state of emergency' amounts to a choice between the 'biological death' and 'economic death' for the working class.

BIBLIOGRAPHY

Anadolu Ajansı (2020) 'Ekonomik İstikrar Kalkanı', https://tinyurl.com/y5296ac4 (accessed 25 March 2020).

Atesci, U. (2020) 'COVID-19 Spreads among Ford Workers In Turkey', https://tinyurl.com/yxlrjtjt (accessed 15 June 2020).

Aysoy, A. M. (2021) 'Kod 29 kılık değiştirdi!', https://tinyurl.com/y3k8e5cv (accessed 20 May 2021).

Bakır, O. (2021) 'The Swamp of Insecurity in the Mirror of Covid-19 and Code-29!', https://tinyurl.com/2zfpc36c (accessed 20 May 2021).

Burgin, A. (2020) 'The Pandemic, the Working Class and the Left', https://tinyurl.com/y48tyh4h (accessed 30 March 2020).

CNNTURK (2021), www.cnnturk.com/yazarlar/guncel/prof-dr-derya-uluduz/sonunda-covid-19-meslek-hastaligi-olarak-kabul-edildi (accessed 28 May 2021).

DİSK-AR (2020a) *İşsizlik ve İstihdam Görünümü Raporu*, https://tinyurl. com/y6cwrmuf (accessed 13 July 2020).

—— (2020b) *COVID-19 Döneminde Kadın İşgücünün Görünümü Raporu*, https://tinyurl.com/yy466khq (accessed 25 June 2020).

—— (2021a) İşçiler Büyümeden Pay Alamıyor, http://disk.org.tr/2021/06/ isciler-buyumeden-pay-alamiyor/ (accessed 4 June 2021).

—— (2021b), İşsizlik ve İstihdamın Görünümü, http://arastirma.disk. org.tr/wp-content/uploads/2021/05/DISK-AR-Issizlik-ve-Istihdamin-Gorunumu-2021-1.-Ceyrek-19-Mayisa-Ozel-Genc-Issizligi-Bulteni.pdf (accessed 5 June 2021).

Evrensel Daily (2020a), www.evrensel.net/haber/421101/erdogan-esnafa-buyuksehirlerde-750-tl-kira-destegi-verilecegini-acikladi (accessed 5 June 2021).

Evrensel Daily (2020b) 'Fabrikada Mess-Safe Dağıtılmaya Başlandı', https:// tinyurl.com/xs6p86de (accessed 5 June 2021).

Evrensel Daily (2020c). 'Dardanel Workers "Taken Hostage" in the Factory after Covid-19 Outbreak', 3 August 2020, https://tinyurl.com/yyykfssj (acessed 7 August 2020).

Saad-Filho, A. (2020) 'Coronavirus, Crisis, and the End of Neoliberalism', *Monthly Review Online*, 18 April 2020, https://tinyurl.com/y66awbsj (accessed 23 April 2020).

Financial Times (2020) 'Pandemic Crisis: Global Economic Recovery Tracker', https://tinyurl.com/y4nczrl7 (accessed 20 July 2020).

Fuchs, C. (2020) 'Everyday Life and Everyday Communication in Coronavirus Capitalism', https://tinyurl.com/y2b49wf7 (accessed 24 April 2020).

Gıda-İş Sendikası (2020) 'Gıda Sektöründe Koronavirüs Sürecinde Yaşananlara Dair Rapor', https://tinyurl.com/y4xq2wmq (accessed 12 June 2020).

Gökay, B. (2020) 'Turkey Tries to Keep Wheels of Economy Turning Despite Worsening Coronavirus Crisis', *The Conversation*, https://tinyurl.com/ y2txcpa2 (accessed June 2020).

Gökten, K. (2020) 'Post Korona ve Olasılıklar', https://tinyurl.com/y29r8c8e (accessed 14 July 2020).

Guterres, A. (2020) 'We Are All in This Together: Human Rights and COVID-19 Response and Recovery', United Nations, https://tinyurl.com/ y8m46vts (accessed June 2020).

Gürsel, S. and H. Mutluay (2020) 'Korona Salgını Şokunun İşgücü Piyasasına Etkisi: İşgücü ve İstihdamda Büyük Düşüş, İşsizlikte Artış', https://tinyurl. com/y4ae4xgx (accessed 10 June 2020).

Harvey, D. (2020) 'We Need a Collective Response to the Collective Dilemma of Coronavirus', https://jacobinmag.com/author/david-harvey (accessed 6 June 2020).

ILO (2020a) 'ILO Monitor 2nd Edition: COVID-19 and the World of Work: Updated Estimates and Analysis', ILO, 7 April 2020, https://tinyurl.com/ya3hwqar (accessed 18 June 2020).

—— (2020b) 'Young Workers Will Be Hit Hard by COVID-19's Economic Fallout', https://tinyurl.com/y2spyd47 (accessed 12 June 2020).

IMF (2020) 'World Economic Outlook', *April 2020: The Great Lockdown*, https://tinyurl.com/yyug6fgs (accessed 10 June 2020).

—— 'World Economic Outlook Managing Divergent Recoveries, April 2021', www.imf.org/en/Publications/WEO/Issues/2021/04/06/World-Economic-Outlook-April-2021-50308 (accessed 4 June 2021).

İŞKUR (2020) 'Kısa Çalışma Ödeneği', https://tinyurl.com/y4mdfa2e (accessed 12 May 2020).

Law No. 4447 'İşsizlik Sigortası Kanunu', https://tinyurl.com/y3594v4o (accessed 24 April 2020).

OECD (2020) 'Turkey Economic Snapshot', https://tinyurl.com/y3uyjgnk (accessed 10 June 2020).

Özveri, M. (2020) 'Fırsat Bu Fırsat', *Evrensel Gazetesi*, 10 Haziran, https://tinyurl.com/y4plxkbv (accessed 10 June 2020).

Pitel, L. (2020) 'Turkey's Logistic Providers Adjust to the Strains of Covid-19, Financial Times, Special Report: Coronavirus and Logistic', https://tinyurl.com/y2n6j8sq (accessed June 2020).

Resmi Gazete, (2021), 3998 Sayılı Cumhurbaşkanı Kararı, www.resmigazete.gov.tr/eskiler/2021/05/20210521-8.pdf (accessed 28 May 2021).

SGK (2020) '96597630-010.06.02-E5852699 Sayılı Koronavirüs Genelgesi', www.turmob.org.tr/mevzuat/Pdf/17715 (accessed 9 June 2020).

Strateji ve Bütçe Başkanlığı (2020) 'Türkiye Ekonomisinde Haftalık Gelişmeler ve Genel Görünüm', https://tinyurl.com/yxmrpsuc (accessed 10 June 2020).

Taymaz, E. (2020) 'COVID-19 Tedbirlerinin Türkiye Ekonomisine Etkisi ve Çözüm Önerileri', https://tinyurl.com/y63oghnn (accessed 10 June 2020).

TBB (Türkiye Bankalar Birliği) (2020) 'TBB Risk Merkezi Aylık Bülten Nisan 2020', https://tinyurl.com/y53b4lem (accessed 12 July 2020).

TCMB (2020) 'Kredi Kartı Kullanımdaki Değişim', https://tinyurl.com/y683qylf (accessed 12 June 2020).

—— (2021), Döviz Kuru İstatistikleri, www.tcmb.gov.tr/wps/wcm/connect/TR/TCMB+TR/Main+Menu/Istatistikler (accessed 4 June 2021).

Voyvoda, E. and Yeldan, E. (2020) 'COVİD-19 Salgının Türkiye Ekonomisi Üzerine Etkileri ve Politika Alternatiflerinin Makroekonomik Genel Denge Analizi', https://tinyurl.com/y6kq7kfz (accessed 12 June 2020).

World Bank (2020) 'The Global Economic Outlook during the COVID-19 Pandemic: A Changed World', https://tinyurl.com/ycpxn4lb (accessed 9 June 2020).

Worldometers (2021) 'COVID-19 Coronavirus Pandemic', https://www.worldometers.info/coronavirus/ (accessed 28 May 2021).

Yeldan, E. (2021), 'Türkiye'nin Büyüme Serüveni', https://yeldane.files.wordpress.com/2021/06/yeldan776_02haz2021_buyumeseruveni.pdf (accessed 6 June 2021).

PART III

Resistance

12

Reconsidering Workers' Self-Management in Turkey: From Resistance to Workers' Self-Management Possibilities/Constraints

Berna Güler and Erhan Acar [1]

12.1 INTRODUCTION

Workers' self-management (WSM) experiences have an important place in today's labour relations and struggles. The WSM practices that were implemented in various forms and specificities in many countries can be considered as attempts to go beyond *challenging* capitalism; they rather attempt to *change* capitalist exploitation and achieve workers' dream of a classless society without exploitation of labour. However, the question arises: Can we speak of a real WSM at the global scale where capitalism's economic, political and cultural domination is unquestionably present? Without doubt, WSM experiences may contain, though not fully, many features inherent in capitalism, marked by the dominance of capitalist economy, politics and culture. However, when WSM experiences provide an alternative model and vision emerging with the initiative of the working class and their ideology against various capitalist social relations, then we are confronted with the fact that WSM itself will blossom at the heart of capitalism.

In the 2000s in Turkey, when capitalist relations of production permeated everywhere through unprecedented neoliberal policies of the AKP governments, one significant WSM practice was the 'Kazova worker self-management factory'. It started at the end of March 2013 and coincided with a moment of popular uprising – the Gezi Park Protests that erupted in late May and the subsequent establishment of the 'Taksim Commune'. These developments in the first half of 2013 unsettled the ruling classes and manifested the aspirations of the people against neoliberal authoritarianism, and their art, culture and struggle practices were witnessed in all areas of daily life.

The focus of this chapter, the Kazova factory workers, were fired by their employers on 31 January 2013, and they began to organise a resistance in the factory. On 28 April 2013, the workers occupied the factory and started production. Gezi Park Protests, which erupted a month later, further encouraged the workers and strengthened the occupation, resistance and co-production, and contributed to organising a WSM experience and solidarity. However, Gezi Protests came to an end through brutal police repression because of 'security reasons' as claimed by the AKP government. Following this, the Kazova WSM experience entered a different phase and they still exist in different forms as of 2020.

The aim of this chapter is therefore to shed light on a historically specific WSM experience introduced by Kazova factory workers. Our purpose is to trace the roots and expound the narrative of their struggle by sharing their rich experiences and show how they moved forward collectively and learned from each other throughout the struggle, rather than focusing solely on the successes and failures experienced by the workers in their WSM and occupation practices.

12.2 UNDERSTANDING WORKERS' SELF-MANAGEMENT: THEORY AND METHOD

The fact that workers do not own the management of the economic unit they work for constitutes the main reason of alienation to the product they produce, to the production process, and to the use of income earned. In this way, workers turn into a living being who sell their labour power to capitalists for production under conditions that they do not determine. As the workers are excluded from the decision-making processes and they gradually turn into machines in terms of their contribution to the production, this phenomenon ensures the survival of the capitalist ideology. However, historically, as the capitalist mode of production has developed and become widespread, it has also brought about its opponent as well. The capitalist mode of production gives birth to the working class while the working class develops and advocates their own mode of production through various practices and experiences.

From the employers' perspective, the generalisation and spread of the capitalist form of production means bringing workers under control and managing them in order to get maximum output at the minimum unit of time, seizure of more surplus value and achieving a constant increase in the value of capital. The capitalist property relations disempowered the workers in terms of controlling and managing the profit made through the products/goods/services produced by the worker. Employers regard workers as a sole production input, and thus the commodification of the labour power of the workers. Commodification is not limited to the production process in terms of labour, however; it also appears with alienation as a phenomenon that affects all areas of life. As a result, as the workers are alienated from internal decisions and their contribution to the production resembles a machinery, this process gives rise to specific consequences that are contradictory with the aims of the capitalist system (Işıklı, 1983: 25). Where these contradictions between workers and employers evolve into conflicting processes, a desire for a more equal and democratic production model for the workers (not only limited to the production process) comes to the fore. The most common of these production models is the WSM. As Vanek (1971: 368) explains: 'a whole and pure WSM (or workers' control) exists only in the cases where all owners of property are workers and where all workers are also the owner of the property and they participate equally in the management's election boards of the organisation and the distribution of the economic surplus of it'.

Despite the fact that WSM practices emerge within and include some aspects inherent in capitalism, they constitute a contrast with the essence of capitalist social relations, and attempt to develop an alternative organisation regardless of the development level of a country (for a detailed comparative study see Bayat, 1991). Unlike employee stock ownership plans (ESOP), the practices of WSM usually occur where capitalist production relations come to a deadlock, or in times of economic turmoil and crises and usually start with an occupation. For instance, the WSM practices started with factory occupations in Argentina and turned into a network of businesses when bankruptcies became a daily routine during the 2001–02 crisis (see Kabat, 2011; Atzeni and Vieta, 2014). Many other cases in several Latin American countries were also discussed later as the 21st Century Socialism (see Lebowitz 2006; Harnecker, 2015). The financial crisis of 2007–08 has also triggered this tendency, and the WSM as a possibility emerged from sit-down strikes during the financial collapse of 2008 in Chicago (see Ness, 2011: 313–19). Similarly, in Greece, they emerged as a response to austerity policies that were implemented in the wake of economic crisis (Kokkinidis, 2014).

Self-managed factories have a historical place in Turkey as well. The examples of WSM in Turkey date back to an experience that took place in September 1923, with the participation of 100 workers as a reaction to long working hours and working conditions at a printing house (Narin, 2017: 51–2).[2] Other major historical cases which started with direct actions and occupations were Alpagut Lignite Mine (Çorum) in 1969 and Yeni Çeltek Lignite Mine (Amasya) in 1980. The most recent wave of workers' discontent in Turkey which manifested itself through various factory occupations came to the fore in late 2012/early 2013 (see Erol, 2014). These were complemented by the Gezi uprising and the 'Taksim Commune' later in 2013. These developments made the AKP show its true colours, once the 'shining example' of prosperity and democracy, in the eyes of the Western media and mainstream commentators. Specifically, the subject matter of this chapter, the occupation of the Kazova factory is the most prominent and long-lasting example of the recent wave. The workers started their resistance on 27 February 2013, and continued with the occupation of the factory on 28 April 2013, establishing the cooperative.

As far as the method is concerned, we contend that the most effective way to reveal the facts in order to achieve a holistic way of understanding and explaining the functioning dynamics of self-managed factories is an in-depth analysis based on a critical social scientific approach, using qualitative research method techniques; specifically, an in-depth interview method (Chirban, 1996;

Kümbetoğlu, 2005: 72). Hence, we conducted face-to-face, in-depth interviews with seven people between 2016 and 2017: three workers from Diren Kazova Cooperative, two workers from Özgür Kazova Textile Cooperative and one lawyer and one activist from an NGO.[3]

12.3 KAZOVA TEKSTIL TRICOTAGE INC.: HISTORICAL DEVELOPMENT IN THE CONTEXT OF TURKEY'S POLITICAL ECONOMY

Kazova Tekstil Tricotage Inc. was founded by Mustafa Somuncu in 1947 as a small workshop manufacturing flannels (underwear). Thanks to the protective and incentive policies towards the industry, brought by the inward-oriented capital accumulation regime in the 1960s, Kazova factory increased their product range, using new machinery imported from the US. This also coincides with the period when the raw material problem was resolved and the factory started to process wool. Afterwards, new machinery was imported from Switzerland and the UK. The factory started to manufacture woollen textiles for women and menswear. In the 1960s, for the first time in Turkey, a big fashion show was held in the Municipality Entertainment Hall of Taç, and Kazova Tekstil Tricotage Inc. products were introduced in the Hall (Yeşilbaş, 2002). Thus, 'Kazova Tekstil Tricotage Inc.' became established within the market with their products.

As Turkey started to implement an outward-oriented capital accumulation strategy in the 1980s as part of the neoliberal transition, ready-made garment manufacturing was incorporated into international markets. Due to the challenging conditions because of international competition, Kazova factory was downsized after the 2000s. The number of workers was reduced and the product range was limited. Especially after 2010, there were delays in the payment of wages for the workers. As the workers could not receive their regular wages, they were forced to work for advance payments worth 100–150 Turkish lira. A.A., one of the employees of Özgür Kazova Textile Collective who used to work in the factory, makes the following comment concerning the troubles they faced in their daily lives because of the delays in the payments:

My son was taken to the ER. I asked my friends for money. I went to the accounting department. The boss said: 'It's not my business, he is your son. If he is sick, he is sick. You should have saved for these days.' I had not been paid for four months. On the same day, my spouse also got sick in the workplace. She was also taken to the ER. One in Şişli Etfal Hospital and the other in Taksim Emergency Hospital; but I had only two liras in my pocket. I did not even have the chance to take the bus. (Gezer, 2014)

There were 96 unorganised workers in total working in the factory in January 2013, and when the workers were fired, the factory became insolvent, and operational machinery and raw materials were removed. The workers were left with a four-month pending payment, together with their unpaid severance and notice pays. Following this, workers got in touch with some left-wing organisations and NGOs (such as DİH – Revolutionary Workers Movement, HHB – People's Law Bureau, and ÇHD – Progressive Lawyers' Association) and started the legal process as legitimacy was important during the resistance. The Nakliyat-İş Union, a member of the Confederation of Progressive Trade Unions (DİSK), was the only supporting union of the Kazova workers. Nakliyat-İş's various actions helped to mobilise and popularise Kazova resistance, such as marching with them to the factory and celebrating the 47th anniversary of the DİSK with the workers in front of the Kazova factory (Nakliyat-İş, 2013). In short, even though they were unorganised before, they gained support from both progressive organisations and a union which organised logistics workers. It could be argued that this support and solidarity with the Kazova workers triggered the notion of *self-management* rather than just compensation of unpaid wages.

In January 2013, a group of workers occupied the abandoned factory as an act of resistance to help reclaim their salaries. While they were waiting for the lawsuits concerning their salaries and severance payments to come to trial, one worker repaired the non-operational machinery and they started to produce their own jumpers using hundreds of rolls of yarn of various colours and the pieces of jumpers abandoned at the factory and started selling them at a shop they rented in Şişli area (Dinler, 2018: 232).

12.4 RESISTANCE AND PROTEST REPERTOIRE
IN KAZOVA FACTORY

When the resistance started only 18 of the 96 workers were left in the factory. Initially, the resistance was in the form of marches from the Şişli Mosque to Bomonti on every Wednesday, where the factory was located. During these marches, workers shouted slogans explaining their current condition and tried to shape public opinion by handing out leaflets. Gradually, the Kazova workers enriched their repertoire of demonstrations. For example, workers located three different addresses where their employers were living. Kazova workers then went to these houses of their employers on every Sunday to make statements and speeches to the press to demonstrate the unlawfulness that the workers faced because of their employers. There were joint demonstrations with 'Hey Tekstil'[4] garment workers who were trying to claim their rights as they had also been fired with no legal basis. On every Saturday, they organised marches from Taksim Square to the Galatasaray High School together with the 'Hey Tekstil' workers.

Following the rumours that the employer of the Kazova factory was removing the machinery from the factory, the workers set up their tents in front of the factory to prevent the goods being 'stolen' from them. Although some workers objected to this decision, the resistance tents were set up in front of the factory as there was no other way to prevent the removal of the machinery and the goods by the employer. However, as some workers did not want to confront the security forces, only 12 workers took part in the resistance.

12.5 GEZI PROTESTS AND THE FIRST SIGNS OF WORKERS'
SELF-MANAGEMENT EXPERIENCE

As the resistance of the Kazova workers was continuing, one of the biggest public protests in modern Turkey's history emerged. The *Gezi Resistance* was a decisive moment for Kazova workers and triggered the occupation of Kazova factory, which later turned into a production cooperative experience (Interview 1, 2016). When heavy-duty machinery was sent to Taksim Gezi Park on the night of 27 May 2013 in the context of the 'Taksim Pedestrianisation Project' of the AKP government, a small group of people who were against the demolition of Gezi Park stood against the machinery. After the first attack on Gezi Park, a group of 70 people, including MPs, started to wait and protect Gezi Park. The next day, the group that the security forces were trying to disperse with brutal intervention showed determined resistance. In particular, social media networks were one of the most important elements that helped the spread of Gezi Park protests to many cities in Turkey, as over 2 million tweets were shared on 30 May 2013 with the hashtags #direngezipark #resistgezipark (Yıldırım, 2014: 24).

On 2 June, people from various segments of the society came together and established the 'Taksim Commune'. Following this, 'Forums' and 'People's Councils' were established in many parts of the country in mid-June. People discussed many issues about the political situation and the future of these Councils and Forums. These platforms also functioned as a bridge for the Kazova workers to pursue their WSM experience. Indeed, the Gezi Park Protests encouraged the Kazova workers to decide not to leave the factory until the workers got their rights. D.C., a worker from Diren Kazova Cooperative, expresses the connection between the Gezi Park Protests and the occupation process of Kazova as follows: 'Everywhere Taksim, everywhere resistance! Our beginning was like this slogan, and the truth is we occupied thanks to Gezi Park protests. Taksim Gezi Park protests have an important role in the occupation process of Kazova. I can say 99 percent' (Gezer, 2014). Similarly, G.I., an activist from a labour-centred organisation, reveals the relationship between the occupation and the Gezi Park protests and the impact of the Forum and the Councils in shaping the workers' struggle practices at Kazova:

> Tatavla Forum was the closest one to us. We met with friends there and told them about our problems. Merkez Neighbourhood Forum was also close to us. We met them as well. Then we met people from Kocamustafapaşa Forum who offered important support. They organised visits. They took our leaflets and distributed them to the people who went to the forums. (Gezer, 2014)

Setting up a tent in front of the factory on 28 April 2013 was a turning point for the occupation process. This led Kazova workers to prevent evasion of goods from the factory by the employer. On 28 June at 8:00 am, Kazova workers occupied the factory and expanded the practical dimension of the resistance. Kazova workers decided not to leave the factory until the employer negotiated with the workers and accepted their demands.

However, when workers entered the factory, they found nothing but scrapped machinery and a nearly ruined building. After a while, the workers found unfinished sweaters in the factory's roof, and they sewed these sweaters. These sweaters were then sold with the help of a solidarity and cooperation network established in the Forums. With the revenues earned, workers purchased parts such as motors and needles for machines, and they also fixed a broken machine. In this way, they continued production and sales; and through the revenues received over time, the workers fixed three more machines and started using them.

12.6 THE RIGHT TO SELF-MANAGEMENT OF THE WORKERS FROM ALPAGUT TO KAZOVA

Among various working-class experiences mentioned by DİH members (Acar, 2019: 162), Kazova workers were mostly influenced by the Alpagut WSM experience in Turkey in 1969 (Narin, 2010). Following non-payment of their wages, workers of Alpagut occupied the coal mine, and planned and kept the production of the mine themselves until the military operations started (see Tür, 2009: 3; Gürcan and Mete, 2018: 4–5). The resistance practices of Kazova workers and the Alpagut WSM experience have many things in common and this clearly had an effect on the Kazova workers. Indeed, the way of thinking of the Kazova workers changed after learning about the Alpagut experience.

Following this change, Kazova workers started to sell the products they produced, relying on solidarity in the Forums, and met their needs by continuing production. Thus, they strengthened the notion that 'not only they can produce but also they can self-manage', thanks to the debates they participated in within the organisations and

Forums. In addition, labour market issues of the working class faced not only in Turkey but globally, that is, the insecurity, exclusion of workers' health and safety measures, negative factors and conditions such as working for lower wages, further encouraged the decision of Kazova workers in terms of the transition to a WSM experience. As the Kazova workers continued the production, the possibility of WSM became increasingly clear in their minds.

Meanwhile, Kazova workers watched a documentary entitled *Patronsuzlar* ('Workers Without Bosses', directed by labour activist Metin Yeğin) about factory occupations in Latin American countries. Thus, they had the opportunity to find answers to questions they had from a comparative perspective (Interview 1, 2016). Kazova workers aimed to produce sweaters for the public which are affordable and of good quality, and set an example of an alternative organisation and way of life beyond capitalist domination, and without a boss. As such, the workers established a cooperative based on a non-profit production model that relies on cooperation and solidarity, where the workers self-manage and have wages above market conditions. The workers also continued their debates on how and for what purpose the cooperative will produce; and issues of wage distribution and sharing the profits equally.

12.7 AGAINST THE CAPITALIST CULTURE: CULTURE AND ARTS COMMITTEE OF KAZOVA RESISTANCE

The practices of the Kazova workers were not limited to the organisation of an alternative mode of production against the capitalist form of production. Hence, in order to overcome the alienation that the capitalist culture creates, a Culture and Arts Committee was established with the participation of Kazova workers and various artists and groups related to Kazova resistance directly or indirectly. These included music bands such as 'Grup Yorum', and initiatives such as 'İdil Kültür Merkezi' and 'Ötekiler Kültür ve Sanat'.

The first event of the Culture and Arts Committee of the Kazova resistance was the organisation of Kazova Resistance Film Festival. During the three-day film festival, movies on workplace occupations were shown. In addition, the Committee organised music concerts with the bands which were in solidarity with the workers. Meanwhile, a store named 'Diren Kazova-DİH' was opened in Şişli province of İstanbul for the purpose of promoting and selling the products produced by Kazova workers. The decoration of the store was designed by a group of artists (Kazova İşçileri Direniş Günlüğü, 2016: 22).

Thanks to the activists who had connections with different cooperatives in countries outside of Turkey such as Italy, France and Spain, Kazova resistance managed to attract an international audience.[5] These activists successfully facilitated expanding sales to European exhibitions and cooperatives and also introduced international experience to the Turkish context. A group of artists were invited to do an art workshop for the design of the summer collection of Free Kazova t-shirts, some of which quickly became popular. An Italian academic/activist designed several jumpers, the design names of which were derived from workers' names. Musicians performed in solidarity evenings and a group composed a special song for Kazova resistance. Workers enjoyed spending time with people with unique skills and backgrounds (Dinler, 2018: 233–4).

Thus, the cooperative demonstrated that it can be an alternative not only to the mode of production that exists in working life but also to the dominant culture and art arising from the current capitalist mode of production. Working and producing on the axis of class-culture brought a sense of closeness between the Kazova Cooperative and the masses while contributing to working-class history and consciousness to create an alternative experience in all areas of life. Thus, the cultural aspect of the cooperative pertaining to 'class' was as important as the economic production.

12.8 DISSENT AND CONFLICT IN KAZOVA

An interesting development was the emergence of disagreements among Kazova workers. After the discussions between the workers and the decision to establish a cooperative, five workers decided to leave. One reason for this disagreement was related to the name of the store that was opened in Şişli. These five workers demanded the removal of the word 'DİH' from the name of the store, while the remaining seven workers opposed them. In this context, dissident workers stated that 'DİH' represented an ideology and representation of a particular group. The other reason for the criticism was that they claimed a group of workers were not going to the factory and not taking part in the production with the excuse that strikes and resistances started in various cities in Turkey. The most important reason argued by a group of workers was that the money collected within the framework of solidarity did not reach them and they criticised the lack of transparency. As a result of these disagreements, five workers broke up with the group and founded Özgür Kazova Textile Collective (Interview 2, 2017). Meanwhile, the other group stated that workers who criticise them for not being transparent acted with self-interest and ambition to gain more. Thus, seven workers established the Diren Kazova Cooperative and continued on their way (Kazova İşçileri Direniş Günlüğü, 2016).

12.9 THE TRANSFORMATIVE POWER OF WORKER SELF-MANAGEMENT: WORKING LIFE AT DIREN KAZOVA COOPERATIVE AND ÖZGÜR KAZOVA TEXTILE COLLECTIVE

Özgür Kazova Textile Collective workers started production on 17 November 2014 with the slogan of 'sweaters without boss' (Özgür Kazova Tekstil Kolektifi Pamphlet). The plant was established as a business on paper but organised as a cooperative. As the cooperative's efforts to develop solidarity with international cooperatives continued, workers adopted the principles of the International Cooperative Association.[6] These principles are: (1) democratic workers' self-management among members; (2) a structure based on willingness and openness to new members; (3) an economic model based on fair sharing; (4) independent production based on workers' self-management; (5) continuous education, teaching and knowledge sharing; (6) cooperation between cooperatives; (7) solidarity with all social struggles (Özgür Kazova Tekstil Kolektifi Pamphlet). These principles adopted by Özgür Kazova Textile Collective also give us some clues about the working life at the cooperative.

As of 2017, there were three workers working in the cooperative. Two of the workers are from the process of Kazova resistance and the other worker joined after the establishment of the Özgür Kazova Textile Collective on a voluntary basis. Because of the economic problems after splitting up, the transition phase of the workers to production was painful. Workers did not have sufficient support to establish a new workshop, for repairing and maintaining machinery, and the requirements for the establishment of the cooperative. Although the desired level of occupational health and safety measures could not be achieved, some measures were taken. The lack of insurance for the workers due to the economic problems of the cooperative transformed into 'self-exploitative' work without insurance to provide the continuity of the organisation.

The recruitment of workers to Özgür Kazova Textile Collective is carried out according to certain criteria. These criteria are that the worker has a sacrificing and productive character that priorities unity and solidarity. The cooperative is open to all workers who meet these criteria, regardless of language, religion, culture or gender. The distribution of income in the Özgür Kazova Collective is made within the framework of equality. In addition, workers have information about profit and loss. For future investment, 2 lira is added to the cost of every sweater produced. The cooperative produces an average of 800 sweaters every month. As a principle, the working day was limited to six hours in the cooperative. However, it varies according to the volume of the work. If the orders received are increased, the flexible run-time is used to deliver the orders on time (Interview 2, 2017).

On 29 May 2015, following the split-up, Diren Kazova Cooperative was opened (Kazova İşçileri Direniş Günlüğü, 2016: 26). Firstly, they produced sweaters only. But they started to produce bags and socks later in order to increase the product variety. The most important principle for the cooperative workers is that supporting resistances that take place in other parts of the country is as valuable as producing. Efforts to establish a solidarity network were made not only within the country but also internationally. Diren Kazova Cooperative faced rapid transformations on many issues related to working life. In the first instance, the workers took measures to ensure health and safety. One of the most important criteria of the cooperative is ensuring full occupational health and safety in the cooperative. Stands were set up in the neighbourhoods and concerts held for the sale of the products produced by Diren Kazova Cooperative. In certain neighbourhoods, shopkeepers who want to support the cooperative take the products of the cooperative and try to deliver them to the public. The products produced for the orders made via the internet are delivered to the public directly.

With the establishment of the cooperative, an assembly was formed with the participation of Diren Kazova workers and activists from DİH and HHB. Decisions were made in the assembly, which held meetings regularly every week. The assembly can be defined as the reflection of the collective will and the democratic functioning at the political level. The assembly, which was established on the basis of criticism/self-criticism, constructive and integrative principles, also plays an effective role in the transformation of social relations.

F.V., a worker from the Diren Kazova Cooperative, explains the sharing of earnings as follows:

> Kazova has its own cooperative account. We put all our profits there. Our first goal is to purchase raw materials. Now we wait for a payment, after we have this payment, we will pay our pending payments such as rent, insurance costs and salaries. All the remaining money in Kazova's account will be used for the purchase of raw materials. Because we do not have a fixed income, we keep the excess money in the bank to use it in the months when we have difficulty. According to our needs, we buy raw materials and machinery. For example, we bought our digital machines two months ago for 80 thousand liras. We bought our machines thanks to the power given to us by our organisation. However, because of a fire we could not produce for 40 days. In our country, it is very difficult for us to be small tradesmen without capital. We face and overcome these challenges with our organisation. Raw material prices are volatile; sometimes the price of raw materials can change from one day to the next, so it is hard to survive as small tradesmen.

Another phenomenon encountered in the above-mentioned statements is how the difficulties and problems faced by the cooperative are resolved. The most significant of these problems is the sustainability of the cooperative, which emerged as an alternative within the market mechanism dominated by the logic of capital. Cooperative workers deal with the sustainability of the cooperative in two spheres: the first one is organisation and the second one is the strengthening of solidarity economy. Thus, as long as solidarity and organisation are strengthened, the cooperative can continue production.

Not only for Diren Kazova Cooperative or for Özgür Kazova Textile Collective but for most of the historical and contemporary WSM experiences, solidarity and organisation are the prerequisites for establishing and maintaining an alternative production and a way of life in and against free-market conditions.[7]

12.10 CONCLUSION

One finding of this chapter is that the limits of the self-emergent resistance practices of the working class are directly related to the effectiveness of the vanguard workers' participation in the resistance. Another argument of this chapter is that there were two factors in terms of shaping the struggle of Kazova workers, especially the occupation and WSM practices. The first one is the Gezi Park protests that emerged in the first months of the resistance. Gezi Park Protests become the turning point for the workers of Kazova, in which fear was overcome and the resistance gained a social dimension. Establishment of the Taksim Commune, People's Councils and Forums were seen as determining factors in the occupation and self-management initiative by Kazova workers. Kazova workers participated in the Forums that were established in different neighbourhoods and regions during and after the Gezi protests to discuss the problems in public and take decisions. Finally, Kazova workers became familiar with the Forum practice during the occupation and self-management.

The split-up which came to the fore after eight months from the establishment of Kazova WSM is a problem not only seen in Kazova practice but also in many self-managed operating factories around the world (Yeğin, 2015: 28). Although that disintegration is seen as a phenomenon that reduces the motivation of the workers, it simply shows that the workers have the right to self-determination within the framework of the democratic principles.

According to our interviews with the Kazova workers, the cooperative-based production is different in many ways from the capitalist mode of production. These differences may be listed as follows:

1. As the ownership of the means of production is in the hands of the workers, the hierarchical management approach of the capitalist enterprises is completely eliminated.
2. The fact that workers are assigned to different departments for certain times and the rotation of those who are involved in management processes at brief intervals ensure that everyone is informed about all processes.
3. Workers do not have to be paid on piecework, and this works as a compensation mechanism for the flexible working time and long working hours.
4. Recruitment is not based on the classical qualification criteria, but rather the evaluation of the needs of production and the principle of solidarity.
5. Occupational health and safety is the most sensitive and prioritised issue that the cooperatives are primarily concerned with.

In a world where the capitalist mode of production is permeated globally, the conditions to maintain the working principles of the Kazova Cooperative need to be raised. Two principles emerged from our interviews with workers and representatives of civil society organisations. The first principle is the importance of organisation and the second one is solidarity. Strengthening and improving the relations of organisation and solidarity is tested by practices that will strengthen the cooperatives against capitalist enterprises and ensure the sustainability of cooperatives. For this purpose, to create an opportunity for workers to be organised by developing solidarity relations is of vital importance, not only on a national scale but also on an international scale. Under conditions where organised relations and solidarity can be strengthened, workers can keep their right to self-determination and ensure the sustainability of their production. Not only for Kazova Cooperative's experience, but in many experiences in different countries in the world, by organised mobilisation and strong solidarity, the self-managed factories can be transformed into institutional alternative structures.

However, in the market conditions where the capitalist mode of production and hegemony of this mode of production dominates, as in many cooperatives, the unhealthy relationship that workers establish with the means of production can make the workers move away from the class consciousness and align them with the logic of capitalist production. This is also a red line for self-managed factories. In such cases, it is one of the most important problems to determine how the self-managed factories will be sustained in capitalist market relations. Given that the self-managed factories will proceed within the capitalist market conditions in the first place, there is nothing wrong with using capital opportunities in circulation in the short term. However, in the long term, it is necessary to create and develop the structure of self-management and to create alternatives by developing relations of organisation and solidarity.

BIBLIOGRAPHY

Acar, E. (2019) *Çalışma Hayatında Özyönetim Deneyimleri: Kozava Örneği*, İstanbul: Sosyal Araştırmalar Vakfı Yayını.

Atzeni, M. and Vieta, M. (2014) 'Self-management in Theory and in the Practice of Worker-recuperated Enterprises in Argentina', in Parker, M., Cheney, G., Fournier, V. and Land, C. (eds), *The Routledge Companion to Alternative Organization*, London: Routledge, 47–63.

Bayat, A. (1991) *Work, Politics and Power: An International Perspective on Workers' Control and Self-Management*, New York: Monthly Review Press.

Chirban, J.T. (1996) *Interviewing in Depth: The Interactive-relational Approach*, London: Sage.

Dinler, D.Ş. (2018) 'New Workers' Struggles in Turkey since the 2000s: Possibilities and Limits', in Azzellini, D. and Kraft, M.G. (eds), *The Class Strikes Back: Self-organised Workers' Struggles in the Twenty-first Century*, Leiden: Brill, 217–37.

Erol, M.E. (2014) '(Re)Radicalization of the Working Class in Turkey? An Appraisal of Recent Workplace Occupations', *The Bullet*, https://socialist-project.ca/2014/04/b972/ (accessed March 2020).

Gezer, F. (Director) (2014) *Kazova Direnişi, 'Diren, İşgal Et, Üret*, Documentary.

Gürcan, E.C. and Mete, B. (2018) 'The Combined and Uneven Development of Working-class Capacities in Turkey, 1960–2016', *Labor History*, 60 (3), 268–86, doi: 10.1080/0023656X.2019.1537027.

Harnecker, M. (2015) *A World to Build: New Paths Toward Twenty-first Century Socialism*, trans. F. Fuentes, New York: Monthly Review Press.

Işıklı, A. (1983) *Kuramlar Boyunca Özyönetim ve Yugoslavya Deneyi*, First edn, İstanbul: Alan Yayıncılık.

Kabat, M. (2011) 'Argentinean Worker-taken Factories Trajectories of Workers' Control under the Economic Crisis', in Ness, I. and Azzellini, D. (eds), *Ours to Master and to Own: Workers' Control from the Commune to the Present*, Chicago, IL: Haymarket Books, 365–81.

Kazova İşçileri Direniş Günlüğü (2016) *İşçi Sınıfı Tarihinde Bir İlk: Kazova Direniş İşgal Üretim!* First edn, Istanbul: A.T İstanbul Teknik Ofset.

Kokkinidis, G. (2014) 'Spaces of Possibilities: Workers' Self-management in Greece', *Organization*, 22 (6), 847–71.

Kümbetoğlu, B. (2005) *Sosyolojide ve Antropolojide Niteliksel Yöntem ve Araştırma*, İstanbul: Bağlam Kitapevi.

Lebowitz, M. (2006) *Build It Now: Socialism for the Twenty-first Century*, New York: Monthly Review Press.

Nakliyat-İş (2013) 'DİSK'in kuruluşunun 47. yılını Kazova Direnişçi işçileriyle birlikte kutladık', https://tinyurl.com/y4f8vuea (accessed 20 October 2019).

Narin, Ö. (2010) 'Uzay *Çağında* Sosyal Adalet Savaşı: 1969 Alpagut Olayı', in Kurt, S. (ed.), *Almanak 2009 Analizleri*, Istanbul: SAV Sosyal Araştırmalar Vakfı, 312–28.

—— (2017) 'Türkiye İşçi Sınıfı Tarihinde İşçi Özyönetim Deneyimleri ve Kriz Dönemlerinde Özyönetim Olanakları', Disk-Ar, 2014, 11 (3), 48–61, https://tinyurl.com/y3jyahm8 (accessed 21 January 2017).

Ness, I. (2011) 'Workers' Direct Action and Factory Control in the United States', in Ness, I. and Azzellini, D. (eds), *Ours to Master and to Own: Workers' Control from the Commune to the Present*, Chicago, IL: Haymarket Books, 302–21.

Özgür Kazova Tekstil Kolektifi Pamphlet. (no date).

Pişkin, C. (2019) 'Sentences Totalling 159 Years 2 Months for 18 Lawyers', https://tinyurl.com/y69kjow2, 23/03/2019 (accessed 27 August 2019).

Söylemez, A. (2014) 'Kazova Factory to Make Jerseys for Cuba, Basque Country', *Bianet* English, https://tinyurl.com/y6sznnug (accessed 1 October 2019).

Tür. Ö. (2009) 'Turkey, Working-class Protest, 1960–1980', *The International Encyclopedia of Revolution and Protest*, 7, 3350–4, doi:10.1002/9781405198073.wbierp1487).

Vanek, J. (1971) *The Participatory Economy: An Evolutionary Hypothesis and a Strategy for Devolopment*, New York: Cornell University Press.

Yeğin, M. (2015) *Patronsuzlar*, Second edn, Istanbul: Öteki Yayınevi.

Yeşilbaş, G. (Director) (2002) *Bir Uygarlık Öyküsü: Sanayi*, Documentary.

Yıldırım, B. (2014) *Sanki Devrim Bir Devrim Gezi'sinden Notlar*, First edn, Ankara: Notabene Yayınları.

Interviews

Interview 1 (2016). Interview with K. Worker of Diren Kazova Cooperative, Date: 24 September 2016.

Interview 2 (2017). Interview with S.G. Worker of Özgür Kazova Collective, Date: 25 April 2017.

13

Organised Workers' Struggles Under Neoliberalism: Unions, Capital and the State in Turkey

Çağatay Edgücan Şahin

13.1 INTRODUCTION

This chapter aims to discuss the interrelations between the state, capital and unions in the neoliberal era in Turkey with a specific focus on the 2000s. The discussion will be based on the changing material condition of the working class in Turkey and its various effects on the bargaining power of the organised labour. The chapter aims to make sense, analyse and underline the possibilities and limitations of the organised labour movement in Turkey through the discussion pursued. Conceptual framework broadly draws upon Erik Olin Wright's types of 'working class power' (2000) and Beverly Silver's (2003) distinction of Polanyi-type and Marx-type labour movements. The chapter provides a general overview rather than a systematic empirical investigation; however, some findings obtained from face-to-face semi-structured interviews will be used for the understanding of the condition of unions and working class in contemporary Turkey.

13.2 AN OVERVIEW OF THE CHANGING MATERIAL CONDITIONS OF ORGANISED LABOUR UNDER NEOLIBERALISM

To analyse the capacity of the union movement and the complex relations between unions, capital and the state in the neoliberal era, several macro-level dynamics which have direct effects on unionism and the labour movement should be highlighted. These could be discussed in terms of state-union relationships and the overall structure of labour markets. For the former, first of all, it is safe to argue that a significant characteristic of union-government relationships is that they are increasingly based on a corporatist philosophy under the AKP rule. This corporatist relationship is complemented with various authoritarian strategies such as union busting aiming at deunionisation and strike bans and executive authority's position against the strikes in an increasing number of sectors. The negative effects of the time-consuming judicial procedure of labour court cases on unionised workers is another obstacle.

The latter aspect is the structure of the labour markets, as mentioned. A significant rate of informal employment standing at 34.52 per cent as of 2019 (SGK, 2020) is combined with high levels of unemployment, especially for the youth. Moreover, long working hours are observed as one in three workers are working over 50 hours a week on average in 2019. Apart from these, widespread precarious employment and subcontracted work are drawing attention. Concomitantly, in recent years, there has been an expanding reserve army of cheap and precarious irregular migrant workers; however, mainstream unions either remained inefficient or did not show any willingness to organise them. Finally, the overall effects of the Covid-19 pandemic on industrial relations and labour markets is yet to be seen and will be significant.

These neoliberal labour market dynamics have gradually developed in the last 40 years, and they were of vital importance for the establishment of a capital-friendly investment environment. For the organised labour and unions, this era can be analysed under three sub-periods: the 1980–89/91 period is a restructuring process of industrial relations under the capital-oriented logic of neoliberalism. The labouring classes, namely private sector workers, public workers, civil servants and some peasants, experienced significant income losses as manifested in the share of labour in GDP during this period. The local elections in 1989 marks the beginning of the process that brought an end to the right-wing single-party rule of ANAP, as the voting share of this party decreased to 21 per cent. Finally, with the

1991 general elections, ANAP lost elections to the opposition parties (Nişancı, 2006: 125). Despite revitalisation of organised labour in the late 1980s, the overall key features of the 1980–89/91 period are the depoliticisation process experienced with the military coup and the elimination of politicised generations of the working class in various ways and their replacement with rural-oriented, first generation migrant workers in industrial cities.

The crisis-ridden late 1990s and early 2000s neoliberal agenda was concentrated, among other things, on privatisation of big scale state-owned enterprises. Under IMF conditionality, coalition governments aimed to implement privatisation, which steadily caused more unemployment. Against this, unions mostly pursued a 'legal' strategy – taking privatisation implementations to the courts, to defend primarily rights of their members only via lobbying in the capital city Ankara, while taking advantage of wage increases as a result of 'a number of cracks' among the ruling class. While the 1980–2002 period can be called an establishment of neoliberal policies under unstable conditions especially in the 1990s, the post-2002 period saw the intensification of neoliberal policies, and can be called the 'mature' phase of neoliberalism (Bahçe and Köse, 2016).

Indeed, these cracks have been gradually eliminated after 2002 with a single-party rule under the AKP, and the two biggest union confederations transformed into 'ideological state apparatuses', thus the organised working-class movement became paralysed. Through various processes and changes such as 'the unions and collective bargaining law' of 2012, the state of emergency rule between 2016 and 2018, and finally, with the presidential regime in 2018, the apparatus position of the unions has been consolidated. 2020s Turkey can be described as a country which is dominated by business logic and its manifestations[1] at all levels, such as a rise of indirect taxes and tax amnesties for the rich, further commodification of labour and jobless growth. This logic is also compatible with decreasing real wages, a rapid proletarianisation of small-scale farmers while agricultural firms becoming more profitable (see Orhangazi, 2019), late retirement, high unemployment especially for the youth, rise of business unionism and inter-union competition, widespread poverty and indebtedness experienced by the working class (Koç, 2019: 507–11).

After this general framework on the material conditions of the working class, what follows is a discussion of the notion of the 'power of the working class', with reference to Turkey, in order to conceptualise resistance tendencies against this 'material condition'.

13.2.1 The Power of the Working Class

According to Wright (2000: 962), working-class power can be analysed in two concepts; associational power and structural power. The associational power refers to various forms of power that result from the formation of collective organisations of workers, such as unions, political parties, works councils. However, the concept of structural power refers to a power that results simply from the location of workers within the economic system. Wright states two determinants of structural power as follows: (1) the power of workers as individuals that results directly from tight labour markets, and (2) from the strategic location of a particular group of workers within a key industrial sector. Silver (2003: 13) develops Wright's approach further and describes three main forms of marketplace bargaining power: (1) the possession of scarce skills that are in demand by employers, (2) low levels of general unemployment, and (3) the ability of workers to pull out of the labour.

In order to have a picture of the bargaining power of the working class in Turkey, an analysis of the main labour market indicators would be useful. Without doubt, the possession of scarce skills that are in demand by employers varies between workers, and between industries. As a general observation, the low level of general unemployment rate which leads to marketplace bargaining power of the working class does not exist for Turkey. Indeed, the unemployment rate of Turkey was 12.8 per cent as of July 2020, with a striking 27.1 per cent youth unemployment rate in 2019. While the employment rate decreases to 41.1 per cent, the unemployment rate actualised as 12.8 per cent, the broad definition of unemployment rate was 23.1 per cent, and youth unemployment was 24.4 per cent by July 2020.

Another important aspect, the ability of workers to pull out of the labour, should be analysed with reference to the alternative income sources such as interest income, rent, stock ownerships or small-scale land-based revenues. While 42 per cent of workers are employed at minimum wage level, and 34 per cent of the population receives social assistance (DW, 2020), household saving rates dropped from 17.5 per cent in 2003 to 6.6 percent in 2012 (Tunç and Yavaş 2016; Özsan et al. 2017). Considered with the rapid dispossession of small-scale farmers in the 2010s, it is hard to argue that labourers in Turkey have a chance to pull out of their labour from the market. To sum up, a large proportion of the working class in Turkey does not have an advantageous position in terms of structural bargaining power. This picture has direct effects on all sides of industrial relations, which will be discussed below.

13.3 THE STATE AND THE UNIONS

The society has been designed from top to bottom via the military coup of 1980, which also paved the way for neoliberal policies in Turkey. As a part of this design, the Constitution and also the legislations on unions were changed by the military junta. Thus, the collective bargaining Law No. 275 was replaced by Law No. 2822 in 1983, and the collective bargaining regime has been transformed in order to accelerate capital accumulation by abolishing fundamental struggle tools of unions, such as unions' right to strike due to employers' abrogation of the collective agreement (Talas, 1992: 295–6). Besides, the unions needed to gain a simple majority of the workers in the workplace (50 per cent + 1 worker), they were also obliged to organise 10 per cent[2] of all workers in a specific branch of activity with Law No. 2822. These changes are supported with the postponement of strikes by statutory decrees[3] and strike vote etc. so the bargaining power of unions diminished significantly. Since there is no mechanism to continue a postponed strike other than applying to the High Board of Arbitration to solve disputes, these postponements can be considered de facto strike bans. These are the most common ways of the state's direct intervention in the industrial relations system in favour of capital in Turkey.

Apart from its traditional regulatory role in industrial relations, the state has an employer role in Turkey both in the service sector and various industries, despite its gradual withdrawal from this role via privatisations since the 1980s. For this reason, the emphasis on a coherence between union administration and various governments in terms of political orientation 'operates as a key' to success in organising in the public entities. These 'success stories' have become more visible than ever under the AKP governments since 2002, as can be seen in Table 13.1. The main dynamics of these developments could be understood within the context of the concept of corporatism, which constitutes one of the peculiarities of the mainstream unionism in Turkey (see Büyükuslu, 1994: 48–60, 103–18). These dynamics led to debates about the concept of 'ideologically compatible unions', especially in the last two decades in Turkey.

The concept of 'ideologically compatible union' refers to a union which acts in line with the ruling political power. The cases of main union confederations provide excellent examples for this. Following the military coup of 1980, two right-wing confederations, TÜRK-İŞ and HAK-İŞ,[4] continued to organise and become stronger, with very good relations with the military junta. Sadık Şide, who was the general secretary of TÜRK-İŞ at the time, has become the minister of social security of the military junta government just after nine days of the coup. However, the radical left-wing DİSK Confederation was dissolved for eleven years; and its managers arrested, properties confiscated, and its ongoing strikes ended by force. The former DİSK members had to organise under the TÜRK-İŞ unions in the 1980s, because only these unions had the authority to sign collective agreements.

The TÜRK-İŞ unions are traditionally organised in public entities (SOEs) since its foundation in 1952, thus its administration developed 'an organic relationship' (Akalın, 1995: 5–3; Baydar, 1998: 16) with the governments, in their administrator's own words. However, TÜRK-İŞ's position on the coup did not prevent destructive effects for the organised labour movement in Turkey. TÜRK-İŞ unions were also affected by deunionisation in the mid-1990s and especially in the 2000s with massive privatisation waves under the AKP rule. When the AKP came into power in November 2002, it also established an 'organic relationship' with the HAK-İŞ Confederation, and HAK-İŞ competed with TÜRK-İŞ and DİSK. Table 13.1 shows the change in the number of the union members for the biggest three confederations since the year 2000, both for the public and private sectors.

According to the data shown in Table 13.1, it can be stated that the working class in Turkey is widely deunionised under neoliberalism. We can also state that, while the subject of ideologically compatible union changes, the clientelist relationship remains as another peculiarity of mainstream unionism in Turkey. This could be observed from the gradual shift from TÜRK-İŞ to HAK-İŞ, while the total number of union members decreased since 2002. There is also a phenomenal jump in civil servant union confederations, from KAMU-SEN and KESK to MEMUR-SEN during the AKP era. While the total number of civil servants has increased only about 188 per cent from 2002 to 2019, the MEMUR-SEN has increased its members by a striking 2435 per cent in the same era. Under the harsh conditions of neoliberalism such as high unemployment, precarity and indebtedness of labour, this unique phenomenon can be best understood by the concepts of clientelism and ideological compatibleness.[5]

Despite this negative outlook, there are mobilisations against public employers or subcontractors of the state. For instance, the TEKEL workers forced their union Tek-Gıda-İş (member of TÜRK-İŞ) into 78 days of industrial action in the capital city Ankara,[6] setting up tents in the streets between November 2009 and February 2010 to keep their existing rights. Turkish Airlines' workers went on strike in 2013 with Hava-İş Union (member of TÜRK-İŞ) to protect their wage levels and establish better working conditions. Türkiye Denizciler Sendikası (member of TÜRK-İŞ), a sailor's union, organised in maritime transportation which had not taken strike action for 66 years, initiated a strike in Izmir ports in 2017, interrupting intercity ferry services (T24, 2017). In 2018, 401 workers, organised by Dev-Yapı-İş Union (member of DİSK) and independent and militant İnşaat-İş Union, organised an industrial action to end inhumane labour practices at the construction site of the new İstanbul Airport (operational since 6 April 2019). The construction of the airport was subcontracted by the state to Kalyon – Cengiz – Mapa – Limak Joint Venture (see Bianet, 2020). The airport is considered to be a symbol of Turkey's rising regional capitalist power status. It also manifests neoliberalism-cum-cronyism through ongoing connections of

Table 13.1 Changes in Population and Confederation Members: 1980–2019/20

Year	Population	Employment	Union Members (Workers)	TÜRK-İŞ	DİSK**	HAK-İŞ	Total Civil Servants	Union Members (Civil Servants)	KAMU-SEN**	KESK**	MEMUR-SEN**
1980*	44 736 937	18 522 000	5 721 074* / 1 500 000	1 100 000*	300 000*	135 000*	1 170 224	–	–	–	–
1990	56 473 035	18 539 000	1 997 564	1 567 501	–	189 090	1 542 433	–	–	–	–
2002	65 022 300	20 584 000	2 717 326	1 915 560	368 505	302 804	1 357 326	650 770	329 065	262 348	41 871
2009	72 561 312	21 277 000	3 232 679	2 239 341	426 232	431 550	1 767 737	1 023 362	375 990	224 413	376 355
2019 & 2020	83 154 997 (2019)	25 614 000 (2020)	1 946 165 (2020)***	1 021 952 (2020)	190 659 (2020)	687 790 (2020)	2 549 094 (2019)	1 702 644 (2019)	413 339 (2019)	137 606 (2019)	1 019 853 (2019)

Source: Data collected by the author from official data of various years.

Notes:

*Since the workers can be a member of more than one union at the same time, and due to lack of a central database at the Ministry of Social Security back in 1980, the total number of unionised workers is lower than stated. However, there are studies that roundly calculate the number as 1.5 million (see Koç, 2019: 372–3).

**The KAMU-SEN was founded in 1992, KESK and MEMUR-SEN were founded in 1995. DİSK reopened in 1992.

***Around 727,000 of these workers, roughly 39 per cent, are not covered by a collective agreement (DİSK-AR, 2020).

the biggest contractors with the regime. However, this process also showed the limits of the regime's ability to turn unions into its loyal partners, as manufacturing workers' consent is becoming more difficult especially under the harsh economic conditions. When the rank-and-file workers push the unions to actions to defend rights, even the most bureaucratic ones mobilise.

13.4 CAPITAL AND UNIONS

The capitalists also have a right to be unionised in Turkey; with examples including the Turkish Textile Employer's Union (TTSİS) in the textile industry and the Turkish Employers Association of Metal Industries (MESS) in the metal industry. The Turkish Confederation of Employer Associations (TİSK) is the only confederation which represents employer's unions. As observed elsewhere, the capitalist class of Turkey has differing interests, which compete with each other but also unify around common interests from time to time. As such, since the 1970s, there have been prominent common interests of capitalist classes of Turkey. These interests can be summarised as (Koç, 2019: 395): (1) flexibility at all levels; (2) regular tax breaks; (3) regionally based minimum wage rather than nationally based; (4) productivity-based wage increases; (5) resolution of disputes through labour courts rather than strikes after the collective labour agreement process; (6) high board of arbitration for postponed strikes; (7) sectoral threshold for the unions; (8) increased retirement age; and finally (9) a fund-based seniority indemnity system, rather than one month's pay for one year's labour at the same workplace. The capitalists achieved seven of these interests in the post-1980 coup era. For the remaining ones, a de facto regionally based minimum wage is implemented in various regions, and transforming seniority indemnity system to a fund is currently on the agenda of the AKP government. On the other hand, one major competing interest between capitalist classes is the proportional distribution of public incentives between different fractions of capital.

Looking closely at the relations between capital and unions, the phenomenon of ideological compatibleness as a problem solver arises again. Even though there are exceptions such as the metal and cement industries, in which companies pursue a de facto union shop policy, the employers in Turkey generally try to keep workers unorganised through violation of various rights and various union busting strategies such as changing the branch of activity to deunionise workers, objecting to the threshold and re-enumerating the number of workers by appealing to the labour court (Şahin & Tepe, 2018), employing illegal migrants, and finally blacklisting policy since the 1970s. Blacklisting is a long-established tradition of the capitalist class in Turkey. For example, the MESS created and mimeographed 335 pages and two volumes of 'workers on strike list' in 1980 (Akkaya, 2002: 84). The employers also take advantage of the time-consuming judicial procedures during the union's authorisation process. For example, between 1983 and 2009 the employers busted the unions during the lawsuit, which lasted an average of 424 days (Birelma, 2018: 4). Thus, these cases became a part of the daily routine of the industrial relations system in Turkey.

The complex relationships between the capital and unions of the 'new Turkey' become crystal clear when a labour dispute occurs at critical industries for the capital accumulation regime. These include the metal sector (which also includes the auto industry and durable goods) or the mega-scale infrastructure projects under public-private partnership, such as multibillion transport investments including a new bridge over the Bosphorus and the new İstanbul Airport. For instance, on 14 September 2018, 401 striking workers at İstanbul Airport issued a list of basic demands, including improved safety measures, more shuttle buses, better living conditions, stopping unfair dismissal of striking workers and payment of delayed wages. While the Dev-Yapı-İş Union (member of DİSK) has played a role in the industrial action, the protests were forcefully suppressed, the workers were detained by the police, and they were transported to the police stations by the buses of subcontractor companies (Bilgiç & Ersoy, 2018; Koca & Dikmen, 2018; Garner-Purkis, 2019).

If it is not possible to prevent unionisation, or if the employers need another oppressor force to discipline workers, then they welcome ideologically compatible unions to their company. In this context, one other major case is the '2015 Wave of Strikes' in the metal industry, or 'the metal storm' in automobile, durable goods and accessories industries. There is a status quo in the metal industry which has been established under the leadership of the biggest union, Türk Metal (member of TÜRK-İŞ). It has been challenged several times, and the 2015 Metal Storm constituted the last and the largest case to state the structural problems inherent in the sector. It was a wave of wildcat strikes against the status quo of low wages, aggravated working conditions, and Türk Metal's authoritarian, bureaucratic, centralised, oligarchic and pro-employer union mentality of unionism.

This emergence of strikes and protests in May 2015 in leading automotive companies of Turkey was due to the reaction of workers against the three-year collective agreements concluded between Türk Metal and MESS. The most crucial development during the process that triggered the unrest was the separate collective bargaining agreement concluded between Türk Metal and MESS in the Bosch factory in Bursa. The Bosch factory was the subject of an ongoing dispute since 2012 as 3500 workers who had resigned from Türk Metal became members of Birleşik Metal-İş (member of DİSK) in the same factory. However, a considerable number of workers turned back to Türk Metal as a result of the pressure from the employer and Türk Metal. The legal dispute could not be resolved for years. Eventually, a group collective agreement in the metal industry was concluded between Türk Metal and MESS in December 2014, then a more satisfying collective agreement signed in Bosch a few months after, in April 2015, due to the delay of the agreement and also to prevent workers from joining Birleşik Metal again. The agreement caused around 500 lira difference per month in favour of Bosch Inc. workers. The remaining workers in the industry demanded the same rights as Bosch workers. In addition to their request for a wage rise, the workers also requested the basics of workplace democracy; free choice of unions, abandonment of Türk Metal from their workplaces, and the ability to choose their own shop stewards freely. After the workers' demands regarding the implementation of the Bosch collective agreement were refused, they began to resist by leaving work in the biggest automotive factories of Turkey; Renault, Ford and Tofaş (Fiat-Chrysler). As the protests escalated to other major factories of the country, a group allegedly affiliated to Türk Metal attacked the insurgent workers who resigned from the union by claiming that there were provocateurs among the workers. This attack helped spread the workers' resistance against union-capital collaboration (Çelik 2015; Taştekin, 2019).

While the strike wave escalated, the employers followed a pattern of actions against the workers' demands: first 'wait and see', then 'using the tools of oppression'. The Human Resources Directorate of Tofaş auto factory announced a statement on 9 May and declared its decision 'not to improve the group collective agreements', and employers became harsher against the workers. The statement accused the workers of 'harming industrial peace' and indicated that the company would have 'taken necessary precautions', i.e. mass layoffs, if the protests were not stopped. Especially after the decision of the High Board of Arbitration, employers and their organisations such as TİSK, MESS and Automotive Industrialists Association (AIA) made recurrent declarations during the resistance which insistently labelled the resistance illegal and the strike unlawful, since Turkey's labour legislation defines only one legal type of strike: 'interest' strikes following the disagreement during the collective bargaining process. However, peaceful resistances and work stoppages are the fundamental rights guaranteed by the ILO (International Labour Organization) conventions, which are also ratified by Turkey. On 14 May, a message was sent to the workers' mobile phones in the morning by MESS and it was stated that the group collective agreement would be valid and binding for Türk Metal and MESS for three years. With this message, the employer tried to curtail the hopes to amend the contract and to halt the workers' attempts, but the message triggered a new phase in the struggle of workers. Hence, it is difficult to argue that the arguments of the union and employers persuaded workers (Çelik, 2015; Korkmaz, 2015; Koç, 2019: 568–9; Taştekin, 2019: 65–73). To sum up, movements of unionised workers against both their union and employers started as a reaction to their union's awkward bureaucracy and passiveness. The resistance of metal workers is the peak of this kind of resistance (Çelik, 2015: 14).

13.5 WORKING CLASS AND THE UNIONS

The established order of unions in Turkey has its own peculiarities, in terms of their relationships with each other and the rank-and-file workers. Hence, some weaknesses and strengths of the established order should be underlined to grasp the potential of current union movement, and organised labour. Firstly, for the weaknesses, it is important to emphasise that the rate of unionisation and the collective bargaining coverage in Turkey are the worst among the OECD countries, 11.4 percent and 7 percent, respectively (OECD, 2017, 2018). Secondly, yellow unionism is a common phenomenon in Turkey in almost all branches of activities, and yellow unions work as a centre of oppression on the workers. Thirdly, unions in Turkey are mainly male-dominated organisations.[7] Fourthly, union bureaucracy and decades-long leadership are common in most cases, which leads to various problems such as nepotism in union management and corruption.

On the other hand, two strengths can be underlined. The first is related to the capability of a grassroots working-class mobilisation which has the potential to limit or destabilise the political power, as observed in various cases in the neoliberal era. These include the April 1989 'Spring Mobilisation', January 1991 General Strike and Miners March, November 2009–February 2010 TEKEL Struggle, and June 2013 Gezi Uprisings. Second, strength is related to the newly established and promising rank-and-file unions and escalating worker militancy, despite all preventive efforts and oppression from all three actors of the industrial relations system: state, capital and ideologically compatible or yellow unions.

Against the background of these weaknesses and potential strengths, the union movement in Turkey could be analysed under two main dynamics such as struggles against privatisation of state economic enterprises such as PETKİM (petrochemicals), SEKA (cellulose paper), TEKEL (tobacco and alcoholic beverages), TÜRKŞEKER (sugar and alcohol) cases, and struggles against various private companies. However, both struggles have a common tendency in terms of protecting pre-existing rights and mostly occur in big-scaled enterprises. Silver (2003: 18) categorises these unrests as Polanyi-type labour unrests, to the extent that they are backlash resistances against the spread of a global self-regulating market. These unrests are particularly developed by working classes that suffer from the global economic transformations as well as by those workers who had benefited from previously established social compacts that are being abandoned from above.

2000s neoliberalism gradually decreased the capabilities of unions to pursue struggles via state interventions: (1) postponement of legal strikes by the government based on 'national security' as an ongoing strategy since the 1980s; (2) widening strike prohibitions by law, such as aviation in 2012 and the banking and transportation sector in metropolitan municipalities since November 2016; and (3) oppression worker revolts by force. The existence of ideologically compatible unions with the capital and the state makes things worse. There are several major unsuccessful industrial actions reflecting the co-opted position of ideologically compatible unions in Turkey – some of them even ended with great losses for workers. For instance, in 2009, a collective labour agreement signed by Türk Metal (member of TÜRK-İŞ) and Çelik-İş (member of HAK-İŞ) for the two biggest integrated steel plants in Turkey, respectively, Erdemir Inc. and İsdemir Inc. As a rather unexpected result of this collective agreement, wages decreased by 35 per cent for 16 months. Union leaders stated that this was necessary to prevent layoffs during the crisis (Radikal, 2009). These agreements are considered a source of shame for Turkish labour history, and also made an example of 'unique shades of yellow unionism', which preferred to sign such an agreement, rather than resisting with the workers against layoff threats by employers. Another striking example of this type of unionism is Şeker-İş Union (member of TÜRK-İŞ). In 2018, Şeker-İş decided to organise a collective protest against the government's attempt to privatise 25 sugar factories in Turkey. In a very strange move, the union protested the government *by working an additional two hours for a month with no compensation* (Evrensel, 2016), rather than organising a more radical protest or a wave of token strikes etc. in all 25 factories.

Another characteristic of unionism in Turkey, inter-union competition, makes things worse. The transportation industry, for instance, has striking examples of inter-union competition. The following quote is taken from an interview with the public relations specialist of Demiryol-İş Union (member of TÜRK-İŞ) in 2017:

Demiryol-İş Union signed six collective labour agreements in a row in Konya Metropolitan Municipality. While the last one was still in operation workers were transferred to Öz Taşıma-İş Union (member of HAK-İŞ), thus there was a contract, but there were no workers to benefit from it ... In another case the employer registered its enterprise in the food industry branch to defeat the union organisation, but actually it is in logistics. (Interview No. 1)

When the unions move away from the essentials of unionism, some workers may experience discouragement and act rather selfishly, while some others become more militant. There are interesting cases in unionisation which we can associate with the term corrosion. For instance, some workers choose the most challenging union in logistics 'Nakliyat-İş' (member of DİSK) for some other reasons. The union's leader summarises these other reasons:

When a worker calls to union and says 'please inform the employer that I am a member of your union', which is not normal at all until we have the majority at the workplace, then we see an opportunist who tries to get a legal compensation from his near future firing because of unionisation! This type of worker behaviour has become frequent in the industry, especially in recent years ... (Interview No. 2)

However, there are also promising developments for the future of the working class in Turkey. Establishing union alliances under the name of platform unionism such as the Labour Platform (1999–2008) was an important experience. Novamed Strike (2006–08), which was the first strike in a free-trade area conducted by Petrol-İş Union's (member of TÜRK-İŞ) women workers, ended up with a collective labour agreement. In recent years, Plaza Workers Action Platform (since 2008, unionisation at IBM), and rising numbers of independent unions and increasing worker militancy such as Tomis Union (independent, automotive industry, 'Metal Storm'), İnşaat-İş Union (independent, construction, 'İstanbul Airport Resistance'), Bağımsız-Maden-İş (independent, mining, 'Soma Resistance') created significant moments of resistance and drew the attention of the wider public. These unions and many others are organised by rank-and-file workers, as a result of the escalating tension between the official union structure and the workers, and also showed the fragile structure of bureaucratic unions.

Other important waves of worker actions are pursued by the migrant workers, which set good examples for Marx-type labour unrest, discussed by Silver (2003: 20) as 'the struggles of newly emerging working classes that are successively made and strengthened as an unintended outcome of the development of historical capitalism, even as old working classes are being unmade'. Indeed, the shoe-uppers (saya) workers resisted against harsh working conditions, low pay and child labour which are the core components of the industry. Since most of the Syrian shoe-upper workers do not have work permits, they established committees and associations along with the local workers, struggled together in 2012, 2017, and finally in 2019 for 50 per cent wage increases, to ban child labour in the industry, and to decrease the workday which was up to 17 hours. All these struggles have ended in success.

13.6 CONCLUSION

As demonstrated in this chapter, unionised workers constitute a small proportion of the working class in Turkey. Atomisation and the lack of organisation of labour can be considered both cause and effect of flexibility, indebtedness and precariousness in the labour process, which undermines the power of the unions. Even though the reasons for the weaknesses of union organisation in Turkey have been established by direct and indirect interventions of the state to promote capital accumulation, the position of ideologically compatible unions which eschew the struggle made the problems greater for the working class in Turkey. Mainstream unionism has problems with union bureaucracy, corporatism as an inherent tendency, clientelism, yellow unionism, ignoring migrant workers and a male-dominated structure, and these characteristics do not help in solving working-class problems that have become more visible with the economic woes since 2018 and during the Covid-19 pandemic. While the mainstream unions remain within the legal framework, a rising number of worker unrests, some of which ended with success, demonstrate the limits of the mainstream unions.

The organised worker struggles across industries, as happened in 1989, 1991, 2009/10 and 2013, caused instabilities at the state level. Since worker struggles have the potential to destabilise political power, it is not surprising that the governments want to neutralise worker movements or take them under control. With change in political power in the biggest metropolitan municipalities in 2019, new cracks occurred in the ruling classes and the determining power of the government over the unions would potentially diminish. Yet, we should note that there is no unified struggle for atomised and unorganised working class in Turkey, which would be essential to counterbalance the neoliberal policies of the last four decades. As Erol noted in 2019, the AKP enjoyed significant support from the working class and urban poor with the help of specific and mostly successful economic and political containment strategies, including ideological manipulations via controlled media that helped shift the focus away from economic and class issues and contradictions to identity-based issues. However, economic recession and decreasing purchasing power, rising tax burden via indirect taxes and rising inequality in income distribution, wastage and corruption debates in society, and thriving militant unionism create a solid base for new worker struggles.

BIBLIOGRAPHY

Akalın, İ. (1995) *DİSK: Kısa Tarih (1960–1980)*, Ankara: Öteki Yayınevi.
Akkaya, Y. (2002) 'Türkiye'de İşçi Sınıfı ve Sendikacılık – II', *Praksis*, 6, 63–101.
Bahçe, S. and Köse, A.H. (2016) 'Financialisation/Borrowing Circle as a Solution to an Unpleasant Conundrum: Observations from the Mature Neoliberalism in Turkey', *Research and Policy on Turkey*, 1 (1), 63–74.
Baydar, O. (1998) *Türkiye'de Sendikacılık Hareketi*, İstanbul: Friedrich Ebert Stiftung.
Bianet (2020) 'Public Tenders Won by Pro-government Companies Exceed Turkey's 2020 Budget', *Bianet*, https://tinyurl.com/yuuxxwnp (accessed 10 November 2020).

Bilgiç, T. and Ersoy, E. (2018) 'Turkey Security Forces Quash Airport Protest, Detain Workers', *Bloomberg*, 17 September 2018, https://tinyurl.com/y8834qm4 (accessed 10 June 2019).

Birelma, A. (2018) *Trade Unions in Turkey 2018*, Berlin: Friedrich Ebert Stiftung.

Büyükuslu, A.R. (1994) *Trade Unions in Turkey: An Analysis of Their Development, Role and Present Situation*, Thesis Submitted for the Degree of PhD at the University of Warwick, November 1994, http://wrap.warwick.ac.uk/53866/ (accessed 10 June 2016).

Çelik, A. (2013) *A General Evaluation of Turkey's New Act on Trade Unions and Collective Agreements*, Friedrich-Ebert-Stiftung, https://tinyurl.com/y26ztf46 (accessed 15 August 2017).

—— (2015) 'The Wave of Strikes and Resistances of the Metal Workers of 2015 in Turkey', IV (10), London: Centre for Policy and Research on Turkey, 21–37.

DİSK-AR (2020) *Covid-19 Salgını Günlerinde Türkiye'de Sendikalaşmanın Durumu Araştırması*, Türkiye Devrimci İşçi Sendikaları Konfederasyonu Araştırma Dairesi, https://tinyurl.com/y5256whd (accessed 16 May 2020).

Duran, B. and Yıldırım, E. (2005) 'Islamism, Trade Unionism and Civil Society: The Case of Hak-İş Labour Confederation in Turkey', *Middle Eastern Studies*, 41 (2), 227–47.

DW (Deutsche Welle) (2020) 'Türkiye'nin Yüzde 34'ü Sosyal Yardım Aldı', https://tinyurl.com/y8zowmx8 (accessed 10 July 2020).

Erol, M.E. (2019) 'State and Labour under AKP Rule in Turkey: An Appraisal', *Journal of Balkan and Near Eastern Studies*, 21 (6), 663–77.

Evrensel (2016) 'Şeker-İş'ten "Eylem": İşçiler 2 Saat Ücretsiz Çalışacak', 29 April 2016, https://tinyurl.com/y64od4k9 (accessed 13 May 2017).

Garner-Purkis, Z. (2019) 'Life "in the Cemetery" – Uncovering Istanbul Airport's Dirty Secrets', *Construction News*, https://tinyurl.com/y6y4md6s (accessed 20 December 2019).

Koca, İ. and Dikmen, Y. (2018) 'Turkish Police Detain Hundreds of Protesting Airport Workers', *Reuters*, 15 September 2018, https://tinyurl.com/y6h83eww (accessed 10 July 2019).

Koç, Y. (2019) *Türkiye İşçi Sınıfı Tarihi Osmanlı'dan 2019'a*, İstanbul: Tek-Gıda-İş Sendikası Yayını.

Korkmaz, E.E. (2015) *Unexpected Wave of Strikes in Turkish Automotive Industry*, Friedrich-Ebert-Stiftung, https://tinyurl.com/yalureag (accessed 10 August 2018).

Nişancı, E. (2006) '1980 Sonrası Dönüşümde Devlet-Sermayedar İlişkilerinin Rolü Üzerine', *Toplum ve Bilim*,106, 110–36.

OECD (2017) 'Collective Bargaining Coverage Statistics, 2012–2016', https://tinyurl.com/yxvcr82w (accessed 10 August 2019).

——(2018) 'Trade Union Density Statistics, 2012–2017', https://tinyurl.com/yxvcr82w (accessed 10 August 2019).

Orhangazi, Ö. (2019) '2000'li Yıllarda Yapısal Dönüşüm ve Emeğin Durumu', *Çalışma ve Toplum*, 60, 325–48.

Özsan, A.G., Pektaş-Erdem, B. and Ata, S. (2017) 'Türkiye'de Yurt İçi Tasarrufların ve Tüketimin Gelişimi', https://tinyurl.com/y8sodbsw (accessed 10 March 2020).

Özuğurlu, M. (2011) 'The TEKEL Resistance Movement: Reminiscences on Class Struggle', *Capital & Class*, 35 (2), 179–87.

Radikal (2009) 'Ücrette Yüzde 35 İndirim Oldu, 1400 kişi Çalışmaya Devam Edecek', https://tinyurl.com/y5rvm3h7 (accessed 21 August 2016).

Reuters (2018) 'Turkey's Erdogan Says Emergency Rule Good for Economy as Stops Terrorism, Strikes', 21 April 2018, https://tinyurl.com/y565y89e (accessed 21 August 2019).

Şahin, Ç.E. and Tepe, P.B. (2018) 'Logistics Workers' Struggles in Turkey: Neoliberalism and Counterstrategies', in Ness, Immanuel and Alimahomed-Wilson, Jake (eds), *Choke Points Logistics Workers and Solidarity Movements Disrupting the Global Capitalist Supply Chain*, London: Pluto Press, 179–95.

SGK (2020) 'Kayıtdışı İstihdam Oranı', https://tinyurl.com/yykpu22w (accessed 20 April 2020).

Silver, B. (2003) *Forces of Labor: Workers' Movements and Globalization since 1870*, New York: Cambridge University Press.

T24 (2017) '66 Yıl Sonra Bir İlk: İzmir'de Deniz Ulaşımını Durduran Grev', https://tinyurl.com/y4qbm755 (accessed 12 July 2020).

Talas, C. (1992) *Türkiye'nin Açıklamalı Sosyal Politika Tarihi*, Ankara: Bilgi Yayınevi.

Taştekin, U. (2019) *The Metal Storm: 2015 Wave of Strikes in the Turkish Automotive Sector*, MA Thesis, The Department of Political Science and Public Administration. METU, http://etd.lib.metu.edu.tr/upload/12623543/index.pdf (accessed 20 January 2020).

Tunç, C. and Yavaş, A. (2016). 'Not All Credit Is Created Equal: Mortgage vs. Non-mortgage Debt and Private Saving Rate in Turkey', *Central Bank Review*, 16 (1), 25–32, https://tinyurl.com/y8ecueq8 (accessed 20 January 2020).

Urhan, B. (2014) *Sendikasız Kadınlar, Kadınsız Sendikalar: Sendika-Kadın İlişkisinde Görülen Sorun Alanlarını Belirlemeye Yönelik Bir Araştırma*, İstanbul: KADAV.
Wright, E.O. (2000) 'Working-class Power, Capitalist-class Interests, and Class Compromise', *American Journal of Sociology*, 105 (4), 957–1002.
Yalman, G.L. and Topal, A. (2017) 'Labour Containment Strategies and Working Class Struggles in the Neoliberal Era: The Case of TEKEL Workers in Turkey', *Critical Sociology*, 1–15, https://doi.org/10.1177/0896920517711489.

Interviews

Interview No. 1. 16 March 2017, Ankara.
Interview No. 2. 17 February 2017, İstanbul.

Notes

1. NOT-SO-STRANGE BEDFELLOWS: NEOLIBERALISM AND THE AKP IN TURKEY

1. With the outbreak of the Covid-19 pandemic which triggered a deep recession and showed the fragility of the 'free market' neoliberal political economy, this debate once again came to the fore (see Saad-Filho, 2020).
2. Shortly after the coup, a three-year standby agreement was signed with the IMF, and Turkey had five *Structural Adjustment Loans* from the World Bank in 1980–84 (Öniş and Webb, 1992: 27).
3. For instance, the cabinet formed after the 2018 elections was a 'cabinet of businessmen' as various capitalists were appointed to various ministerial posts.

2. TURKEY'S LABOUR MARKETS UNDER NEOLIBERALISM: AN OVERVIEW

1. For the details of this process see Öngen (2004: 82–5).
2. As a result, Turkish Lira loses value in nominal terms but it gains value in real terms. In this way a precondition for short-term capital inflow was created. This implementation is in accordance with the general preference of the international financial circles and institutions that do not want to face the risk of devaluation (Oyan, 1998: 27–8). The other essential part of the macroeconomic policy is about the real interest rate. It is necessary that the domestic interest gain is higher than the speculative foreign exchange earnings. A high interest, overvalued national currency spiral discourages fixed capital investments and exports (Yeldan, 2004: 135–6).
3. The ANAP government had to leave fiscal austerity, one of the most obvious political preferences. In 1989, public sector workers were given a 42 per cent raise. This was followed by civil servant hikes (Boratav, 2004: 175–6).
4. See data for OECD Data at https://data.oecd.org/emp/labour-force-participation-rate.htm (accessed 12 February 2017).
5. These assessments were made using the World Bank Open database.

6. According to the World Bank data, as of 2019, it is 13.7 per cent against 5.9 per cent.
7. Forcing resignation, asking for a resignation letter when starting work, taking the same worker out of work frequently and then hiring back, etc.
8. Pension reform is based on reducing the role of the state and conventional intergenerational income transfer. The redefined pay and go scheme aims to provide a basic income. More clearly living in prosperity in old age has become an individual responsibility (Oran, 2017: 51–2). As Oran has stated, 'this signifies a neoliberal paradigm shift within the pension provision from state to market and from social to individual' (2016: 35).
9. As a result of neoliberal policies, the states retreat from fields of healthcare, education, pensions. Due to the release of these fields to the market forces, the cost of reproducing labour power has increased. For the increased borrowing needs of workers and the 'financial expropriation' relationships they create see Soederberg (2014).

3. COMMODIFICATION AND CHANGING LABOUR IN TURKEY: THE WORKING CLASS IN THE PUBLIC SECTOR

1. The declaration of the former Minister of Labour Mehmet Müezzinoğlu on 27 October 2016, https://tinyurl.com/y4ardnhz (accessed 2 May 2020).
2. The analyses of professional labour and indirectly and directly social labour are based on Gouverneur (2005).
3. This draft law is associated with the US-based 'Great Middle East Project' by Güler (2005: 70).

4. NEOLIBERAL TRANSFORMATION OF TURKEY'S HEALTH SECTOR AND ITS EFFECTS ON THE HEALTH LABOUR FORCE

1. See Yenimahalleli-Yaşar (2011).
2. Official Gazette, Number: 29007, 22 May 2014.
3. See Kablay (2012) and Kablay (2014a) for the differences based on different employment models in the public sector.
4. Official Gazette, Number: 25178, 10 July 2003, 'Law on the Employment of Contracted Personnel Where Problems Occur During Recruitment and Modifications in Certain Laws and Decree'.

5. Official Gazette, Number: 25983, 20 October 2005, 'Law on the Employment of Contracted Personnel Where Problems Occur During Recruitment and Modifications in Certain Laws and Decree'.
6. See Chapter 11 for the condition of the working class during the Covid-19 pandemic.
7. WHO data: https://covid19.who.int/region/euro/country/tr (accessed June 2021).

5. BETWEEN NEOLIBERALISM AND CONSERVATISM: RECENT DEVELOPMENTS AND NEW AGENDAS IN FEMALE LABOUR POLICIES IN TURKEY

1. Indeed, with a presidential decree in March 2021, Turkey withdrew from the Istanbul Convention (The Council of Europe Convention on preventing and combating violence against women and domestic violence).

6. THE MAKING OF THE RURAL PROLETARIAT IN NEOLIBERAL TURKEY

1. Agricultural work is seen as 'female work' in Turkey as in most parts of the Global South. Since the 2000s, as a result of the massive male proletarianisation, female members of rural households started to maintain the agricultural production that was previously done by the whole family. Therefore, family farming which had historically been the dominant form of farming in the countryside of Turkey has become women's work in this period (for a detailed analysis see Çelik and Balta, 2017; Çelik, 2019).
2. For E.P. Thompson, as a historical category, class is derived from the observation of social process over time. Therefore, he conceptualises class as something which happens in human relationships (Thompson, 1963: 9; Thompson, 1978: 147). His analysis of 'class as a process and relationship' (Wood, 1995) explains class formation processes in inter-class and intra-class relations instead of mapping class locations.
3. Forced migration of the Kurdish population was due to skirmishes between Turkish security forces and the Kurdistan Workers Party (PKK) in southeastern provinces. The state announced State of Emergency Rule in 1987, following which forced migration was put into effect. The goal was to prevent providing money, shelter or food to the PKK from these villages. Thus, many Kurdish villages were evacuated, resulting in an immense wave of migration from eastern and southeastern provinces to western Turkey (Pelek, 2010; Yüksel, 2015).

7. BURDEN OR A SAVIOUR AT A TIME OF ECONOMIC CRISIS? AKP'S 'OPEN-DOOR MIGRATION POLICY' AND ITS IMPACT ON LABOUR MARKET RESTRUCTURING IN TURKEY

1. While informality is widespread within the garment industry, large-scale enterprises function under formal entities in which the working conditions and work relations are regulated and protected by law. Furthermore, these large-scale textile enterprises are often subcontracted by foreign companies, thus, also subject to scrutiny or inspections. In that sense, those enterprises hardly employ immigrants without working permits or underage workers. Nevertheless, there is no inspection mechanism that would detect those violations when those subcontractors further subcontract some parts of their production to the informal sweatshops where immigrant and child labour are employed.

8. SOCIAL ASSISTANCE AS A NON-WAGE INCOME FOR THE POOR IN TURKEY: WORK AND SUBSISTENCE PATTERNS OF SOCIAL ASSISTANCE RECIPIENT HOUSEHOLDS

1. Göçmen's (2014, 2018) works can be examined on this subject. Also see Kutlu (2015: 249–58).
2. Income test criteria are determined as one-third of the remaining part after the minimum subsistence allowance of one single worker is subtracted from monthly net minimum wage. It is reported to Social Assistance and Solidarity Foundations by the Ministry, Labour and Social Services.
3. Those who receive alimony or are able to receive.
4. Those who receive an allowance according to the Social Services Law No. 2828.
5. For similar findings, see Sallan-Gül and Gül (2006: 26–33).

9. A VIEW OF PRECARISATION FROM TURKEY: URBAN-RURAL DYNAMICS AND INTERGENERATIONAL PRECARITY

1. This chapter is based on research conducted for my PhD thesis: 'Precarity Experiences in the Working Class Map in Turkey' (Hacısalihoğlu, 2014).
2. One of the striking examples in these debates is Munck's argument (2013), which states that the type of work characterised by precarity is

anchored in the Global North whereas this type of work has always been the norm in the Global South. Through a similar perspective, Mitropoulos (2005) also points out that precarity is not a novel phenomenon: 'The experience of regular, full-time, long-term employment which characterised the most visible, mediated aspects of Fordism is an exception in capitalist history. That presupposed vast amounts of unpaid domestic labour by women and hyper-exploited labour in the colonies.'

3. For examples of the studies on this topic see Çerkezoğlu and Göztepe (2010: 67–95), Oğuz (2011), Özuğurlu (2011), Savran (2010), Yalman and Topal (2017).
4. The rural ties have continued in the city in a different form: through townsmanship, a relationship of communality and solidarity is constructed to ward off the harsh experience of precarity. However, studies dated after 2000 indicate that those relationships of communality and solidarity have weakened as well. For relevant studies, see Işık and Pınarcıoğlu (2011) and Suğur et al. (2010).
5. Based on the findings from a field study conducted in İstanbul, Özatalay (2016) also argues that the shared relationships between the employer and the worker such as kinship, townsmanship and ethnicity constitutes a feeling of trust. According to Özatalay, the avoidance of legal arrangements particularly in the informal sector leads to unpredictability for both sides. This mutual unpredictability creates insecurity for both parties. Hence, such relationships make it possible to achieve 'a common understanding based on trust' in the context of this insecurity (Özatalay (2016: 156–7).
6. In her book *Psychogeneology*, Ancelin-Schützenberger describes her client's participation in therapy as 'unpacking the locked baggage from the past in order to deal with the devastation caused by traumas, effects, consequences, possible outcomes, wounds, mistakes etc. of a bad family history' (2017: 5). While tracing precarity and intergenerational transmission, I was inspired by this description of Schützenberger to see what is transmitted from previous generations in the proleterianisation process as a locked baggage from the past.

10. WHEN THE LAW IS NOT ENOUGH: 'WORK ACCIDENTS', PROFIT MAXIMISATION AND THE UNWRITTEN RULES OF WORKER'S HEALTH AND SAFETY IN NEW TURKEY

1. In October 2014, the number of deadly work accidents with more than three deaths at the same time rose to 22 incidences.

2. It is stated in the İSGM Work Murders Report 2015 (first term) as follows: 'The common opinion of our council is all work accidents are preventable. We describe the given life events as capitalist "work murders" instead of "work accidents, destiny and natality" as being the most basic result of the opinion of death of workers are preventable.' See İSİG Council of Turkey (2015a).
3. The last SGK data available to the public is for the year 2018. However, the ISIG Council detected 1736 workers died at work accidents for the year 2019, and 732 more until May 2020. See ISIG (2020b) for related years' summary reports in English.
4. For instance, see Durmuş (2012): 'As we attach more importance to the law, many things will change automatically in the country.'
5. The pheonemenon of 'ideologically compatible unions' can be seen in almost all branch of activities.

11. ARE WE ALL IN THE SAME BOAT? COVID-19 AND THE WORKING CLASS IN TURKEY

1. The declaration of Covid-19 as a pandemic has had a deepening effect on the structural problems of neoliberal order, which could not eliminate the 'long stagnation' that has existed since 2008. Stock market declines that started on 19–20 February and the accompanying oil prices decline were not the worst, but only the first wave. The Saudi Arabia-Russia dispute, which marked the OPEC+ meeting held in the first week of March, triggered the new wave. On 20 April, it was recorded as a historical day when oil prices fell to negative numbers for the first time. The MSCI World Index, which measures the performance of global capital, fell by 34 per cent between 19 February and 23 March (Gökten, 2020).
2. It is applied if the weekly working hours in the workplace are reduced by at least a third because of general economic, sectoral, regional crisis or challenging reasons or if the activity stops completely or partially for at least four weeks. However, I limit the application that provides income support to companies for the period when they cannot work for their insured workers to three months. See İŞKUR (2020).
3. In May 2021, Covid was accepted as an occupational disease (CNNTURK, 2021). For the effects of Covid-19 on healthcare workers, see Chapter 4.
4. According to TurkStat's unemployment definition, a person must look for a job for the last four weeks to be considered unemployed. Because of the dismissal prohibitions implemented in conjunction with Covid-19, short-time working allowance and unpaid leave allowance are imple-

mented. These workers are considered to be in employment even though they do not work in the actual sense. Therefore, there is a difference between TurkStat data and DISK-AR data.

12. RECONSIDERING WORKERS' SELF-MANAGEMENT IN TURKEY: FROM RESISTANCE TO WORKERS' SELF-MANAGEMENT POSSIBILITIES/CONSTRAINTS

1. This chapter is broadly based on a revised and developed version of Erhan Acar's MA.thesis titled 'Çalışma Hayatında Özyönetim Deneyimleri: Kazova Örneği', under the supervision of Associate Professor. Berna Güler. The thesis was published as a book in Turkish by SAV Publications in 2019.
2. According to official records, the first workers' self-management experience in Turkey was by typesetting workers in September 1923. On the other hand, a different form of self-management is mentioned in the newspapers printed during the self-management experience of the typesetters. Between 1900 and 1901, press workers went on strike due to poor working conditions and non-payment of wages. As they could not get a result from the strike, they started printing their own newspapers by seizing the printing house against Abdul Hamid's oppressive regime (http://isikdahacokisik.blogspot.com.tr, accessed 27 August 2019).
3. These democratic mass organisations include Revolutionary Worker's Movement (Devrimci İşçi Hareketi), Contemporary Lawyer's Association (Çağdaş Hukukçular Derneği) and Legal Bureau of the People (Halkın Hukuk Bürosu). Among these organisations, ÇHD and HBB were closed down through Statutory Decrees No. 677 and 678 issued under the State of Emergency and published in the Official Gazette dated 22 November 2016. On 19 March 2019, 18 lawyers, members and administrators of ÇHD and HBB received a prison sentence for 159 years two months in total for 'commanding a terrorist organisation' (see Pişkin, 2019).
4. 'Hey Tekstil' workers started their resistance and demonstrations when the factory with 3000 workers declared its bankruptcy in 2012 and the workers were fired without their previous payments and rights given.
5. In 2014, Kazova Workers announced that they would be producing jerseys for Cuba and Basque Country football teams for the upcoming friendly game in Havana on 15 February 2014 (Söylemez, 2014).
6. See 'Cooperative Identity, Values & Principles', www.ica.coop/en/cooperatives/cooperative-identity (accessed 15 January 2020).

7. In the book *Patronsuzlar* written by the activist Metin Yeğin, the workers state that the trade union confederation in Uruguayan self-management experiences and MST (Landless Workers' Movement) in Brazil was the pioneer in the workers' self-management in these countries and that it is effective in the organised movement of the workers. Argentinean workers express themselves as 'self-managed'. In interviews with workers who produce in self-managed factories in these countries, it is stated that self-managed factories can be sustained in free-market conditions, especially through solidarity.

13. ORGANISED WORKERS' STRUGGLES UNDER NEOLIBERALISM: UNIONS, CAPITAL AND THE STATE IN TURKEY

1. In President Erdoğan's words on 15 March 2015; 'Turkey should be governed like a corporation.' As such, the minister of health, minister of education, minister of culture and tourism, minister of trade, minister of transport and infrastructure who are appointed following the 2018 elections either have a private sector background or are capital owners.
2. The threshold decreased to 1 per cent with Law No. 6356 in 2012. The unions shall carry out their activities in the branch activity of their establishment according to Article 3 and some of the branch activities have been combined with Law No. 6356. Thus, the number of branch activities is decreased from 28 to 20, and that caused an increase in the number of workers in these newly combined branches. Hence, some unions could not reach the new 1 per cent threshold, while they reached 10 per cent just before the regulation (see Şahin & Tepe, 2018).
3. As Çelik (2013: 6) stated: 'For example strikes in the tire and glass industries were postponed for national security reasons. What is more, the new law in 2012 – 6356 – abolishes the possibility of judicial appeal, which existed with the old law. While the old law contained a provision making it possible to appeal to the supreme court against the postponement decree, the new law does not. In this way, strike postponement turns into a strike ban.' The state of emergency also served to strike bans with decrees (see Reuters, 2018; Koç, 2019: 567).
4. HAK-İŞ has an Islamic political orientation, and promotes cooperation between classes (see Baydar, 1998: 18; Akkaya, 2002: 82; Duran & Yıldırım, 2005).
5. MEMUR-SEN is a pro-government union confederation which promotes social unionism.

6. For detailed analyses of the Tekel Workers Struggle see Özuğurlu (2011) and Yalman and Topal (2017).
7. According to the data obtained by official web pages of the biggest three Confederations by 2019: (1) TÜRK-İŞ has an all-male central executive committee, supreme boards, and regional and local representatives; (2) HAK-İŞ also has all-male central executive committee, supreme boards, and only two women presidents of the 81 cities, and 'a women committee'; (3) DİSK has a first and only woman general secretary, and she is also the only woman member of the executive committee. There is only one of five women on the disciplinary board, two of 31 on the board of presidents, and 19 of 148 on the broader board of presidents, yet none in the city and regional representatives. See Urhan's detailed qualitative study based on the data obtained by face-to-face, in-depth interviews (2014: 33–48), which shows the main determinants of the male-dominated structure of Turkish unions.

Contributors

Erhan Acar holds an MA in Labour Economics from Marmara University, Turkey. His research interests include social policy, workers' self-management, labour organisation and trade unions. He is the author of *Workers' Self Management Experiences in Labour Relations: The Case of Kazova* (SAV Publications, 2019, in Turkish).

Coşku Çelik is a Visiting Assistant Professor in the Department of Political Science at York University, Canada. She holds a PhD in Political Science from the Middle East Technical University. She has worked extensively on the extractive investments, rural transformation and patterns of proletarianisation in the countryside of Turkey. Her research interests broadly include feminist political economy, labour studies and political economy of the natural resource industries. Her current research addresses the relationship between extractive investments and transformation of women's productive and reproductive work in the Global South.

Ertan Erol is an Assistant Professor at Istanbul University, Faculty of Political Sciences. He holds an MA and a PhD in International Relations, both from the University of Nottingham, UK. His research interests are on critical international relations theory, comparative political economies of Mexico and Turkey, and Latin American politics. He was part of a research team that investigated migrant labour in the garment industry in Istanbul in 2017. He is the author of *Historical Sociology of Peripheral Capitalisms in Mexico and Turkey* (Tarih Vakfı Yurt Yayınları, 2020, in Turkish).

Mehmet Erman Erol is an Affiliated Lecturer at the University of Cambridge, Department of POLIS and a Postdoctoral By-Fellow at Churchill College, Cambridge. Previously he held a lecturer position at Ordu University, Turkey. He holds an MA in International Political Economy and a PhD in Politics, both from the University of York, UK. He has contributed to journals, books, political economy blogs and newspapers on the political economy of Turkey & Middle East.

Kerem Gökten is an Associate Professor at Ömer Halisdemir University, Turkey. He holds an MA in International Political Economy and a PhD in Economics, both from the Gazi University, Turkey. His research interests include globalisation and developing countries, China's transformation and

Contributors

labour studies. He is the author of *Understanding Chinese Century: China's Transformation from Opium Wars until Today* (NotaBene Publications, 2012, in Turkish).

Yeliz Sarıöz Gökten is an Associate Professor at Ömer Halisdemir University, Turkey. She holds an MA in Economic Theory and a PhD in Economics, both from the Gazi University, Turkey. Her research interests include hegemony, economic policy and labour studies. She is the author of *Past, Present and Future of Hegemonic Relations: A Neo-Gramscian Perspective* (NotaBene Publications, 2013, in Turkish).

Berna Güler is an Associate Professor in the Department of Labour Economics and Industrial Relations at Marmara University, Turkey. She is the author of *The Economics of Contract Manufacturing: Shoe Production in Gedikpaşa* (Bağlam Publications, 2005, in Turkish) and various articles. Her research interests include social change of modern Turkey, social policy, female labour politics, informal labour and trade unions.

Elif Hacısalihoğlu is an Assistant Professor in Labour Economics at Trakya University, Turkey. She holds an MA in Labour Economics from Marmara University, Turkey, and a PhD in Labour Economics from Ankara University, Faculty of Political Sciences, Turkey. Her research interests include precarity, unions and industrial relations.

Sebiha Kablay is a Professor in the Department of Labour Economics and Industrial Relations at Ordu University, Turkey. She holds a PhD in Labour Economics from Ankara University, Faculty of Political Sciences. Her research interests include neoliberalism and the transformation of the health sector and labour relations in the education sector, and child labour. She is the co-author of *Neoliberal Policies and Health Workers* (Nobel Publications, 2012, in Turkish).

Denizcan Kutlu is an Assistant Professor at Namık Kemal University, Turkey. He holds an MA and PhD in Labour Economics, both from Ankara University, Faculty of Political Sciences, Turkey. His research interests include flexibility and labour markets, social assistance regime, social policy and poverty. He was a visiting scholar at SOAS Development Studies in 2013. He is the author of *Establishment of Social Assistance Regime in Turkey: Accumulation, Control, Discipline* (NotaBene Publications, 2016, in Turkish).

Murat Özveri is a union lawyer in Turkey, and a part-time Lecturer at Kocaeli University, Department of Labour Economics and Industrial Relations, Turkey. He also holds a PhD in Labour Relations from Kocaeli University. He has published several books on democracy and unions, privatisations and working class, social security legislation, collective labour law, and also a number of articles and book chapters on these subjects. He is the editor of the journal *Çalışma ve Toplum (Labour and Society)*.

Çağatay Edgücan Şahin is an Associate Professor at Ordu University, Department of Labour Economics and Industrial Relations, Turkey. He holds an MA and PhD in Labour Economics, both from Marmara University, Turkey. His research interests include labour history of modern Turkey, social policy, trade unions, political economy and human capital. He is the author of *Human Capital and Human Resources: A Critical Approach* (Tan Publications, 2011, in Turkish).

Demet Özmen Yılmaz is an Associate Professor in the Department of Economics at Ondokuz Mayıs University, Samsun, Turkey. She holds an MA and PhD in Development Economics, from Marmara University, Turkey. She was a visiting scholar at SOAS Development Studies Department in 2012. Her research interests include development, gender, social policy, female labour and family policies. She is one of the contributors to *Polarizing Development* which was published by Pluto Press in 2015. She is on the editorial board of *Praksis Journal*.

Koray R. Yılmaz is a Professor in the Economics Department at Ondokuz Mayıs University, Samsun, Turkey. He holds an MA and PhD in Development Economics from Marmara University, Turkey. His research interests include economic thought, development, social theory, Marxian critique of political economy and Turkish capitalism. He is the author of *From Grocery Store to a Global Agent Arçelik Joint-Stock Company: A Marxian Perspective on Business History* (SAV Publication, 2010, in Turkish). He was awarded Young Social Scientist by the Turkish Social Science Association with this book in 2011. He was a visiting scholar at SOAS in 2012. He translated *An Introduction to the Three Volumes of Karl Marx's Capital* by Michael Heinrich into Turkish in 2017. He is on the editorial board of *Praksis Journal*.

Index

Thanks to our Patreon Subscribers:

Lia Lilith de Oliveira
Andrew Perry

Who have shown generosity and
comradeship in support of our publishing.

Check out the other perks you get by subscribing
to our Patreon – visit patreon.com/plutopress.
Subscriptions start from £3 a month.